Citizen Internees

Citizen Internees

A Second Look at Race and Citizenship in Japanese American Internment Camps

Linda L. Ivey and Kevin W. Kaatz

PRAEGER™

An Imprint of ABC-CLIO, LLC

Santa Barbara, California • Denver, Colorado

Library of Congress Cataloging-in-Publication Data

Names: Ivey, Linda L., author. | Kaatz, Kevin W., author.
Title: Citizen internees : a second look at race and citizenship in Japanese
   American internment camps / Linda L. Ivey and Kevin W. Kaatz.
Description: Santa Barbara, California : Praeger, an Imprint of ABC-CLIO, 2017. |
   Includes bibliographical references and index.
Identifiers: LCCN 2016052235 (print) | LCCN 2017000568 (ebook) |
   ISBN 9781440837005 (alk. paper) | ISBN 9781440837012 (ebook)
Subjects: LCSH: Japanese Americans—Evacuation and relocation, 1942–1945. |
   World War, 1939–1945—Japanese Americans. | United States. War Relocation
   Authority.
Classification: LCC D769.8.A6 I89 2017 (print) | LCC D769.8.A6 (ebook) |
   DDC 940.53/1708956073—dc23
LC record available at https://lccn.loc.gov/2016052235

ISBN: 978-1-4408-3700-5
EISBN: 978-1-4408-3701-2

21 20 19 18   2 3 4 5

This book is also available as an eBook.

Praeger
An Imprint of ABC-CLIO, LLC

ABC-CLIO, LLC
130 Cremona Drive, P.O. Box 1911
Santa Barbara, California 93116-1911
www.abc-clio.com

This book is printed on acid-free paper ∞

Manufactured in the United States of America

To Doug and Elizabeth, as always.
To Jim for his support, Liv for the smiles, and Marcella for always being there during times of writing.

Contents

Preface

In the summer of 1990, an unidentified man entered the Redwood City Public Library in California. He explained to the librarian at the front desk, Jeanne Thivierge, that he had in his possession some documents from the local branch of the bank that at one point he was asked to destroy after the war. He had thought better of it and had confiscated the papers in question. Today he was there in the library to turn those documents over to the public.

It sounds a bit like the beginning of a spy novel, and to be truthful, it is difficult to know how risky his actions were, if daring at all. But despite the likely romanticization of this act—our hero's secretly absconding with highly classified documents—what he delivered was enough to hook the interest of a group of historians working in the San Francisco Bay area. The man had delivered more than two thousand previously unread World War II–era documents, primarily correspondence between the vice president of the First National Bank, J. E. Morrish, and the interned citizens of Japanese descent from Redwood City. The act of saving these documents from the dustbins of history was heroic—with so many oppressed voices of our past silenced or missing, this was an act worth dramatizing. Plus, it's a heck of story with which to start a book of historical documents.

The following pages serve as an introduction to this collection of documents—from this point forward referred to as the Morrish Collection. We weren't sure what we would find in this collection, and some preliminary skimming of the documents seemed less than promising. Mr. Morrish wrote to someone to inform them that he had paid their taxes. That person wrote back to say thank you. Maybe this is why our unnamed man was asked to destroy them.

But as we immersed ourselves deeper into the collection, the narratives of families and experiences began to emerge. More than that, through the correspondence with their banker, we witnessed these families adapt to their circumstances in an effort to go about their business as usual. In one sense, the very mundane act of paying taxes takes on a different meaning when the taxpayer is being detained without due process. There were properties to be managed, rents to collect, business associations to attend to. They had to plan for their future, despite its uncertainty. The internees were not prisoners in the legal-status sense of the word. So what was their legal status? They could vote. They could collect social security. They could serve in the military, and they could collect survivors benefits. In some cases, they could accept work outside of the camps but had to go through a lengthy petition process to leave. But they could not live in their homes. They lived behind barbed wire. How does one continue the business of being a resident of the United States while being forcibly removed not only from your home, but from your properties, your businesses, your bank accounts, your entire manner of living, playing, engaging, and existing as a contributing member of American society? How does one function as a *citizen internee?*

The legal status was never clearly defined; there was never a recognizable process of law. Nonetheless, the decision to intern was given a collective pass by the public and the government. A structure began to develop around the act of removal, operating via the War Relocation Authority (WRA), a civilian organization at once supporting the internees and supporting the internment. The WRA, along with white liberal supporters of the Japanese and Japanese Americans (like Morrish), facilitated as best they could an open flow of communication and money. Morrish, for one, became a caretaker of people and their places. The WRA was determined to make the internment work smoothly by doing "the job as a democracy should." But the WRA, while guided by a pledge to operate humanely, in fact, succeeded in creating a structure and a language to legitimize, on a federal level, an elastic definition of citizenship in which ethnic and racial minorities in the United States continue to operate. It was a normalizing, legitimizing process of a very un-normal act.

Within these pages lie testaments to the "life goes on" experience of internment. Logically, students of the internment should know that those interned did not simply wallow as victims, voiceless and without thought for over four years. They also may intuitively sense that there was more to their lives than baseball games and camp newspapers and makeshift kindergartens. The documents herein expose details of financial, political, personal, and civic reality. Moreover, they begin to unwrap how Japanese and Japanese Americans operated within the structure of the internment as landowners, property owners, and, in a majority of the cases, as U.S.

citizens. They prompt us to pose questions about how such a structure to allow and support the stripping of constitutional rights and human dignity in a modern, stable, and oft-claimed "exemplary" democracy could develop. Ultimately, they remind us that the possibility of abrogating the rights of citizenship remains perhaps dormant but needs vigilant watch.

Citizen Internees was really an organic process of thinking and writing, as we paced ourselves in figuring out what this collection could offer in terms of adding complexity to the narrative of the internment during World War II. We had many more documents to choose from than could make it into the book, so we found ourselves cherry-picking the meatiest—or at least most meaningful, as we saw them—for inclusion. The book provides a familiar chronological narrative of internment but aims to focus specifically on these documents and these people, and to write about this with attention to the collaborative construction of the role of "citizen internee."

We would like to thank the Redwood City Public Library, and specifically Derek Wolfgram, the Library Director, and the staff and board of the Local History Room in Redwood City, for granting us full access to the documents and allowing us to share them with the world. Specifically, we want to thank Jean Thivierge for her support from the beginning of the project. California State University, East Bay rewarded us with grant money for the time and support of graduate students in tackling the digitizing process. Two MA candidates (now graduates), Michael Burton and Moriah Ulinskas, allowed us to rely on their tremendous talents as historians to digitize, archive, and analyze the potential value of what we had in front of us. They are contributors to many of the ideas in this book and were likely the first to wrestle with and analyze the meanings of what the Morrish Collection could tell us. Finally, I would like to thank my co-author, Dr. Kevin Kaatz, who was sitting on the Board of the Redwood City Library Local History Room and realized that what was available in that collection was worth dragging the rest of us into. Further, he remained the lead of this project, steering us toward completion and devoting an admirable amount of time immersing himself in the narrative of the internment to give these documents a chance to tell their story.

Linda Ivey
Hayward, California

PART 1

The Idea of the Citizen Internee

CHAPTER ONE

Citizen Internees

In the final year of his presidency, Ronald Reagan signed the Civil Liberties Act of 1988, a historically extraordinary gesture on behalf of the federal government of the United States. It was, in essence, an apology "on behalf of the nation" for the actions taken against civilians of Japanese ancestry during World War II. Within the text of the act, Congress noted that "a grave injustice was done to citizens and permanent resident aliens of Japanese ancestry" and that the individuals and families "suffered enormous damages for which appropriate compensation has not been made." The act provided "for restitution of positions, status, or entitlement lost during the internment period" and generally acknowledged the missteps of the government in condemning a population residing legally within the United States without proof of security risk or wrongdoing.[1]

The apology within the 1988 act is an essential part of the conversation about the evacuation and internment of more than 120,000 legal residents of the United States without due process. It is an acknowledgment that in spite of the language within the standing Supreme Court opinion in *Korematsu*,[2] the decision to deprive those of Japanese descent on the West Coast of their liberty and property was a mistake. It moves the conversation past *whether* this should have happened and allows us to explore *how* it happened. How did the military, the government, and the public participate in the construction of the internment process and its support mechanisms? How did it function? What compromises did U.S. leadership conscientiously make in the face of war and public fear, and what language and structure was used to justify and facilitate these compromises?

The documents of the Morrish Collection—especially when read in conjunction with the literature produced by the civilian agency at the helm of the internment, the War Relocation Authority (WRA)[3]—provide glimpses of the *structure* of internment. Beyond the decision to intern, there needed to be the structure: the buildings and camps, on the one hand, and the functioning bureaucracy that comes with supporting the lives of 120,000-plus persons within those buildings and camps, on the other. The collection also addresses further aspects of the structure and language of internment through experiences that are relatively under-researched, including opportunities to leave camp during the war and the process of returning home—or relocating somewhere else—after the war. These threads work together to help us examine how the guarantees of citizenship and legal-resident status were interpreted rather fluidly at this time, and to the detriment of one racial group in particular. The general acceptance in U.S. society of this fluidity of citizenship rights—and the rights of noncitizens who were nonetheless legal residents—allowed the process and structure to thrive.

Actions led by the U.S. military, the federal government (including the concurrently established WRA), fearful public opinion, and, in some sense, the Japanese community itself, all contributed to the facilitation of the process and the culture of acceptance. And then there is Morrish, the centerpiece of this collection, the banker aiding (and abetting?) internment from his home base in Redwood City, California. Within the letters, he exists as a contact and a confidant, a reference and a referee. But what do we, as historians, make of Morrish? And to that point, what do we make of the hundreds of Caucasian Americans like Morrish who helped with navigating the removal order and perhaps sympathized with the Japanese and Japanese American evacuees who were previously their neighbors, their business associates, their landlords, their clients, their friends. Morrish is our hero in this story, but he is also, in some senses, our foil. He is a figure that helps us look critically at the society that existed alongside internment. The voices from within this correspondence are overwhelmingly grateful for the assistance that this man provides. But we know little of his motives, or politics for that matter. Was he simply doing his job as vice president of the bank? Had the federal government or the WRA instructed the bank to aid the internees in this manner? Or was he appalled by the treatment of his clients in the California Chrysanthemum Growers Association and determined to limit the damage done by their sudden evacuation? Do his motives matter? Morrish supported the interned, but in doing so, he also supported the functionality of the intern-ment. His role and others like it are critical pieces in understanding how something like the internment was able to happen, and how it was able to work.

New Questions About the Internment

As a result of the Civil Rights Act of 1988, the official word on the internment is that it was a grave error in judgment and execution. Histori-cal studies of the internees themselves have since flooded bookshelves and websites alike, largely attributed to the lifting of a "veil of shame" among survivors that came with the reparations. The internment-as-abrogation-of-civil-rights narrative has since been deservedly given significant atten-tion, and both primary literature and secondary analysis address the loss of freedom, property, and dignity in what was an essentially racist act.

Keeping in mind this narrative of injustice, historians have begun to carve out new areas of inquiry concerning the motivations, mechanisms, and long-term meanings with regard to the internment. If indeed the documents of the Morrish Collection could help historians approach this event from a new perspective, the first step is to consider what set of questions they might illuminate, and what research exploration they might prompt. The content of the Morrish Collection seemed to over-whelmingly lean toward the facilitation of everyday business in spite of the extraordinary circumstances in which the evacuees found themselves. If those interned were expected to keep up with the duties of citizen-ship, such as paying taxes, how did those involved with the internment—from the architects to the incarcerated—make sense of the altered notion of citizenship and civil rights? The following questions kicked off the inquiry:

- How did government officials process and conceive of this action? How did the government process and conceive of the existence of camps of interned, displaced, relocated citizens?
- How did the internees process their place as interned, displaced, relocated citizens?
- What can these documents tell us about this unique moment of govern-ment action in a representative democracy, with constitutional guarantees in question?
- How can we categorize this specific unique structure of *the state of being interned* in the United States? How did internees continue to function as citi-zens? What was altered in this role?

- How did the architects intend to protect or dismantle the status/identity of "citizens" in the internment camps?
- How did notions of freedom/liberty/citizenship become redefined, and by whom?
- How did allies outside of the camps' structure contribute to the altered notion of citizenship? What was the impact of this on the internees?
- How did these notions of an altered citizenship shape the anticipation/process of relocation after internment?
- How did these notions about altered citizenship impact the sociocultural structure of the internees (e.g., family, gender, generational identity, ethnic identity, national identity, political identity)?
- From what language or structure did the internment borrow to frame this process/action?
- What precedents in language or structure did the internment create with regards to relocating/displacing citizens in the United States? Globally?

In addition to these questions regarding the structure of internment, the Morrish Collection contributes to topics addressed by previous studies, including the role of women in the camps and the impact on family structure, with new perspectives. The documents also provide much more tangible discussions of relocation after the internment, and the multiple paths out of the camps during the war. The correspondence itself serves to flesh out the story of how the incarcerated dealt with the loss of freedom in the camps and envisioned their future—and how this shaped their notions of loyalty in terms of both cooperating with the U.S. government but resisting victimization as well. Most significant, however, is the theme subtly underlining the very existence of the collection: the collective establishment that supported the functioning of the process and sustained it throughout the war.

These are certainly not the only new questions about the internment to have emerged recently. In the past ten years historians have dug more deeply into the social-justice and civil-rights narrative to think about the complexity of this federal action. The first wave of these studies focused on the institution of "the internment" itself. Some studies have sought to understand the place of the internment in the United States as part of a global response during wartime toward enemy nationals within their boundaries. Others have focused on the role of the executive branch in order to understand why President Franklin D. Roosevelt may have supported—or at least tolerated—the decision to evacuate Japanese and Japanese Americans. Slowly, studies have emerged concerning allies outside of the camps, including radicals, African Americans, Jews, and white liberals.[4]

Seventy-five years after the fact, perhaps one of the most unnerving aspects of the internment lies not only in the evident racism underlying the decision, but in the appearance of general complacency among non–Japanese Americans throughout the process.[5] There are stories, still somewhat isolated in the literature of the internment, about the actions of allies outside of the camps—various civil-rights-advocacy groups, the Quakers, community leaders, and even bankers. In the case of Bainbridge Island, a small community outside of Seattle, a husband/wife team who owned the local paper became well known for their defense of the islanders of Japanese descent who had been among the first communities forced to evacuate. With clever forethought, they hired locals from within the camp to send back reports for the newspaper—reports that had the long-term effect of keeping the interned families close in the community's thoughts, continuing to make their story a local story. In a sense these bits of camp news, in conjunction with a strong liberal editorial voice, served as an antidote to the ghettoization of the internees from their hometown. The community had among the largest percentage of evacuees returning home after the war. In this story, the newspaper editors are framed as anomalies, in a sense: an unusual Caucasian couple who would speak out against the injustice of their neighbors' internment. As voices such as these are emerging from the historical record, we find a place for the banker in our collection, Mr. Morrish, as one of the Japanese Americans' allies.

Conversely, the vociferous pro-internment voices have been well documented in history: the fervor of anti-Japanese public opinion in the West; the ultimate decision by the federal government to evacuate; and the military leadership who equated national loyalty with race, rather than culture or politics or even legal status. That last sentiment is perhaps most aptly summed up in the famous quote from the general at the helm of the internment, John L. DeWitt: "A Jap's a Jap. It makes no difference whether the Jap is a citizen or not."

Indeed, DeWitt's quote is remarkable in that in fact it *clearly* equates loyalty with race, directly brushing aside the guarantees of citizenship. This leads to another facet of the internment that begs attention in light of the Morrish Collection: the very *language* of internment. What language was used to make sense of this action in the United States? Historians have discussed the language of this era extensively, primarily in the sense of the words used to (a) refer to the camps—evacuation center, relocation camps, concentration camps—or (b) refer to the Japanese and Japanese Americans in question—evacuees, internees, the incarcerated. These and similar terms have been debated as to which are appropriate, which are anachronistic, and which are spot-on in terms of their evocative impact.

Within the documents of the WRA and, to an extent, the Morrish Collection, the language is more subtle, where words act as signifiers in the attempt to normalize the act. At best, we can begin to trace the *fluidity* of the concept of citizenship during this time, specifically in how it applies to Americans of Japanese descent and their families.

As a Democracy Should

At its most insidious, the official language of the internment had the intent of normalizing this action. As we critically examine such language to see how it subtly removes the protections of citizenship, we should also keep in mind the basic problem of the internment, as historian Emily Roxbury so clearly articulated in her recent work:

> (The) subtle but no less insidious violations that made up the everyday lives of internees, such as the total lack of privacy that plagued every aspect of camp life, including toilet facilities, and the utter degradation resulting from assigning inmates numbers and lining them up in dehumanized masses for every conceivable purpose.[6]

At its very core, the internment was constructed in such a way to result in a generally demoralizing experience, from the day-to-day life in relocation centers and camps, to the overarching experience of the loss of freedom and property. Various sources contemporary to the internment reveal a discomfort with the essentially unconstitutional nature of the action. This comes clear even in the government propaganda generated during the war. For example, a 1941 film produced by the WRA references the "normal" things found in the areas of detention: democracy by voting, Boy Scouts, Girl Scouts, parades. This was a common strategy in making peace with the establishments of the camp: life went on as usual, and everyone was kept safe—both inside and outside the camps. The film's narrator, however, reminds the audience not to indulge the sense of the normal, stating, in fact, that "relocation centers are not normal" and that "the people are not under suspicion, they are not prisoners. They are not internees. They are merely dislocated people—the unwounded casualties of war."[7] One might assume that official pronouncements from the vehicles of the internment, such as the WRA, would unapologetically defend the necessity of such a course of action. The historical record reveals traces of ambivalence, however, as witness to a nation struggling in its decision to execute such a mass removal and incarceration.

That being said, it was not solely conflicted moral consciences that propelled such introspective remarks. The perception of the United States as a haven of democracy was an important message to maintain, both at home and abroad. According to the same Department of War film, the WRA promoted permanent relocation "out of the backwaters of the relocation centers" and "into the mainstream of American life" so that their labor could contribute to the war effort, reducing the cost to taxpayers, and so "there can be no question of the constitutionality of any part of the action taken by the government to meet the dangers of war. So no law abiding American need to fear for his own freedom."[8] The documents of the WRA also reveal that those in this organization were not entirely comfortable with the actions they were orchestrating. The overall report from the WRA described a shared feeling at the incipience of the action:

> "Many of the members of the WRA staff," the Solicitor of the agency told a general meeting of the Washington office personnel in the summer of 1942, "are walking around these days with heavy constitutional consciences." It was an apt phrase and it summarized a great deal of early WRA thinking. Almost from the start, the key personnel of the agency—the policy formulators—were acutely aware that the job they had to do was one which raised grave and delicate legal and constitutional issues. They also realized that the resolution of these issues in WRA program and policy could have far-reaching implications for the future of American democracy.[9]

The WRA further acknowledged the international implications in terms of what the Allies were ostensibly fighting for, and the possible repercussions of the nation's reputation, describing the WRA actions as "an acid test of American democracy's ability to handle a racial minority problem justly and humanely in wartime and that it would be watched and evaluated as such by freedom-loving peoples in every quarter of the globe."[10] The public-relations problem of incarcerating citizens and legal residents during a war posited to fight oppression of freedoms globally was not brushed under the rug. From the beginning, those in charge acknowledged the human element, while assuring the public that the United States would proceed with all due respect, despite the difficulties of the decision. Milton Eisenhower, the first director of the WRA, clarified this ostensibly mindful approach:

> Neither the Army nor the War Relocation Authority relished the idea of taking men, women, and children from their homes, their shops, and their farms. So the military and civilian agencies alike determined to do the job as a democracy should: with real consideration for the people involved.[11]

Interestingly, a letter-writer in the Morrish Collection expressed a similar sentiment when his family was adjusting to life in the Tanforan Assembly Center, noting, "The situation here is very well organized, a certain credit to the democratic American way of doing things."[12] This language is meaningful in its tone of accommodation. One shared sentiment that emerges across the many communities affected by the internment is that this is simply what needed to be done. In a time of war, in the name of national security, in order to protect American residents of Japanese ancestry, the removal was simply an unfortunate necessity. During the internment itself, the historical record shows consistent mentions of how life proceeded onward, schooling resumed, make-shift communities emerged, and any inconveniences endured by those in camp were not all that different from the sacrifices the average American was asked to make.

Regardless of the degree of accuracy of such pronouncements, or the degree of acceptance, the ability to craft language to foster a sense of normalcy or propriety, and to disseminate that language successfully, is an aspect of the internment that needs careful attention. In the end, these words and sentiments created a language of justification. It was a language that permeated the home front during the war. And it was a language that remained a relatively uncontested idea in U.S. history, at least until the field of Asian American Studies emerged in the late 1960s, and largely until the passage of the Civil Liberties Act of 1988.

Does the appearance of more and more critical analysis of the internment since that time signal that the precedent this action might have established will be discredited? The lessons of the internment seem to have become more integrated into national conversations on the protection of civil rights in times of global tension. The internment was referenced frequently in the weeks following the World Trade Center and Pentagon attacks on 9/11. The continued tension over immigration and terrorism in the United States in the early 21st century has called upon the internment story as a lesson in what could happen if fear gets the best of our society. And yet, the language of the U.S. Supreme Court ruling *Korematsu v. US* (1944) remains legal precedent, and in the words found in the dissenting opinion, a frightening precedent that "validated the principle of racial discrimination." In essence, the court's decision upholds the notion that concerns of national security outweigh the guarantees of equal rights promised in the Constitution. But who is to determine the severity of the national-security concern and the severity of the actions that need to take place? And how quickly could our society revert to this sort of policy?

In the aforementioned propaganda film sponsored by the WRA, the narrator notes with candor that "Americanism . . . loses much of its meaning in the confines of a relocation center."[13] The central premise of this book is to examine the ways in which the people of the United States cooperatively allowed "Americanism" to lose its meaning during World War II. In the pages that follow we will walk through a chronology of the internment, integrating some of the voices found within this collection as we go. At each step of the way, we will remind you to consider how the concept of citizenship has been treated as a flexible category, with the promise of protections often dependent upon racial or ethnic identities. *Citizen Internees* is not a definitive work on the internment. Rather, it is an invitation—an invitation to explore these letters and consider the ways in which people functioned as citizens and legal residents within a state of incarceration. We challenge you to think critically about the role of those like Mr. Morrish—on the outside, but participating in the functioning of the internment itself: were they compassionate, complacent, or complicit? It's a tough question to entertain. Perhaps it is naïve to assume altruism, yet it is somehow comforting when looking back at a time when the abrogation of civil rights seems impossibly egregious. At the same time, contemporary cynicism should not inappropriately obscure the understanding of past actions. Along these lines, we urge you to consider the ease in the architecting and functioning of these internment camps as a cautionary tale of sorts. How did this happen so quickly and so efficiently—and has the United States established a precedent for this kind of mass removal and incarceration to happen again?

The world in 2016—the time of the writing of this book—is witnessing a great deal of tumultuous social division along the lines of race, religion, sexuality, and politics. We are witnessing migrations replete with fear and devastation, and the sense that erecting barriers—political, social, or physical—is a way to either protect or divide our communities, depending on your point of view. Revisiting the motives and mechanisms of the Japanese and Japanese American Internment is thus a timely endeavor. The story of the internment is, after all, one about a nation in crisis, a world in crisis. It is a story about how fear ran roughshod over basic legal rights, constitutional rights, and human rights. But it is also, we hope, the story of what happens after the war—a story about recovering, healing, recognizing our missteps, and, hopefully, learning.

Notes

1. The Civil Liberties Act of 1988 (Pub.L. 100–383, title I, August 10, 1988, 102 Stat. 904, 50a U.S.C. § 1989b et seq.).

2. *Toyosaburo Korematsu v. United States* (1944), http://caselaw.findlaw.com/us
-supreme-court/323/214.html.

3. The WRA was the civilian organization created to oversee the internment process. When the Executive Order was lifted in January of 1945, the WRA was primarily responsible for the resettlement of the Japanese and Japanese American internees. For more information, see Richard Drinnon, *Keeper of Concentration Camps: Dillon S. Myer and American Racism* (Berkeley: University of California Press, 1987).

4. Allan W. Austin, *From Concentration Camp to Campus: Japanese American Students and World War II* (Urbana: University of Illinois Press, 2004); Nancy Nakano Conner, "From Internment to Indiana: Japanese Americans, the War Relocation Authority, the Disciples of Christ, and Citizen Committees in Indianapolis," *Indiana Magazine of History* 102, no. 2 (June 2006): 89–116; Hilary Conroy and Sharlie Conroy Ushioda, "A Review of Scholarly Literature on the Internment of Japanese Americans during World War II: Toward a Quaker Perspective," *Quaker History* 83, no. 1 (Spring 1994): 48–52; Louis Fiset, "Thinning, Topping, and Loading: Japanese Americans and Beet Sugar in World War II," *The Pacific Northwest Quarterly* 90, no. 3 (Summer 1999): 123–39; Cheryl Greenberg, "Black and Jewish Responses to Japanese Internment," *Journal of American Ethnic History* 14, no. 2 (1995): 3–37; Brian Masaru Hayashi, *Democratizing the Enemy: The Japanese American Internment* (Princeton, NJ: Princeton University Press, 2004); Eric Muller, *Free to Die for Their Country: The Story of the Japanese American Draft Resisters in World War II* (Chicago, IL: University of Chicago Press, 2001); Mae M. Ngai, "Asian American History: Reflections on the De-centering of the Field," *Journal of American Ethnic History* 25, no. 4, 25th Anniversary Commemorative Issue (Summer 2006): 97–108; Greg Robinson, *By Order of the President: FDR and the Internment of Japanese Americans* (Cambridge, MA: Harvard University Press, 2003); and Charles Wollenberg, "'Dear Earl': The Fair Play Committee, Earl Warren, and Japanese Internment," *California History* 89, no. 4 (2012): 24–55, 57–60.

5. This idea was thoroughly explored in an unpublished paper by one of the researchers on this project: Moriah Ulinskas, "New Narratives of Internment: The Letters of Joseph Elmer Morrish, Jr." (Graduate Seminar at California State University East Bay, Hayward, CA, June 9, 2015).

6. Emily Roxworthy, *The Spectacle of Japanese American Trauma: Racial Performativity and World War II* (Honolulu: University of Hawai'i Press, 2008).

7. "A Challenge to Democracy," War Relocation Authority, with the Office of War Information and the Office of Strategic Services, producers, 1942, https://archive.org/details/gov.fdr.21, accessed September 27, 2016.

8. "A Challenge to Democracy."

9. U.S. War Relocation Authority, U.S. Department of the Interior, *WRA: The Story of Human Conservation* (Washington, D.C.: U.S. Government Printing Office, 1947), 15.

10. *WRA: The Story of Human Conservation*, 17–18.

11. "Japanese Relocation," Office of War Information, Bureau of Motion Pictures producer, with the War Activities Committee of the Motion Picture Industry, 1942.

12. 14_Nakano_038 Undated, 1942, Morrish Collection.

13. "A Challenge to Democracy."

CHAPTER TWO

History of the Japanese and Anti-Japanese Sentiment in California

Introduction

On February 19, 1942, in response to the Japanese attack on Pearl Harbor and the subsequent declaration of war, President Roosevelt issued Executive Order 9066 to separate out the Japanese American citizens and people of Japanese ancestry from the western part of the United States. Government and military officials scrambled to determine how this almost inconceivable plan could be carried out. Ultimately, this executive order led to the mass evacuation and incarceration of approximately 120,000 people, over half of whom were U.S. citizens. Contemporary voices cited military necessity, the danger of espionage, and protection of the evacuees themselves as the reason for the drastic action of removal. More recently, leading internment historian Roger Daniel, after years of research, instead arrived at these three reasons for the action: "race prejudice, war hysteria, and a failure of political leadership."[1] In the 2010s, as the United States faces renewed tensions at the nexus of race and politics, perhaps it is time to look critically at how we as a nation allowed this chapter in our history to occur.

One way to approach this inquiry is to examine how the structure of the internment itself was supported and facilitated. In the years since Daniel first began publishing on this topic, scholarship on the internment has exploded. Most focus on what led to the internment, what happened during the internment, and how the U.S. government handled this situation during the war. Not much has been written on the reality of living through the internment as a resident of the United States, including what the Japanese Americans were doing to protect their houses, property, and businesses when they were forced into these camps. Historian Wendy Ng, in her book *Japanese American Internment during World War II,* notes: "The evacuation notices were issued so quickly that most people had little time to make the necessary arrangements for their personal property. Many were forced to store or sell their personal property and make sure that their finances and other aspects of their personal lives were in order within a few weeks' time."[2] The Japanese Americans documented in the Morrish Collection were certainly rushed out of their homes and businesses, but most were able to organize their businesses, homes, and personal property in many cases before they departed. These were hard-working Americans (most of them were American citizens—some were long-term residents, excluded from citizenship because of their race) who worked, played, and had families. They also had their own businesses and had to pay their property taxes, state and federal taxes, and any insurance premiums like property and life. Although the American government took away their freedom, they still had to pay their bills.

While their lives were turned upside down when they were forced out of their communities, they had to plan ahead. Generally, the internees—and most Americans—assumed that the war would not last forever, and those evacuated hoped ultimately to be allowed back home. But what would they come home to? This book looks at one community's response to their internment and what they did to preserve their homes and livelihoods. There were, of course, many who helped the Japanese Americans during their imprisonment.[3] In San Mateo County, California, a small group of Japanese Americans found that they could rely on a banker at the First National Bank (later taken over by Wells Fargo) named J. E. Morrish to help them navigate between their internment and what they were forced to leave behind. Perhaps the place to start in our inquiry is with the question of how U.S. society got to a point at which this action appeared reasonable if not optimal. This chapter looks at the history of Japanese Americans on the West Coast of the United States, starting in the late 1800s.

Conditions in Japan in the 1800s

Primarily because of the emigration-restrictive policies of Japan up through 1885, and then because of the restrictive immigration policies of the United States in the early 1900s (especially with the "Gentlemen's Agreement" of 1907–1908), the population of Japanese in the United States had remained relatively small since its inception, hovering at around 127,000 at the time of the internment.[4] Japan, for the most part, was a relatively inward-looking country up until the middle of the 1800s. The Japanese government restricted its people from leaving Japan, and it also restricted the number of non-Japanese coming into Japan. There are a few reasons for this isolationist policy, but foremost in the minds of the Japanese was what was happening in China. China had been battling with an influx of western traders for centuries, and in particular, during the early 1800s with the English who were causing major disruptions in Chinese society with the export of opium. This drug was devastating to the native Chinese population as it was highly addictive, and as more and more people became addicted, some parts of Chinese society began to break down. The Chinese government tried to resist this influx by outlawing opium, but since it was a highly profitable product, the English fought back; this ultimately led to two wars (the Opium Wars). The Chinese lost these wars, and the country then became economically controlled by England and other European and American powers when it could not resist.

The Japanese government, knowing what was happening to its neighbor, tried to restrict the interaction between westerners and the Japanese. This isolation was broken with the near-forced entry of the Americans, under the command of Commodore Matthew C. Perry, in 1853. Perry appeared in Tokyo Bay with four warships and discussed forming a trade treaty with the Japanese government. The Japanese did not want to give an immediate answer, and Perry then returned later with a larger fleet. The might of the U.S. Navy pushed the Japanese into accepting the Treaty of Kanagawa. This allowed, among other things, the exchange of ambassadors and the establishment of a U.S. consulate in Japan, thus introducing the Japanese to the Americans, and as Kiyu Sue Inui wrote in 1921, Japan was introduced to the United States "at the point of a 'muzzle.'"[5]

Conditions in California

Japan eventually changed its emigration policies, allowing the departure of Japanese laborers out of the country—and many left for Hawaii and the West Coast of the United States. The Japanese were not the first migrants from Asia to come to the United States. The Chinese had been coming to the mainland United States since the mid-1800s. Primarily drawn by the promise of the mid-century gold rush, their population increased quickly; it is estimated that their numbers reached 10 percent of the entire population of California by 1870.[6] Local, primarily Anglo-led labor groups in the San Francisco area took notice. One of the most vocal opponents of the Chinese was Dennis Kearney, himself an immigrant from Ireland. Buoyed by Kearney's insidiously catchy slogan "The Chinese Must Go!" the anti-Chinese groups made enough noise to be noticed by the federal government. Soon Congress itself passed legislation (in 1879) that would exclude the Chinese from immigrating to the United States, but President Rutherford B. Hayes vetoed the legislation (H.R. 2423). It then went through Congress again in 1882, and the current president, Chester A. Arthur, signed the Exclusion Act. It stated that the Chinese were prohibited from immigrating to the United States for ten years, but this prohibition was then extended in 1892, and in 1902 it was made permanent.[7] Not surprisingly, anti-Chinese sentiments among the white population in California made Chinese lives very difficult.

As the title suggests, the main goal of this legislation was to limit and hopefully stop the immigration of Chinese workers into the United States. The introduction and the first section of the legislation states:

> An Act to execute certain treaty stipulations relating to Chinese.
>
> Whereas in the opinion of the Government of the United States the coming of Chinese laborers to this country endangers the good order of certain localities within the territory thereof: Therefore,
>
> Be it enacted by the Senate and House of Representatives of the United States of America in Congress assembled, That from and after the expiration of ninety days next after the passage of this act, and until the expiration of ten years next after the passage of this act, the coming of Chinese laborers to the United States be, and the same is hereby, suspended; and during such suspension it shall not be lawful for any Chinese laborer to come, or having so come after the expiration of said ninety days to remain within the United States.[8]

It was not repealed until 1943, perhaps ironically in the middle of the internment, when the United States and China were fighting on the same side in World War II. The 1882 law, while working to keep out the Chinese, had the side effect of producing a labor shortage in Hawaii and the United States, especially in agricultural areas such as California. Business owners were desperate for workers, and they requested that Japan send over its men to work the fields. Ultimately, the Japanese government allowed (mostly) male citizens to leave Japan on work contracts, leading to a large influx of Japanese laborers in Hawaii. Like the Chinese before them, they were attracted to the West Coast of the United States and soon made their way there in hopes of earning some money, and then ultimately going back to Japan.

The flow of Japanese immigration into the United States fluctuated over time. It progressed very slowly in the late 1800s, rose rapidly to 30,000 persons in 1907 alone, dropped after the so-called "Gentlemen's Agreement," began to rise again by 1918, and was virtually cut off by the federal immigration restrictions introduced in 1924. It finally declined to a mere 522 Japanese workers in 1928.[9] When the Japanese first arrived in the United States to work, it appears that many of them were not planning on staying, especially since they were not allowed to become citizens, primarily because of the Naturalization Act passed in 1870. This stated that anyone who was white, or of African descent could become naturalized citizens, but since the Japanese did not fit into any of these categories, they were forever blocked from becoming citizens. This, however, did not stop them from arriving in the United States to make their fortunes. There were only a few large ports on the western coast of the United States for them to pick from, and many Japanese workers landed in San Francisco, primarily because of the stories they had heard about the wealth and land in California.[10] They tended to stay in boardinghouses that were run by Japanese men and women who were already in the country. The boardinghouses also acted as a conduit to employment, with the owners farming out the Japanese to do work mostly in agriculture, at least in California.[11]

Unfortunately, the newly arrived Japanese laborers did not escape the notice of the anti-Chinese movement, which was very active through the early 1900s. The movement moved its attention from one Asian group to another and used similar language and tactics. As Daniels pointed out, the spark that started serious anti-Japanese sentiment once again occurred in San Francisco.[12] The *San Francisco Chronicle* published a piece on February 23, 1905, titled "The Japanese Invasion, the Problem of the Hour." This article then led to a large number of anti-Japanese articles in the newspaper. It was soon after the *San Francisco* article was published that the California State Legislature, on March 1 and 2, 1905, passed an anti-Japanese resolution.

In May 1905, the Asiatic Exclusion League, also known as the Japanese and Korean Exclusion League, became one of the first groups to organize against the Japanese aliens. They were very active, both in and out of California. The group was formed primarily to create statewide legislation against the Japanese. Many labor unions, including the American Federation of Labor, as well as the American Legion and the Native Sons of the Golden West, were also very anti-Japanese. Even the fact that Japan donated $256,000 (more than any other country) to San Francisco to help it rebuild after the earthquake of April 18, 1906, did little to reduce the vitriol against the newly arrived Japanese.[13] While the earthquake helped politicians focus on something other than anti-Asian policies, soon after the devastation, the anti-Japanese forces resumed their activities. There were boycotts called on Japanese businesses, and physical attacks increased.

One specific problem pointed out by the anti-Japanese coalition was that Japanese men were sitting in school classrooms, right beside white girls. This caused such an uproar that on October 11, 1906, the San Francisco Board of Education kicked out all of the Japanese students from the school district, including the Japanese (and Korean) children. However, news of this reached Japan, and Japan soon contacted President of the United States Theodore Roosevelt. He sent Secretary of Commerce and Labor Victor H. Metcalf to San Francisco to see what was going on and to try to convince the board to reverse its decision. Metcalf was unsuccessful, and the conflict eventually led to the Gentlemen's Agreement—an agreement to limit Japanese immigration to the United States (discussed below). In return for this, the San Francisco Board of Education allowed Japanese students to remain in school.

The anti-Japanese ire did not go wholly without response. Many voices pointed out the economic benefit to a large influx of Asian workers (presumably because of the lower pay they were able to demand) and at times extolled Japanese and Chinese workers for "their moral character[,] the rarity of crime among them, and their high sense of honor."[14] In response, the Asiatic Exclusion League emphasized widespread, discriminatory myths categorizing Asians as prone to drugs and vice. One story of what took place in Pendleton, Oregon, exemplifies this familiar script:

> Drunken men, cursing, drinking, telling ribald jokes; women fallen from all that is good and clean; profligate Japs, and sodden, sullen, opium-soaked Chinese. What do you think of such a place being frequented by boys and girls, school children whose ages run from ten to sixteen years? . . . Search the police records of Seattle, Portland, San Francisco, Los Angeles, New York, or any other Mongolian center and you will find—what? Bestiality, vileness, filth. . . . Young women throughout the State are becoming objects of vicious assaults of a felonious nature at the hands of Japanese, and if continued much longer, scenes similar to those of the South will be enacted here.[15]

Even though the San Francisco Board of Education had segregated Japanese children in late 1906, the Asiatic Exclusion League was still concerned about not mixing white and Asian children. The anti-Asian groups were organized enough, and vocal enough, to convince the office of the U.S. President to pen an executive order (March 3, 1907) limiting the immigration of Japanese laborers. Part of the executive order reads:

> And Whereas, upon sufficient evidence produced before me by the Department of Commerce and Labor, I am satisfied that passports issued by the Government of Japan to citizens of that country or Korea and who are laborers, skilled or unskilled, to go to Mexico, to Canada and to Hawaii, are being used for the purpose of enabling the holders thereof to come to the continental territory of the United States to the detriment of labor conditions therein;
>
> I hereby order that such citizens of Japan or Korea, to-wit: Japanese or Korean laborers, skilled and unskilled, who have received passports to go to Mexico, Canada or Hawaii, and come therefrom, be refused permission to enter the continental territory of the United States.[16]

In 1908, on the heels of the executive order, the U.S. and Japanese governments devised a diplomatic agreement that became known as the Gentlemen's Agreement. According to the Gentlemen's Agreement, the Japanese government would cease issuing passports to laborers, but passports were given to people already connected in the United States, including the wives of laborers already resident. This ultimately brought those wives to the United States, and any children they had were U.S. citizens. However, it also severely curtailed the number of Japanese workers who were arriving from Japan.

The Asiatic Exclusion League and anti-Japanese sentiment remained strong through the first part of the 20th century, with the restrictions implemented in 1908 perceived as too limited. Claiming nationwide support, the League continued its campaign for total exclusion.[17] The detailed *Proceedings of the Asiatic Exclusion League* included statistics (although these numbers have been questioned by scholars) and often found support for their ideas in statewide newspapers warning of the dangers of the "yellow peril." Most of them were particularly sensitive to the role of Japanese labor in agriculture, and a perceived labor competition with white Americans. For one pointed example, the Hollister *Free Lance* stated:

> A good move, and one that should be adopted by all labor employers, recently started among fruit-growers to rid themselves of the Japanese who have long controlled the labor situation, is already bringing results.

Hundreds of brown men have been summarily discharged and white men put in their places, and the time is not far distant when white labor only will be employed.[18]

Agriculture in fact played a significant role in the history of the anti-Japanese movement. The Gentlemen's Agreement protected Japanese residents with agricultural interests, perhaps as a nod to the already significant part they played in California's economy by the early 20th century. Long viewed as the special domain of Anglo-Americans, land ownership and successful farming endeavors by Japanese residents hit a particular nerve among California nativists. So while the anti-Japanese movement again found its way into the California State Legislature debates, and tens of anti-Japanese bills were introduced between 1909 and 1911 (with seventeen in 1909 alone[19]), it is worth noting that more and more legislators argued for taking away the right of Japanese aliens (or those who could not become U.S. citizens) to own agricultural land.

There were many tactics to support the passage of such legislation, including spreading the idea that a foreigner in Japan could not own land. Anti-Japanese land restriction advocates argued that if Japan could prevent Americans from leasing land, then so could the United States. The problem, however, is that this claim was untrue. As pointed out by historian Roger Daniels, a foreigner could lease land for up to almost one thousand years (essentially owning it).[20] But this did not stop California legislators from ignoring facts and continuing to push for restrictive covenants. The Asiatic Exclusion League, the labor unions, and, of course, nativist legislators were successful with the passage of the 1913 California Alien Land Law, otherwise known as the Webb-Haney Act. Early conversations about this proposed law included directing it at all aliens in California—which seems logical, considering the xenophobic reasoning at its base. But resistance from the federal government as well as local business owners kept the law focused on Asians in a very specific way: only those ineligible to become citizens were prohibited from purchasing land.

After the change, the government of Japan bitterly complained to Washington about these anti-Japanese laws. There were some protests held in Tokyo in April 1913, and although they were not government sponsored, the U.S. government took notice; Secretary of State William Jennings Bryan contacted Governor Hiram Johnson (who was originally against any anti-Asian legislation[21]) to ask that the governor understand that although the proposed legislation affected only people living in California, it could have an effect on international politics.[22] The secretary of state even came out to California to try to sway the legislature into softening the proposed law.

Other voices chimed in to prevent the passage of the act. More often than not, however, these arguments were made in economic terms. Various community groups from across the state requested that the assembly not pass the Alien Land Act, including those represented by the Stockton Chamber of Commerce. On May 1, 1918, they wrote:

> Dear Sir: At a special meeting of the board of trustees of the Stockton Chamber of Commerce held this day, the following resolution was adopted:
>
> Whereas, There is now proposed in the California State Legislature legislation which forbids the leasing of lands to aliens; and
>
> Whereas, A large area of fertile land in San Joaquin County and throughout the delta region is tilled by aliens, and by reason of the nature of the soil and the products grown it is impossible to secure other than alien tenants for such lands; and
>
> Whereas, The products of the delta soils grown by aliens are a source of much wealth to our citizens, and
>
> Whereas, Rentals of land leased by aliens have increased from $5 to $7 an acre in 1902, $10 to $12 an acre in 1905, to $16 to $25 an acre in 1912, and land values have increased to from $50 to $200 an acre; and
>
> Whereas, Much foreign capital has been brought to the State, and is now being brought for the reclamation of land which is susceptible to cultivation by aliens, and not by our citizens; now, therefore, be it
>
> Resolved, That the Stockton Chamber of Commerce protests against legislation forbidding the short term leasing of land to aliens, believing such legislation to be inimical to the best interests of our people; and be it
>
> Resolved, That our representatives in the State Legislature be provided with copies of this resolution. Very truly yours, J. M. Eddy, Secretary, Stockton Chamber of Commerce.[23]

The Fresno County Mass Meeting of Citizens, writing on May 2, 1913, also demanded that the bill not be passed:

> Hon. C.C. Young, Speaker of the Assembly, Sacramento, Cal.:
>
> Mass meeting of Fresno County citizens adopted the following resolution last evening.
>
> Whereas, There is now pending before our State Legislature a bill known as the Webb anti-alien land bill; and
>
> Whereas, Said bill does not meet the necessities of our social economic conditions and is apparently a subterfuge; therefore, be it
>
> Resolved, That we, the citizens of Fresno County in mass meeting assembled, must respectfully protest against the passage of said Webb bill in its present form—First, because in our judgment it will place a cloud upon every title hereafter conveyed in our State; second, because it is a direct

invitation to our Federal Government to naturalize Japanese and Chinese; third, because it is in our judgment in direct conflict with our treaty relation with Japan and will, if enacted into law, be declared void by our courts;

Resolved, That we do here and now request our Legislature—First, to enact a law which will apply to all aliens alike; second, which will not disturb settled land titles; third, which shall make citizenship the basis of land ownership; fourth, which shall apply to agricultural lands only; fifth, which shall not drive capital from our state.[24]

The Stockton Chamber of Commerce and the Fresno County citizens did not want the legislation to pass because it would negatively impact agriculture in these areas. However, there were many other groups and unions that wanted the bill to pass immediately. These included, among others, the Barbers' Union of Stockton, the Oakland Barbers' Union, the Gas Workers of Alameda County, the Cooks and Waiters Union #31, along with Teamsters and butchers, engineers, and bartenders unions.[25] Even groups not particularly local to California, including the Aryan Pure Race Society of America, piped in, demanding the exclusion in more global terms:

Tell Secretary Bryan have the Japanese Mongolians pay back the six hundred millions dollars the Jews, by prejudicing Aryan German, France, England and America, got for these Mongolians to injure Aryan Russian, because Aryan Russians feeding six million Jews. Three hundred millions of this money came from our Aryan people and savings banks. Our earnings should be used and this money should be here to aid our people and help our Aryan farmers produce beet and cane sugar, wheat, corn meal and other foodstuffs, and clothing fibres, wool, cotton, silk, flax, on our own lands, and not be given the low rates who threaten to come six thousand miles across ocean in boats our money paid for, to whip us because we prefer not to let them in our houses to produce grandchildren for us and outrage as the Mongolians and use maraudered and outraged Russia for over two hundred hears[sic] and mongrelized some Aryan Russian families, as they are today mongrelizing and weakening some of our Aryan families. Taft's gentleman's agreement with these Japanese and his veto of the immigration bill for the Jews brings this on us now. So, Aryan statemen, you must purify your race.
Aryan Pure Race Society of America.[26]

On May 19, 1913, the governor of California signed the Land Act into law, even though President Woodrow Wilson had telegraphed the governor asking him to veto it.[27] Its wording was directly adopted from a 1911 treaty that the United States and Japan had that said the Japanese could own corporations and residential property, but not agricultural land.[28] In a nod to the president and the secretary of state, the legislature added to the bill that Japanese aliens could lease agricultural land for up to three years but not own it outright. The Japanese government still protested that it was discriminatory against its own people and continued to let the U.S. government know its position throughout the summer of 1913. It even led to talk of war between Japan and the United States. This clearly did not occur. Many other western states passed their own version of the California Alien Land Act.

Despite the new law, Japanese residents still found ways to work on, and own, California's agricultural land. When the Gentlemen's Agreement of 1908 included a loophole for the wives of those Japanese already in the United States, it inadvertently ushered in the era of the Japanese nuclear family working the land in California. The children of these couples (many of whom were married after 1908) were American citizens by birth, and these citizens were able to be landowners in California. Other loopholes were found: having white Americans technically lease the land and permitting the Japanese to continue working it; or forming agricultural corporations (and the forming and maintaining of a corporation was allowed). On June 12, 1913, a leading Japanese immigrant newspaper, the *Nichibei Shimbun,* actively encouraged farmers to form these corporations. In response, 65 new companies were created in July and August 1913.[29] And of course, they could also lease agricultural land for up to three years (according to the 1913 law). The amount of agricultural land actually being used by the Japanese increased in the period between 1913 and 1920.[30]

The fact, however, that the Japanese aliens were bypassing the law infuriated many Californians, and it had strong repercussions. One person who was definitely not happy with the loopholes in the 1913 law, or with the Asian population in general, was James D. Phelan, the mayor of San Francisco between 1897 and 1902 and then a U.S. Senator representing California between 1915 and 1921. In 1919 he wrote an article for the *North American Review* titled "The Japanese Evil in California." He began by stating: "The farming communities of California are organizing to suppress the Japanese evil." They are "evil," according to Phelan, "because they are a masterful people, of great industry and ingenuity. They have no disposition in California to work for wages, but seek control of the soil by purchase, leasehold or a share of the crops, and under these circumstances, become impossible competitors."[31] He was, in effect, upset that the Japanese were such good workers. He was against the Gentlemen's Agreement because he believed that ships were delivering the Japanese to Mexico (also addressed in Roosevelt's executive order from 1907), and they then proceeded to cross the U.S. border. Phelan was also upset that the Japanese aliens were circumventing the 1913 law, which forbid them to own land. He ended his letter with a demand for an exclusion law, much like the 1882 Chinese Exclusion Law. He also formed a political group called Keep California White and used this as a vehicle for his anti-Japanese sentiments, and as a tagline for his political campaigns.

Due to influential voices like Senator Phelan, a 1920 ballot issue sought to close the loopholes of the 1913 act. As pointed out, the California State Legislature attempted to appease President Wilson by allowing the proposed law to include a statement allowing aliens to lease land for up to three years. This one sentence would lead directly to the 1920 ballot issue, which hoped to close this particular loophole.

The 1920 ballot proposal read:

ALIEN LAND LAW. Initiative act. Permits acquisition and transfer of real property by aliens eligible to citizenship, to same extent as citizens except as otherwise provided by law; permits other aliens, and companies, associations and corporations in which they hold majority interest, to acquire and transfer real property only as prescribed by treaty, but prohibiting appoint thereof as guardians of estates of minors consisting wholly or partially of real property or shares in such corporations; provides for escheats in certain cases: requires reports of property holdings to facilitate enforcement of act; prescribes penalties and repeals conflicting acts.[32]

What is of interest is the phrase "prohibiting appoint thereof as guardians of estates of minors consisting wholly or partially of real property or shares in such corporations." These minors were U.S. citizens, and the ballot, if passed, would take away the rights of U.S. citizens, even minors, from owning property or controlling shares. This particular section of the ballot would lead to rulings by the U.S. Supreme Court (discussed below). As with California ballot issues today, after the initial summary, the actual wording of the ballot was given, followed by the arguments for and against the issue. The argument in favor of this ballot issue, written by notable nativist newspaperman V. S. McClatchy, stated (among other things):

Through the measure California seeks, as is her inherent right, to preserve her lands for Americans, precisely as Japan preserves her lands for the Japanese. Its primary purpose is to prohibit Orientals who cannot become American citizens from controlling our right agricultural lands. . . . The initiative measure simply closes the loopholes in the 1913 law which permit violation and evasion thereof. In addition, it forbids even short leases. . . .[33]

These "short leases" also led directly to a challenge in the Supreme Court (discussed below). McClatchy pointed out that the treaty between the United States and Japan did not give aliens the right to own property. On the other side, in the *Argument against Proposed Alien Land Law*, an opponent using the pseudonym John P. Irish wrote that the treaty with Japan specifically allowed Japanese residents to "own or hire and occupy houses, manufactories, warehouses, shops and premises and lease land for residential and commercial purposes." Toward the end of the argument he stated: "In the forgoing I have stripped the initiative of its cryptic and involved language and technicalities, so that it is naked in its two purposes: First, to forbid the leasing of land to Japanese and Chinese; and, second, to take land-owning minors of those races from the natural guardianship of the parents and commit them to the control of public administrators."[34]

Unfortunately for the Japanese aliens and their children, who were U.S. citizens, the ballot passed with 668,483 Yes votes and 222,086 No votes. Many on the "Yes" side took this as a confirmation that an overwhelming number of Californians endorsed not allowing aliens to own or lease agricultural land, while the Japanese communities, along with their supporters, believed that it showed they had considerable support from California citizens since it was not an "overwhelming" vote as was anticipated. The law took effect on December 9, 1920. It was challenged in the Supreme Court (the case of *Takao Ozawa*), but in 1922 the court found that Japanese aliens were not eligible for citizenship since they were neither white nor of African descent. (The California Alien Land Act was finally ruled unconstitutional by the U.S. Supreme Court, citing the 14th Amendment [the Equal Protection clauses], in 1952.)

Like California, the rest of the country was experiencing a wave of anti-immigration sentiment in the late 1910s and early 1920s, and not just directed at Asians. The country as a whole was trying to limit the number of southern European immigrants because they were believed to have lower intelligences than northern Europeans. In the early 20th century, the U.S. government began to expand upon its restrictive immigration policy. Anti-Japanese sentiment was certainly embroiled in the discussion and continued to thrive in the early 1920s, especially after a number of western states passed their own versions of the 1913 California Alien Land Act and, in particular, after the successful passage of the 1920 anti-Japanese ballot issue. In 1924 the federal government passed its most sweeping anti-immigration legislation, virtually calling a halt to immigration from most Asian countries, in what one significant American historian called "the triumph of old nativism."[35] Still not content with the state and federal anti-Japanese laws, nativist voices did not quiet down, continuing to clamor about the amount of land and resources under Japanese control. For example, Austrian immigrant John Lechner traveled around California to whip up anti-Japanese sentiment. He arrived in California in 1924, and in 1926 he created the Americanism Educational League. Lechner "criss-crossed Southern California, delivering anti-Japanese American speeches and distributing Leaflets."[36] He campaigned for money to send him to Washington so that he could spread his anti-Japanese message even further. It wasn't enough to restrict further entry; many people wanted Japanese residents and Japanese Americans deprived of all of their agricultural holdings.

The legal right to own land meant more than having a place for a home or soil to farm. In the early 20th century this legislation was cultural and politically loaded. In broader cultural terms, the American agrarian ideal was still an influential and coveted cultural construct. Dating back to the country's political origins, farming was considered the ideal American vocation: hard-working, independent, virtuous farmers taming the wilderness and making it productive, building out the nation with Anglo-Americans. Indeed, Thomas Jefferson famously envisioned a nation of yeoman farmers as the key to a vibrant, successful society. But at the close of the 19th century, several factors converged to give a sense that the frontier was "closing," including urbanization, industrialization, and a growing population in part buoyed by significant foreign immigration. In the second half of the 19th century, in the years following the initial boom of the California Gold Rush, the new state of California (with its climate, soil, and sheer acreage) promised significant opportunity for the resurgence of the agrarian ideal. Additionally, from at least the early 20th century, nativist sentiment against foreigners was also experiencing a resurgence—aimed at any number of immigrant groups participating in California agriculture who were perceived to be taking American resources away from American citizens.

It was in this particular context of land, agriculture, increased racial diversity and animosity, and a sense that the opportunities to make it as your own self-made man were dwindling, that laws like the Alien Land Act were passed. Japanese growers were indeed making a significant footprint in California agriculture—and settling down on the land with wives and children, in many senses acting as ideal American citizens. But the expectation for agriculture was still steeped in racial terms. A familiar pattern of anti-Asian sentiment—that complained about the "Asian Invasion" taking over jobs, opportunities, and so on—secured a prominent place in California politics. This extended beyond the agitation about closing the loopholes of the 1913 act to continued pressure for exclusion. When Senator

Phelan ran for reelection, his campaign poster prominently displayed supposedly terrifying statistics as to the amount of land Japanese residents were controlling in California and the Japanese birthrate in agricultural counties. Not every Californian shared this sentiment, but it does speak to the ways in which those of Japanese descent were characterized as not-quite-citizen contributors to the growing California agricultural economy: integral, but not really welcomed.

It should be noted that Japanese citizens and residents did not just accept these anti-Japanese laws. They tried to use the courts to reverse them, and in 1923 a few cases made it all the way to the Supreme Court. Unfortunately for the Japanese, the Supreme Court upheld quite a bit of the California Alien Land Act as constitutional. While it appears that the 1913 Alien Land Act had few negative consequences, the passage of the 1920 ballot issue had many.[37] The amount of land owned and leased by Japanese residents dropped by nearly 150,000 acres, from 458,056 acres in 1920 to 307,966 in 1925.[38] And by 1940 there were 126,947 people of Japanese descent living in the United States. Of these, 60 percent were U.S. citizens, and 90 percent of them lived on the West Coast.[39] By all accounts they were extremely successful in California in particular, despite the repeated attempts to keep them from farming. By 1940, they were growing nearly 35 percent of all commercial crops, were heavily involved in the transportation of these crops, and like those documented in the Morrish Collection, were successful at growing flowers.[40] They owned 5,135 farms that worked 220,094 acres (and it should be noted that this is a significant drop in acreage from the 1925 amount).[41] Things, however, changed rapidly with the entry of the United States into World War II.

Notes

1. Roger Daniels, "Incarcerating Japanese Americans," *OAH Magazine of History* 16, no. 3, World War II Homefront (Spring 2002): 19, quoting the *Commission on the Wartime Relocation and Incarceration of Civilians, Personal Justice Denied* (Washington, D.C.: Government Printing Office, 1982).

2. Wendy Ng, *Japanese American Internment During World War II: A History and Reference Guide* (Westport, CT: Greenwood Press, 2002), 33–34.

3. Shizue Seigel, *In Good Conscience: Supporting Japanese Americans During the Internment* (San Mateo, CA: AACP, Inc., 2006). This book examines the stories of 20 people who devoted their lives during World War II to helping Japanese Americans. The book focuses on those who helped, specifically in the camps. J. Elmer Morrish receives a paragraph in this book (p. 89).

4. J. L. DeWitt, *Final Report: Japanese Evacuation From the West Coast, 1942* (Washington, D.C.: United States Government Printing Office, 1943), 79.

5. Kiyo Sue Inui, "California's Japanese Situation," *Annals of the American Academy of Political and Social Science* 93, Present-Day Immigration with Special Reference to the Japanese (January 1921): 97–98.

6. Roger Daniels, *The Politics of Prejudice: The Anti-Japanese Movement in California and the Struggle for Japanese Exclusion* (Berkeley: University of California Press, 1962), 16.

7. Daniels, *The Politics of Prejudice*, 19.

8. Chinese Exclusion Act, 1882: http://www.ourdocuments.gov/doc.php?flash =true&doc=47&page=transcript, accessed June 28, 2015.

9. Masakazu Iwata, "The Japanese Immigrants in California Agriculture," *Agricultural History* 36, no. 1 (January 1962): 26.

10. See Yasuo Okada, "The Japanese Image of the American West," *The Western Historical Quarterly* 19, no. 2 (May 1988): 141–159, for a description of what the Japanese had heard about California and the American West in general.

11. Daniels, *The Politics of Prejudice*, 7ff.

12. Ibid., 24ff.

13. Ibid., 32–33.

14. Proceedings of the Asiatic Exclusion League, minutes, December 8, 1907, as found in G. N. Grob, ed., *Anti-American Movements in America: Proceedings of the Asiatic Exclusion League, 1907–1913* (New York, NY: Arno Press, 1977), 6.

15. Ibid., 9.

16. http://theodore-roosevelt.com/trexecutiveorders.html, accessed February 29, 2016.

17. Proceedings of the Asiatic Exclusion League, minutes, January 5, 1908, 3.

18. Ibid., minutes, April 12, 1908, 8.

19. Iwata, "The Japanese Immigrants in California Agriculture," 29.

20. Daniels, *The Politics of Prejudice*, 51.

21. See Spencer C. Olin Jr., "European Immigrant and Oriental Alien: Acceptance and Rejection by the California Legislature of 1913," *Pacific Historical Review* 35, no. 3 (August 1966): 303–315.

22. Thomas A. Bailey, "California, Japan, and the Alien Land Legislation of 1913," *Pacific Historical Review* 1, no. 1 (March 1932): 40.

23. *California State Assembly Journal*, 1913, 2401.

24. Ibid., 2463.

25. Ibid., 2461–2463.

26. Ibid., 2461, reproduced here verbatim.

27. Olin, "European Immigrant and Oriental Alien," 313.

28. Bailey, "California, Japan, and the Alien Land Legislation of 1913," 43.

29. Yuji Ichioka, "Japanese Immigrant Response to the 1920 California Alien Land Law," *Agricultural History* 58, no. 2 (April 1984): 159–160.

30. Ibid., 161–162.

31. James D. Phelan, "The Japanese Evil in California," *The North American Review* 210, no. 766 (September 1919): 323.

32. http://repository.uchastings.edu/ca_ballot_props/130/, accessed July 1, 2015.

33. http://repository.uchastings.edu/cgi/viewcontent.cgi?article=1129&context =ca_ballot_props, accessed July 6, 2015.

34. Ibid., accessed July 1, 2015.

35. For details on this sea-change in immigration policy, see Roger Daniels, *Guarding the Golden Door: American Immigration Policy and Immigrants since 1882* (New York, NY: Hill and Wang, 2004).

36. Kevin Allen Leonard, "'Is That What We Fought For?' Japanese Americans and Racism in California, The Impact of World War II," *The Western Historical Quarterly* 21, no. 4 (November 1990): 436.

37. Masao Suzuki, "Important or Impotent? Taking Another Look at the 1920 California Alien Land Law," *The Journal of Economic History* 64, no. 1 (March 2004): 126ff.

38. Ichioka, "Japanese Immigrant Response to the 1920 California Alien Land Law," 170.

39. Roger Daniels, *The Decision to Relocate the Japanese Americans* (Philadelphia, PA: J. B. Lippincott Co., 1975.), 4.

40. Iwata, "The Japanese Immigrants in California Agriculture," 25.

41. Ibid., 32.

CHAPTER THREE

Planning for Relocation and the Protection of Property

When the war came, the anti-Asian movement in California had nearly four decades of organizing exclusionary sentiment on the West Coast of the United States, particularly in California. Nativist leaders had carefully crafted a language of secondary citizenship, cultivating the belief that those of Japanese descent were not quite American, cultural attitudes and legal standing to the contrary. Found in everything from racial stereotypes to constitutional language regarding naturalization, a structure of exclusion preceded the structure of removal and internment. In many ways, the anti-Asian movement engendered and promoted a cultural ghettoization of Asians in America. When the Japanese navy attacked Pearl Harbor in December 1941, the American public was largely ready to distinguish the Japanese as a distinct subset of American residents, and as potential enemy saboteurs. All it would take would be the government and military to draw up the plans to create the largest mass exclusion of people in the history of the United States.

The Concept of Citizenship after Pearl Harbor

While some members of the government had talked about excluding the Japanese from the West Coast before the Pearl Harbor attack, the real discussions and planning started soon after.[1] Western leaders met in late January 1942, including General John DeWitt, head of the Western Defense Command, California's Governor Culbert Olson, and Attorney General Earl Warren. DeWitt made it clear that the public did not trust the Japanese residents living in the state since they were believed to be enemies, and Californians were generally unable or unwilling to distinguish American residents from Japanese combatants.[2] DeWitt himself believed that there were many Japanese organizations in the United States helping the Japanese war aims, that many potential agents lived in areas of high security interest for the United States, and that those Japanese Americans who went to Japan to study were "rabidly pro-Japanese" when they returned. In his own words, he categorized the Japanese people as a "large, unassimilated, tightly knit racial group, bound to an enemy nation by strong ties of race, culture, custom and religion along a frontier vulnerable to attack (and) constituted a menace which had to be dealt with."[3] Governor Olson began to assault Japanese American citizenship rights in a radio address on February 4, 1942, stating that the Japanese who were living in the state were dangerous and were possibly communicating with Japan. He also stated that Japanese residents needed to be secluded from the rest of the public. Ironically, he claimed that the "loyal" Japanese would understand this necessity and would cooperate with officials, both for the safety of the United States and for their own safety "from unfair and abusive treatment." Acknowledging the citizenship of some internees, Olson made the powerful suggestion that complacency would be equated with loyalty.

Many local and national newspapers spread the fear of enemies living within the United States and thus the necessity of drastic measures. On February 12, 1942, renowned journalist Walter Lippmann wrote for the *Washington Post*: "What makes it so serious [the enemy alien problem] and so special is that the Pacific Coast is in imminent danger of a combined attack from within and from without. The danger is not as it would be in the inland centers or perhaps even for the present on the Atlantic Coast from sabotage alone. The peculiar danger of the Pacific Coast is in a Japanese raid accompanied by enemy action inside American territory." Lippmann stated that although there had not been, as yet, attacks from within, it was not because there was "nothing to be feared," but rather, it was a sign that the future attack would be very well organized and would hit with "maximum effect." American-born citizens (really meaning American citizens of Japanese ancestry) were as much a threat as those who were not citizens. He finished his article by stating:

This approach to the question by-passes the problem which, as I see it, has caused the trouble in Washington. For what Washington has been trying to find is a policy of dealing with all enemy aliens everywhere and all potential Fifth Columnists everywhere. Yet a policy which may be wise in most parts of the country may be extremely fool-hardy in a combat zone. Therefore, much the best thing to do is to recognize the Western combat zone as territory quite different from the rest of the country, and then set up in that zone a special regime. This has been done on the Bataan Peninsula, in Hawaii, in Alaska, in the Canal Zone. Why not on the threatened West Coast of the United States?[4]

On February 14, DeWitt submitted his Final Report of the Commanding General, Western Defense Command and Fourth Army, to the secretary of war. Among other things, he made it very clear that all Japanese, aliens or citizens, were the enemy. The distinction was solely racial. The recommendation stated:

The Japanese race is an enemy race and while many second and third generation Japanese born on United States soil, possessed of United States citizenship, have become "Americanized", the racial strains are undiluted. . . . That Japan is allied with Germany and Italy in this struggle is no ground for assuming that any Japanese, barred from assimilation by convention as he is, though born and raised in the United States, will not turn against this nation when the final test of loyalty comes. It, therefore, follows that along the vital Pacific coast over 112,000 potential enemies, of Japanese extraction, are at large today.

DeWitt reinforced the notion that "(t)he very fact that no sabotage has taken place to date is a disturbing and confirming indication that such action will be taken."[5]

Others responded in the same way, showing the influence of Lippmann's article. On February 26, 1942, Portland was hosting the House Select Committee Investigating National Defense Migration (the Tolan Committee). Representative John H. Tolan himself clarified:

So far, there are no cases of sabotage; that is, generally speaking. Well, there weren't any in Pearl Harbor, either, were there, until the attack came. There wasn't any sabotage; it all happened at once. In other words . . . if the Pacific Coast is attacked, that is when the sabotage would come, with attack, wouldn't it?[6]

It is perhaps no coincidence that the day after Lippmann's article was published in the *Washington Post* (February 15, 1942), the "entire Pacific

Coast congressional delegation" asked for the evacuation of all people of Japanese ancestry from California, Oregon, Washington, and Alaska.[7] President Roosevelt then signed his Executive Order 9066 on February 19, 1942. This order set the stage for the mass evacuation and holding of nearly 120,000 people, many of whom were American citizens. The Executive Order states:

> Now, therefore, by virtue of the authority vested in me as President of the United States, and Commander in Chief of the Army and Navy, I hereby authorize and direct the Secretary of War, and the Military Commanders whom he may from time to time designate, whenever he or any designated Commander deems such action necessary or desirable, to prescribe military areas in such places and of such extent as he or the appropriate Military Commander may determine, from which any or all persons may be excluded, and with respect to which, the right of any person to enter, remain in, or leave shall be subject to whatever restrictions the Secretary of War or the appropriate Military Commander may impose in his discretion. The Secretary of War is hereby authorized to provide for residents of any such area who are excluded therefrom, such transportation, food, shelter, and other accommodations as may be necessary, in the judgment of the Secretary of War or the said Military Commander, and until other arrangements are made, to accomplish the purpose of this order. The designation of military areas in any region or locality shall supersede designations of prohibited and restricted areas by the Attorney General under the Proclamations of December 7 and 8, 1941, and shall supersede the responsibility and authority of the Attorney General under the said Proclamations in respect of such prohibited and restricted areas.
>
> I hereby further authorize and direct the Secretary of War and the said Military Commanders to take such other steps as he or the appropriate Military Commander may deem advisable to enforce compliance with the restrictions applicable to each Military area hereinabove authorized to be designated, including the use of Federal troops and other Federal Agencies, with authority to accept assistance of state and local agencies.
>
> I hereby further authorize and direct all Executive Departments, independent establishments and other Federal Agencies, to assist the Secretary of War or the said Military Commanders in carrying out this Executive Order, including the furnishing of medical aid, hospitalization, food, clothing, transportation, use of land, shelter, and other supplies, equipment, utilities, facilities, and services.[8]

A few things to note about the executive order: it is clear that the president and his advisors were thinking about the process of the exclusion itself. The order allows for the U.S. government to help those who were being excluded for military reasons (with transportation, food, and shelter). It is also clear that the order does not refer to either "aliens" or U.S. citizens. While there were certainly discussions about the impact this exclusion order would have on U.S. citizens and their civil rights, many military officers and government officials had decided (or were in the process of deciding) that it was a military necessity to move any threat out of the exclusion zone. General DeWitt was one of these people.

The general went to great lengths to establish sound cause for evacuation. DeWitt's *Final Report* stated, for one example, that a wary public had committed many instances of violence against Japanese residents after December 7, 1941, and that the relocation was necessary for the protection of Japanese civilians. While DeWitt claimed that there was violence against the Japanese in the West, the War Relocation Authority's (WRA) own report questioned this claim. It stated: "Unfortunately, he [DeWitt] does not document his remark about 'numerous incidents.' Writers differ sharply about how much violence was actually suffered by "enemy aliens between December 7 and the Japanese evacuation."[9] The WRA report further stated that "no objective account has been published as yet of the number and nature of verifiable incidents reported to local, state, or national law enforcement officials as distinguished from wild, barroom threats of violence which came to official ears."[10] But DeWitt's exhortations did not end there. To muster support, he asserted that there were many Japanese who were actively helping Japan by means of radios, lights for signaling ships, and the stockpiling of weapons and ammunition. He also claimed that there were numerous pro-Japanese community groups located throughout California. All of these things together told DeWitt that all persons of Japanese descent had to be moved out.

But a sticky constitutional problem remained: what to do with American citizens of Japanese ancestry? The Department of Justice allowed the FBI to search properties and seize contraband without warrants against aliens.[11] However, many of these aliens lived with American citizens, and these houses could not be searched without warrants. DeWitt and his associates were worried that these Japanese Americans (along with Japanese aliens) were helping Japan and were hiding behind their U.S. citizenship to do it. DeWitt, in particular, was worried about the American citizens who were sent to Japan for their education and had moved back home after they were finished (the *kibei*). He believed that they were tainted with pro-Japanese sentiment and that it didn't matter that they were U.S. citizens. Pro-evacuation voices even cited the limits of the Constitution, and American law, in dealing with the unique situation at hand. In one example, the District Attorney of Madera County posited that "our State and Federal laws, supported by a bill of rights are entirely inadequate to meet the situation. If we are not to run the risk of disaster we must forget such things as the writ of habeas corpus, and the prohibition against unreasonable searches and seizures. The right of self-defense, self-preservation, on behalf of the people, is higher than the bill of rights."[12] Others, testifying in front the Tolan Committee, also dismissed the constitutional rights of these Americans. The Portland Legion Post stated in its presentation to the committee:

> This is no time for namby-pamby pussyfooting, fear of hurting the feelings of our enemies; that it is not the time for consideration of minute constitutional rights of those enemies but that it is time for vigorous, whole-hearted, and concerted action in support of the Pacific Coast Committee on Alien Enemies and Sabotage toward the removal of all enemy aliens and citizens of enemy alien extraction from all areas along the coast.[13]

In the end, this sentiment prevailed. American citizens were rounded up, sent off to temporary holding areas, and then finally off to permanent relocation centers. The WRA's *Impounded People* stated: "The greatest mass migration of American residents in history was to follow, far greater than any movement of American Indians from tribal lands to reservations. America had learned something about human engineering since the Indians were moved. The human engineering exhibited in the evacuation of the Japanese from the West Coast was a magnificent tour de force, as different and superior in technique and administrative management from the transfer of Indians as the oxcart differs from the latest bomber."[14]

The Construction of Internment

Despite the potential constitutional problems of rounding up American citizens and detaining them indefinitely without their being accused of any crimes, General DeWitt still wanted all aliens and Japanese American citizens removed from the West Coast.[15] By March 2, 1942, the general was given authority by Secretary of War Henry Stimson to start the process of evacuation by employing associations, firms, or any other group in order to do this. The Secretary of War authorized DeWitt to spend whatever it took to get all of this started: "In order to remove any doubt as to your authority to obligate funds, I specifically authorize you to obligate funds in such amounts as you deem necessary to effectuate the purposes of the Executive Order. . . ."[16] It was also on this day that the Western Defense Command issued Public Proclamation 1, establishing Military Area #1 (the western half of Washington, Oregon, and California). Public Proc-lamation 2 was issued on March 14, 1942, creating more military zones.

Not surprisingly, the evacuation and the thought of evacuation caused huge problems for both Japanese aliens and Japanese American citizens. The WRA report noted: "March was a nightmare period for people of Japanese descent. Some Nisei in the American Army were being discharged, and local boards were referring others; their American citizenship had not protected their civil rights."[17] Throughout the process, the evacuees were reminded of the sentiment espoused by Governor Olson: that they were not "accused of any crime" but rather were "being removed only to protect you and because there might be one of you who might be dangerous to the United States. It is your contribution to the war effort. You should be glad to make the sacrifice to prove your loyalty."[18]

In the first step of devising ways to organize such a large evacuation, the WRA imagined that a volunteer program could be set up, allowing Japanese aliens and Japanese Americans to leave the military zones before they were forced out. This started in early March 1942 (although unofficially it began in February 1942). The government provided a "Change of Residence" document that indicated that residents had complied with military orders. Financial assistance was also given, but many did not take advantage of it. Only 97 applications for assistance were filed and accepted during the voluntary phase, with $10,200 given to these 97 along with 28 people who also left.[19] The government also provided information about possible employment and housing, and about 9,000 people left for other parts of the United States. However, it was noted that many interior states did not receive the evacuees kindly. On March 27, Public Proclamation No. 4 was issued, and this stated that Japanese aliens and Japanese Americans were now not allowed to leave Military Zone #1 after all.[20]

At this point, the powers behind the internment decision and execution were confronting the near absurdity of the task at hand: the colossal undertaking of carrying out a forced migration of more than 100,000 residents. To state the obvious using the language of internment, people were not only being "removed" but were "evacuated" from their homes and "relocated" somewhere else. This action was undertaken in a fury of fear and racism. How could this happen safely, while guaranteeing humanity, decent conditions, and accommodations for property left behind? What would be the overall impact of this many people leaving an area, traveling to a new area, and settling in this new area? How would this massive deportation of citizens and residents affect families, communities, local economies, and the impacted environments?

At least in terms of local economies, the federal agencies involved were not entirely remiss in considering the impact of relocation. Roosevelt's Executive Order 9066 set the stage for the evacuation and, in theory, allowed for the protection of those who were going to be taken away. The WRA did try, at least on paper, to help the people they were about to take out of society, especially in terms of their property. Discussions about the potential economic disruption took place as early as January 1942. On February 14, 1942, five days *before* Roosevelt issued the executive order, DeWitt recommended that the Treasury Department be responsible for the "conservation, liquidation, and proper disposition of the property of evacuees if it cannot be cared for through the usual and normal channels."[21] And the day after the signing of the Executive Order (February 20, 1942), DeWitt received a memorandum from Assistant Secretary of War John J. McCloy giving a list of things that needed to be done to execute 9066. Section 14 of this memorandum had to do with securing the property of the evacuees:

> It will, of course, be necessary that your plans include provision for protection of the property, particularly the physical property, of evacuees. All reasonable measures should be taken through publicity and other means, to encourage evacuees to take steps to protect their own property. Where evacuees are unable to do this prior to the time when it is necessary for them to comply with the exclusion orders, there is always danger that unscrupulous persons will take undue advantage or that physical property unavoidably left behind will be pillaged by lawless elements. . . . Where they [local law enforcement agencies] are unable to protect physical property left behind in military areas, the responsibility will be yours, to provide reasonable protection, either through the use of troops or through other appropriate measures. The appointment by you of a property custodian and the creation by him of an organization to deal with such property in military areas may become necessary. . . .[22]

DeWitt's final report noted, "While the decision was pending, and even after it had been determined to evacuate all persons of Japanese ancestry from the West Coast, no single aspect of evacuation procedure stimulated more discussion than that which related to evacuee property."[23] DeWitt, however, seemed relatively unconcerned with the economic loss to any Japanese aliens or Japanese Americans. He stated that the evacuation process was orderly and "emphasis was placed upon the making of due provision against social and economic dislocation."[24] It is clear from the rest of his statement that he was not referring to the social and economic dislocation of persons of Japanese ancestry, but that of the nation. He said that nearly all farms previously run by the internees were now in production. He further said that people had been found to take over these operations, and in fact, some were reporting that not only land value but also agricultural output had increased during this period.[25]

The degree to which the Japanese internees were deprived of their property varied up and down the West Coast. In one instance, those who were living on Terminal Island in Los Angeles were given very short notice, and despite the goodwill of many who helped them get off the island, quite a bit of their property had to be abandoned.[26] The WRA was fully aware that there would be problems with the evacuation of the West Coast, but because the process was moving so quickly, WRA officials did not have time to set up a policy that would actually be useful to the internees. Ideally, this should have been done before the evacuation orders had been issued. In his department's deliberations on the issue of evacuee property, Secretary of the Treasury Henry Morgenthau Jr. was inclined not to deal with these particular issues. On February 26, 1942, he stated that the issue of personal property during the war was a "social problem" and was the same as if the army had decided to use land for an ammunition dump or a firing range—people living in the area would have to "be resettled in new areas, find new employment, and liquidate at forced sale their immovable property."[27] However, just a few days later, on March 5, 1942, he had a change of heart and sent a telegram to the Federal Reserve Bank of San Francisco and tasked them with assisting evacuees with the liquidation of their property and with handling unscrupulous business dealings (such as pressure sales of land or items the internees could not bring with them). The secretary claimed that he could send out at least 100 men to San Francisco by airplane to help with this program, which, he stated, should be ready by Monday, March 9, 1942.[28] It is clear that the government had been working on assigning the Federal Reserve Bank to the protection of evacuees' property, notifying the bank on March 5, 1942, that it would take over this role; and on March 7 the Federal Reserve Bank of San Francisco was officially given permission to carry out the program. On March 9, two days before Executive Order 9095, titled *Establishing the Office of Alien Property Custodian*, was given, the bank created the Evacuee Property Department, and at its peak, 184 people worked there.[29] One of the main purposes of this department was to provide the evacuees with legal help in dealing with the unscrupulous handling of their property while they were interned. Another part of the program allowed the internees to store their property—in particular, automobiles—in government-run storage facilities at no cost to the internee. Their personal cars could also be sold to the army.

The president signed Executive Order 9095 on March 11, 1942.[30] The main part of the order (Section 3) stated:

> Any property, or interest therein, of any foreign country or a national thereof shall vest in the Alien Property Custodian whenever the Alien Property Custodian shall so direct; and, in the case of any property, or interest therein, subject to the control of the Secretary of the Treasury, when the Alien Property Custodian shall notify the Secretary of the Treasury in writing that he has so directed, the Secretary of the Treasury shall release all control of any such property, or interest therein, to the Alien Property Custodian.

The U.S. government tried to contact, through the press and radio, as many Japanese aliens and Japanese Americans about the evacuation in general and the protections that would be afforded them. Banks in the military exclusion zone were contacted with information about the goals of the evacuation.[31] Unfortunately, the Morrish Collection contains no information on any contact the government might have had with Morrish and what he and his bank should have been doing to help the evacuees. What is clear, however, is that the bank must have given Morrish (and his secretary) time to do what he did, whether this was a part of his expected duties or under direction from the federal government. The description in the *Final Report* of what the banking officials were doing fits some of what we know Morrish did. For example, the *Final Report* states, "Bank agents were so stationed for the purpose of administering such of the evacuee property program problems which remained unsolved at the time of actual evacuation" and "As it was necessary for evacuees to use some household equipment until the day of evacuation, it became necessary for bank agents to remain in contact with evacuees in order to finally settle any pending affairs and to dispose of and store the last of their effects, and for those purposes Bank representatives were maintained at Assembly Centers. In some instances representatives were permanently assigned to the Centers and in others contact was maintained through periodical visits."[32] While we know Morrish was not permanently assigned to Tanforan, he certainly made numerous visits to see his clients in this particular assembly center. For example, on September 10, 1942, Morrish wrote to Ms. S. Adachi,[33] "It is possible that I will be able to get up tomorrow as I wanted to see Ham Honda. I also understand that some of the folks may be moved and I would like to see them before they leave; so should you see any of the Redwood City folks thereabouts in the morning, will you please ask them to be somewhere around the Pavilion around ten thirty."

The *Tanforan Totalizer,* the newspaper printed in the Tanforan Assembly Center, stated that the grandstand was where the internees met with visitors and that as early as late May 1942 there were nearly 1,000 visitors meeting the internees at the grandstand.[34] Morrish also wanted to meet with Mrs. N. Nakata, but a letter he had sent telling her of the date did not arrive. As it turns out, this was very near the closing date of Tanforan, and as he told Nakata, he wanted to say his goodbyes before everyone was shipped out (to Topaz).[35]

Morrish may have been a concerned community man, an active defender of the Japanese American community, or simply a banker managing his accounts. In any case, the attention paid to property and banking interests on the part of the government signaled something important. Those people about to be relocated away from their homes were property owners, business people, and generally engaged members of their community. These were not folks living on the fringe, or in the shadows, and their removal signified a potential destabilizing threat to the places they were leaving. It was clear that a cooperative community structure, both efficient and invested, would be needed to manage the process not only of removal but of internment.

Property and the War Relocation Authority

It was just a week after Executive Order 9095 was issued that President Roosevelt signed Executive Order 9102, which established the War Relocation Authority (March 18, 1942), which would become the overseeing entity of the actual experience of internment.[36] Among other things, the executive order stated:

3. In effectuating such a program the Director shall have authority to

—(a) Accomplish all necessary evacuation not undertaken by the Secretary of War or appropriate military commander, provide for the relocation of such persons in appropriate places, provide for their needs in such manner as may be appropriate, and supervise their activities.

(b) Provide, insofar as feasible and desirable, for the employment of such persons at useful work in industry, commerce, agriculture, or public projects, prescribe the terms and conditions of such public employment, and safeguard the public interest in the private employment of such persons.

. . . (f) Employ necessary personnel, and make such expenditures, including the making of loans and grants and the purchase of real property, as may be necessary, within the limits of such funds as may be made available to the Authority.

While sections 3(a) and 3(b) are directly related to the internees them-selves, section 3(f) was related to setting up the camps and having access to money to buy land. The first director of the WRA was Milton Eisen-hower, followed quickly by Dillon S. Myer, who took over in June 1942 and remained director until the end of the war when the WRA was disbanded.

There is very little indication from the letter-writers in the Morrish Col-lection that they took advantage of the storage program or even discussed the problems of property with the WRA. Neither do they make mention of the Office of Alien Property Custodian, established by Executive Order 9095 to help with issues of property, nor the programs offered by the Federal Reserve Bank, which was also made responsible for the storage of evacuees' property. This was to be done by leasing out warehouses for the duration of the war or leasing out places that could act as warehouses. The evacuees were supposed to crate their own materials, clearly label them, and if they lived in an urban area, the bank would arrange to pick up the crated material at their houses.[37] Automobiles could also be stored, but that was something that the WRA discouraged, primarily because it thought that the cars would be better used if they were sold to the army for the war effort.

Considering that nearly all of the documents in the Morrish Collection concern property and finances, the absence of the use of these programs is a bit surprising. According to the *Final Report*, the Information Division of the Wartime Civil Control Administration—the arm of the military's West-ern Defense Command in charge of evacuation—"secured the support of the press and radio in advising evacuees, creditors, prospective purchas-ers, lessees, operators, and the public, of the services, aims and policies of the government and the Military Establishment in the evacuee property program."[38] It further stated that evacuees' newspapers and organizations were also informed about the program. The program was purely voluntary, and according to the report, more than 41,000 people were represented by the Federal Reserve Bank.[39]

As with the program created to help with financial and property issues, those who took advantage of the governmental storage of property were in the minority, as DeWitt later admitted.[40] The WRA suggested possi-ble reasons why the evacuees did not take advantage of these programs. The first is that the internees were encouraged to take care of their own property issues before resorting to the WRA. It appears that many people in the Morrish Collection had signed over power of attorney to Morrish before they were sent to Tanforan, in effect bypassing much of what the WRA could have done for the internees. They probably did not trust the government to safeguard their property, considering that many were U.S. citizens and were being forced out just because of their race. The second and most probable reason is that they just did not know about the programs available to them, or that they found out about what the WRA was offering too late to take advantage of it. For example, it wasn't until October 17, 1942, that The *Topaz Times* had an article about the governmental program to help protect the property of the evacuees—this was after all of the evacuees were at Topaz. The *Topaz Times* stated what the government would do to protect the agricultural, commercial, and residential properties. It then listed eight services offered by the Evacuee Property Department, which were not developed until August, 1942—months after the evacuation had been completed and when many of the internees, at least at Tanforan, had already been told that they were going off to the relocation camp at Topaz.[41] These services would have been very useful if they had been developed earlier. The services were:

1.   To secure tenants or operators for both agricultural and commercial properties.
2.   To negotiate new leases or renewal of existing leases.
3.   To obtain buyers for real or personal property of all kinds.
4.   To effect settlement of claims for or against an evacuee.
5.   To adjust differences arising out of inequitable, hastily made or indefinite agreements.
6.   To obtain an accounting for amounts due, and to facilitate collections.
7.   To ascertain whether property was being satisfactorily maintained or whether damage or waste was occurring.
8.   To check inventories of goods and equipment, and to recommend utilization of material for the best interests of the evacuee and the nation.[42]

In August 1942, the government began receiving complaints from internees that their property, which had been stored in churches or abandoned buildings for the duration of the war, was going missing. The WRA, in turn, told the internees that they could request the WRA to recover their stored property and move it to government-run warehouses, at the government's expense. Property was then stored in warehouses in the San Francisco Bay area, and moved near Topaz when the evacuees were taken there. For those in Topaz, access to stored property was not given until the end of November 1942, more than two months after people had arrived. However, any internee who had stored their property in a church or other private building could have had their goods shipped to the camps if they paid for it themselves.[43] Nearly everyone in the Morrish Collection paid for the crating and shipping of their own property and did not store their belongings in government warehouses. Because many of them were members of the California Chrysanthemum Growers Association, they decided to store their belongings in the CCGA warehouse, where they almost certainly felt it was safer. For example, Matsuyama wrote on March 29, 1943, from Topaz, noting that his employer, Enomoto, recommended that he store some of his own personal items in the company warehouse. These items included a G.E. washing machine and a Singer sewing machine. He was asking Morrish to "arrange with a transport company in Redwood City to crate the two and send them to the above address Freight C.O.D." After a few difficulties finding someone to do the crating, Morrish wrote back to Matsuyama (June 25, 1943), telling him that the items had been crated and shipped and that Morrish was charging his savings account for the costs.[44] Another example was Rikimaru.[45] Morrish wrote to him on March 25, 1944, telling him he was sending out a typewriter and a trunk for a Mr. Yamane once he could find someone to pack it up. Finally, K. Yamada had asked Morrish to send out a number of items. She wrote:

> Are you in possession of the key to the Association Office? If you are, would you assist us again in getting some of our essential articles. We have a sewing machine and a big wooden box of household goods in the office which we would like to have shipped to us, if possible. There're [sic] ready for shipment and believe they both bear our name. Have some doubt as to our big wooden box bearing our name, but believe it's the only box of its kind in the office. If you have any doubt, as to its owner please leave it there, because we hate to have other's possession sent to us. Hope you can acquire the Wells Express and ask them to be especially [sic] careful with the big wooden box because it is full of breakable or fragile articles. Charge this to our acct. and would you please send us a statement of our account to-date.[46]

As it turns out, Morrish sent the wrong typewriter, but he tells Yamada to keep it, or he could have her return it and he would send out the correct one.[47] Later, Yamada writes to Morrish asking him to send another trunk that was stored in the Association Office. It had her winter clothes in it and that the trunk is labeled with her name and was new. She asks him to send it "by railway express collect." Her final request is to ask Morrish to send along ten 1944 calendars for the Redwood City families. There is a hand-written note on this particular letter (presumably written by Morrish or his secretary) stating that he sent twelve.[48]

FLOWER GROWERS

Many people whose correspondence is part of the Morrish Collection were flower growers before the war broke out. Japanese immigrants started growing of flowers on the San Francisco peninsula in the late 1800s, with cuttings coming from Japan. The flowers were successful enough that the flower growers on the peninsula started the California Flower Growers Association in 1906.[1] It was decided that many of the flower growers in the area should band together to help their individual companies grow. This led to the creation of the California Chrysanthemum Growers Association (CCGA). Toru Yamane was made the director in January 1932, and Joseph Iwasuke Rikimaru was made manager in February 1932, beginning his work in March.[2] The CCGA was created because of the fluctuations in the flower markets, and many individual businesses were suffering, especially with the Great Depression.

Growers' associations had become relatively common in the larger California agricultural industry by the early part of the 20th century. The cooperative nature of the Japanese flower growers represented here was indicative of several trends in the industry at large. First, the wheat market in California busted by the 1870s; following in its wake came the rise of horticulture—flower and truck crops, more specialized, more skill-based, more perishable. As many of these crops were grown on smaller acreages, smaller-scale farming ventures appeared in great numbers. At the same time, agriculture was outgrowing its old clothes. Ventures in horticulture were not intended as an enterprise for local or even home consumption. In 20th-century California, growers were generally capitalists, specializing in and producing one kind of product for widespread consumption. Thus, the growers associations were also born out of the need to market and distribute. Smaller growers—such as cut-flower producers or strawberry growers (typically dominated by Japanese immigrants in the early part of 20th-century California)— needed to work together to make such ventures economically feasible.[3] Associations brokered marketing costs, acquired access to tools and innovations, published emergent techniques in the field, and generally strengthened the position of the association members in the industry.

Although the Depression made it difficult to keep businesses alive, the CCGA was able to survive by a number of different ways. It acted as a cooperative and shared the cost of some items; it organized for shipments of flowers not only to San Francisco but around the country (especially once refrigerated train cars were invented); and it promoted the new use of shade cloth that allowed for multiple crops. These efforts enabled business to thrive into the late 1930s, and the association grew enough that it had to move its new headquarters and warehouse to Horgan Ranch in Redwood City. Many families in the Morrish Collection grew or rented farms on this large ranch.[4] In remarkable foresight, Joseph Rikimaru, the manager, decided to put the second-generation family members (called *Nisei,* and who were also American citizens) in charge of the board, in case there were problems with discrimination against those who could not be American citizens because of their race (the *Issei*).[5]

When in the aftermath of the Pearl Harbor attack the U.S. government began plans to remove all people of Japanese ancestry from the Pacific Coast, the board asked J. E. Morrish, vice president of the First National Bank in Redwood City, to handle the financial affairs of its members' businesses. This occurred on March 14, 1942, six weeks before the evacuation in San Mateo County. Clearly, some people of Japanese ancestry suspected that the government was planning for an internment. Morrish received power of attorney for the CCGA on March 28, 1942. The power of attorney, signed by George Nakano and S. Adachi, gave Morrish wide control over the association, including "to demand, sue for, collect and receive all sums of money, debts, accounts, legacies, bequests, dividends, royalties, annuities, and any other demands whatsoever. . .[he could also] bargain, contract, agree for, store, buy, sell, mortgage, hypothecate, manage, and in any and every way deal in and with, goods and merchandise and all other personal property. . . ."[6] Morrish handled the CCGA's dealings throughout the war. There are 99 letters between the directors of the association (who were mostly evacuated to Topaz) and Morrish, and associated documents (such as bills, requests for payments, deposits), making the CCGA one of the larger groups in the Morrish Collection. Morrish did his job so well that after the war the association members had no trouble starting it back up.[7]

Morrish also received powers of attorney from other growers such as William Enomoto, who owned his own nursery and was part of the California Flower Growers Association. On March 24 the board of directors for Enomoto & Co., Inc., passed a resolution as follows:

A special meeting of the Board of Directors was called by William Enomoto on March 24th at 3 oclock. The subject of evacuation was brought up and it was pointed out by the President that we must have an agent to look after our affairs while we are gone. Therefore, William Enomoto made a resolution: BE IT RESOLVED: That Enomoto & Co., Inc. appoint Elmer Morrish its agent and that he be granted a power of Attorney to conduct business as our representative; with the exception that Elmer Morrish is not given the right to mortgage or convey our real estate properties. Seconded and passed unanimously.

Below the resolution is a hand-written note that the resolution in the Morrish Collection is "a true copy of minutes from the minutes, by Edes Enomoto, Secretary."[8]

Many of the original members of the CCGA are in the Morrish Collection and were taken away during the war, including Nobuo Higaki, Tamakichi Kashima, Seishiro Mayeda, Kaoru Okamura, Joseph Iwasuke Rikimaru, and Toru Yamane. Others who joined the organization after its founding (and who are also in the Morrish Collection) were Sumi Adachi, Iwataro and Tetsuo Kitayama, Shozo Mayeda, George Nakano, George Tsukagawa, and George Tsukushi. Morrish was put in charge of handling the day-to-day aspects of their individual businesses as well as that of the association, including paying their taxes, collecting bills, and keeping various insurances up to date.

Notes

1. Gayle K. Yamada, Dianne Fukami, and Dianne Yen-Mei Wong, eds., *Building a Community: The Story of Japanese Americans in San Mateo County* (San Mateo, CA: AACP, Inc., 2003), 27.

2. Hiroji Kariya, *Kiku Kumiai, 50 Years* (Palo Alto, CA: California Chrysanthemum Growers Association, 1981), 4.

3. For further details on the impact and role of grower associations in California, and with the Japanese enterprises in California, see: Masakaza Iwata, Valerie J. Matsumoto, Douglas C. Sackman, and David J. Vaught.

4. Kariya, *Kiku Kumiai*, 6.

5. Ibid., 7.

6. 28_CA_Chrysthanthemum _Growers_087, March 28, 1942.

7. Kariya, *Kiku Kumiai*, 7, fn.

8. Morrish Collection, Box 2, Enomoto, Archive Room, Redwood City, CA, Public Library.

While many internees stored their property in industry warehouses, a few also kept their belongings at home, in locked rooms or barns. For example, a letter-writer listed the contents of the property's packing shed, including "twenty-three (23) rooms of black sateen cloth; ten (10) rooms of lumber; pipe; three (3) tons of fish meal, wire for black cloth; wire netting."[49] Another letter listed the contents of the "main dwelling house," which included (among other things), a gas range and an electric refrigerator in the kitchen, and a dinner set and two couches in the dining room.[50] Another example was the Nakano family. Morrish had written to them on November 23, 1943, to tell them that someone had broken into their house by breaking a window and that the front door was wide open. Morrish wanted to put up boards on the windows and asked that the family send him their keys. He also stated: "This is the first difficulty of this kind that I have had occasion to check up."[51] In the follow-up letter, George Nakano literally drew a picture of the house and listed the items. He asked Morrish to safeguard the wedding silverware and to send a "pinkish colored comforter, a black woman's coat (in the closet) and some shoes that we would like to have sent up to us if possible. In fact all the clothes in the closet would be quite helpful to us out here as we could use them." He requested that Morrish buy some mothballs and spread them around the rooms. Nakano had boarded up the back windows but not the front because he had been worried about the appearance, but he told Morrish to go ahead with the front windows if he thought it would help and that the key was in the safe-deposit box. Nakano also made it very clear in his letter that his wife was upset about the break-in and that:

> we should have taken greater precautions of security for them but at the time of evacuation our activities were so jumbled and curtailed by the thoughts of impending evacuation that we didn't do many things that we should have done to protect our property. I realize that vandalism will flare up in times like these but I hope the damage done is at a minimum. Will you investigate the circumstances and as you suggest go into the house and check over some of the items of value that are in the house?[52]

The storage and care of personal automobiles became a common point of discussion in the letters between Morrish and the interned. The government wanted people to try to dispose of their cars first or sell them to the military. There were provisions made to store them in government-leased warehouses or in storage lots. The government would also have personal automobiles shipped to the relocation camps. But many people working with Morrish decided either to store their cars at their own property or, if they sold their cars at all, to sell them privately.

Morrish generally initiated the discussion on whether or not the internees should sell their cars. When all of the letters were examined, it seemed as if there was one period during the war when local people were particularly interested in buying these stored cars—between October and December 1943. While this period is not particularly clear, one could venture a guess that both resources and car parts were getting scarce two years into the war.[53] This also may be indicative that many, including Morrish himself, were realizing the internment would not be ending anytime soon. Morrish wrote quite a few letters to the internees to ask if they were willing to sell their cars since people were coming into the bank asking about buying them.

For example, on August 27, 1943, Morrish wrote to K. Yamada: "Regarding your automobile, I believe that it would be a good idea to dispose of it. Most of the boys have disposed of their cars at fairly good advantage. It is hard to store a car for an indefinite period and it does not improve [sic] by not using it, so if you wish to sell, I shall be glad to get a price for you."[54] Then on October 5, 1943, Morrish wrote to Kiniuye Kashima (at Topaz), asking if she would like to sell her car: "Would you be interested in selling your car, if so at what price. Harry Lee is interested in getting a car and if you would like to dispose of it, let me know and I will be glad to take it up with him."[55] Harry Lee was the current tenant at the Kashima ranch. Kashima did not respond to this particular letter, and three weeks later Morrish wrote again, asking about selling two cars: "Recently I have had several inquiries for second-hand cars. If you wish to sell your Chevrolet, put a price on it and let me know, also I think your nephew owns an old Dodge coupe that may be salable. If he has you might speak to him and advise me."[56] Kashima responded that she did not want to sell the car, and that his cousin asked Harry Lee to sell his own car.[57] Then on December 8, 1943, Morrish wrote to T. Kashima (who was living at the same address as K. Kashima), stating that although he recently wrote saying he did not want to sell his car, Morrish had a firm offer of $1,000 if he wanted to rethink selling it.[58] K. Kashima (the son of T. Kashima) wrote back on December 26, 1943, saying that his father now wanted to sell the car, but if Morrish could get more, that would be great.[59] On December 31, 1943, Morrish wrote back to T. Kashima to tell him that he was sending along the pink slip for the car for him to sign, that he had sold the car for $1,050, and that he needed to know which account he wanted the money deposited into.[60]

Morrish also wrote to Mr. Nakano on November 18, 1943, telling him there had been inquires for a car and that Frank Isidoro was interested.[61] He wrote to a few internees (Nakano and T. Kitayama) on December 7, 1943, saying again that several people had been calling about buying cars and in particular, he wrote to Nakano to say that he should think about selling the car since "they are not improving any by storage and the rubber is deteriorating."[62] The next day, on December 8, 1943, Morrish wrote to several other internees (Mayeda, Mori, Adachi, and T. Kashima [see above], all interned at Topaz), also asking whether or not they would like to sell their cars.[63] In the letter to K. H. Mori (in c/o T. Yatabe), Morrish wrote:

I have had two or three inquiries for a car and if your car is still here and if you wish to sell, advise me and I will be very glad to endeavor to dispose of it for you. If interested, give me a price when you reply. Several of the folks

have recently sold cars to good advantage. Continual storage and non use
of the car is not helping it any, so will you please advice [sic] me right soon
about this.[64]

Unfortunately, we don't know if Mrs. Mori kept or sold her car since it wasn't
mentioned again in the remaining letters. His letter to Adachi was similar:

There are several people interested in buying cars and if your car has not
been sold, it might be a good plan to dispose of it. If you wish to sell, let me
know the price and I will see what I can do.[65]

It is also possible that Morrish wrote to M. Enomoto about selling his car
about the same time since Enomoto wrote to Morrish on December 14,
1943, stating that he had sold his cars before the evacuation.[66] It was only
in February 1944 that Nakano responded about selling his car. He said he
had two cars (a 1940 DeLuxe Sedan and a Dodge 1938 half-ton pickup)
he would be willing to sell.[67] It isn't known if Nakano ultimately sold his
vehicles or kept them.

At least one internee took more drastic measures to make sure that the
cars would be safe while they were interned. As mentioned above, Morrish
wrote to K. Yamada in August 1943 about the possibility of selling her car.
She wrote back to Morrish on September 6, 1943, telling him that they
had taken the car apart and hid the various parts:

We wish to sell our automobile and radio, too. The automobile parts are
quite well taken apart so it may be a difficult task to dispose of it at a advan-
tageous price. (The tires are hidden in the foundation of our house, the
distributor points in the inside car compartment and we have the keys!).[68]

Morrish soon wrote back to say that if he could put the car back together,
he should be able to sell it and he wanted to know how much she wanted
for it.[69] On October 5, 1943, K. Yamada wrote, "The wheels to the car are
stored in the back room of the barn right behind the door. The points are
in the car compartment." In a handwritten note she said that she was sending the keys and the pink slip for the car.[70] She wanted $500 for it, and it
ultimately sold to a car dealership for $525.

The automobiles mentioned above were just one of the many types of
property that the interned had to care for and oversee while being detained
away from home. But the link between this particular kind of property
and the state of being interned goes beyond mere ownership. Automobiles
were a symbol of financial achievement and of independence—both key
pieces of autonomy that were taken from these citizens and residents when

they were interned. And the selling of a car may certainly signify a degree of surrender in terms of how long the internment might last—both a sign of needing cash and a sign of an uncertain future.

While structures were indeed put in place to the handle the issues of personal property at the time of the internment, and it seems that they were relatively well advertised, it does not appear that they were widely taken advantage of. In examining the day-to-day functioning of citizen internees, and how an architecture was established to help the internment function, this disconnect is a provocative mystery. What stopped internees from applying for this assistance? Why did Morrish not point them in this direction? What does this signify about the internment of these citizens and resident aliens, and the structures created to facilitate this formidable task of relocation? Many clues in the collection support the idea that many assumed, or at least hoped, that the actual evacuation and relocation would be over quickly, if it happened at all. A quick boarding up of the house, family valuables left behind, and a quick affidavit giving your banker power of attorney perhaps show these early programs were not taken advantage of because those being evacuated could not quite believe it needed to come to that. They held on to normalcy as long as they could, with the help of Morrish.

It is also interesting to explore the idea that these protective property policies —whether provided by the WRA, the Western Defense Council, or the Federal Reserve Bank—functioned in order to give that same feeling of normalcy, to allow people to hold on to their property or personal wealth and thus keep the internment "citizen-friendly." While most of the Morrish Collection internees did not take advantage of the WRA programs, there are some exceptions. Tsukagawa had been renting (or probably his mother was renting) from a Mr. Mockmorton when the evacuation took place, and he was clearly forced to leave early. He had made improvements to the rented property and had left some of his own belongings behind, probably in haste to follow the evacuation order. In early 1943, Tsukagawa had been in contact with the WRA property control director in San Francisco, whom he wanted to start an investigation into the trouble he was having with the rental agreement and the property improvements he had made. He requested that a lawyer be involved and asked that the "WRA property control office . . . be contacted. They are supposed to represent me in matters of this kind."[71]

In a letter dated June 7, 1943, Tsukagawa wrote to Morrish and told him that when he was in Tanforan he had the Federal Reserve Bank write to Monkton about the problems with the lease, but he told Morrish that they could not come to an agreement. The Federal Reserve Bank had been put under the control of the Wartime Civil Control Authority to help the internees with their businesses and property. Tsukagawa then asked Morrish to write to the WRA property control manager.[72] Clearly, Tsukagawa knew of the program and made use of it to help him with the rental issues. One thing to note about Tsukagawa (and it is a bit different from many of the Morrish letters) is that he had not given power of attorney to Morrish. The experience of Tsukagawa and his interactions with the WRA property director/agent fit with the description of the *Final Report* in terms of the problems that internees could have when they were not free to act on their own.

Tsukagawa did not mention where he heard about this program, but we do know (from the *Tanforan Totalizer*) that in June 1942 the internees at Tanforan heard from Edwin Ferguson, the regional attorney for the WRA:

> At a packed Town Hall last Wednesday night, Edwin Ferguson, regional attorney for the War Relocation Authority, explained the functions of the WRA and answered questions on relocation areas. He painted no rosy picture of the relocation areas, but he indicated their potentiality for development. "Each relocation area," he stated, "will be about what you choose to make it. The standards of living, the quality of community life, your own happiness will largely depend on your own initiative, resourcefulness and skill." He pointed out that the task would not be easy, but added, "I am confident that you possess the qualities that will make you come out on top." Ferguson announced 3 new relocation zones, in southeast Colorado, in southeast Arkansas and in Wyoming. All evacuees will be out of the Military Areas 1 and 2 before fall, he reported. Moderator was Henry Tani. Ferguson was accompanied by his assistant, R.R. Throckmorton.[73]

K. Yamana also knew of the Evacuee Property Officer and what he could do for the internees. She was having a number of difficulties with the rental of her house. After Morrish let her know that he was having difficulties collecting the rent, she said she hoped he would not, but "if you should, would you advise writing to the San Francisco Evacuee Property Officer and have a field man sent there and see what he could do?"[74] In the letters by Morrish and K. Yamada there is no further discussion of using the Evacuee Property Officer to settle this problem. In fact, Morrish stated that the new land tenant would be the one now responsible for kicking out the illegal tenants from her house.[75] Like Tsukagawa, it isn't clear in the letters how K. Yamada knew about the Evacuee Property Officer. More than likely she heard about the program when she was held at Tanforan or through the WRA officials at Topaz.

After the end of the war, the WRA itself recognized that it did not do enough to protect the physical assets of the internees at the beginning of the relocation. The WRA's document titled *The Wartime Handling of Evacuee Property* made this explicitly clear at the beginning. It stated that loss of property was "inevitable" because of six factors: 1) people on the West Coast were opposed to giving any rights to this hated minority; 2) the U.S. government waited too long to set up procedures to protect the property of the internees; 3) when the procedures were finally set up, they were inadequate to deal with unresolved issues; 4) the protection of property, at least in the beginning of the internment, was the responsibility of a number of different agencies and was finally taken over by the WRA, but again, this was almost too late; 5) local and state officials did not really care about vandalism, nor did they follow up on reports of property destruction, thus allowing the perpetrators to run free; and 6) the Western Defense Command took no responsibility for protecting the internee's property even though it was clearly stated that this would be one of its responsibilities.[76] The intention behind these property-related services was indeed to "behave as a Democracy should," as was consistently the spoken goal of the WRA. There were shortcomings in these services to be sure. But there is something wildly important about observing the existence of these programs at all. Here is where we see the structure of removal and detainment, for those who are forced to leave behind their world but are not entering a prison system or leaving the country unceremoniously—they were "relocated," for a time, and the protection of *some* basic rights was woven into the process. It was enough to allow the internment to function, and to allow some semblance of citizenship rights within the lives of the interned. But ultimately, the process reeked of a humiliation that the architects could not ameliorate.

Notes

1. Roger Daniels, *The Decision to Relocate the Japanese Americans* (Philadelphia, PA: J. B. Lippincott Co., 1975), 31.

2. Ibid., 31.

3. J. L. DeWitt, *Final Report: Japanese Evacuation from the West Coast, 1942* (Washington, D.C.: United States Government Printing Office, 1943), vii.

4. "Article written by Walter Lippmann for the Washington Post that calls on the U.S. government to take action against persons of Japanese ancestry, aliens and citizens alike, in military zones, Feb. 12, 1942.," *Densho Encyclopedia* http://encyclopedia.densho.org/sources/en-denshopd-i67-00001-1/, accessed February 2, 2016. A copy can also be found in the *Congressional Record*, February 17, 1942, 568–569.

5. DeWitt, *Final Report*, 34.

6. Ellen Eisenberg, "'As Truly American as Your Son': Voicing Opposition to Internment in Three West Coast Cities," *Oregon Historical Quarterly* 104, no. 4 (Winter 2003): 542.

7. Daniels, *The Decision to Relocate the Japanese Americans*, 48.

8. Executive Order 9066, http://www.ourdocuments.gov/doc.php?doc=74 &page=transcript, accessed April 9, 2016.

9. *Impounded People: Japanese Americans in the Relocation Centers* (n.p.: United States Department of the Interior, WRA, 1946), 14.

10. Ibid., 14.

11. DeWitt, *Final Report*, 8. See also p. 24 for the letter from Assistant Attorney General Rowe to General Dewitt.

12. *Impounded People*, 17.

13. Eisenberg, "'As Truly American as Your Son,'" 543.

14. *Impounded People*, 20.

15. DeWitt, *Final Report*, 9–17.

16. Ibid., Letter from Henry Stimson, Secretary of War, to Lt. General DeWitt, March 2, 1942, 31–32.

17. *Impounded* People, 35.

18. Ibid., 37.

19. DeWitt, *Final Report*, 104.

20. Ibid., 43.

21. War Relocation Authority, *The Wartime Handling of Evacuee Property*, vol. II (Washington, D.C.: U.S. Government Printing Office, n.d.; reprinted in New York, NY: AMS Press, 1975), 13.

22. DeWitt, *Final Report*, 29.

23. Ibid., 127.

24. Ibid., ix, section 6.

25. Ibid.

26. *The Wartime Handling of Evacuee Property*, vol. II, 12.

27. Ibid., 19.

28. Ibid., 21.

29. Ibid., 24.

30. Franklin D. Roosevelt, "Executive Order 9095 Establishing the Office of Alien Property Custodian," March 11, 1942, in Gerhard Peters and John T. Woolley, *The American Presidency Project* http://www.presidency.ucsb.edu/ws/?pid=16232, accessed August 1, 2015.

31. DeWitt, *Final Report*, 129.

32. Ibid., 130.

33. 01_Adachi_036, September 10, 1942, Morrish Collection.

34. The *Tanforan Totalizer* 1, no. 3 (May 30, 1942).

35. 16_Nakata_006, Morrish Collection.

36. Franklin D. Roosevelt, "Executive Order 9102 Establishing the War Relocation Authority," March 18, 1942, in Gerhard Peters and John T. Woolley, *The American Presidency Project* http://www.presidency.ucsb.edu/ws/?pid=16239, accessed August 1, 2015.

37. DeWitt, *Final Report*, 134.

38. Ibid., 129.

39. Ibid., 132.

40. Ibid., 134.

41. *Topaz Times*, pre-issue no. 8 (October 17, 1942).

42. *The Wartime Handling of Evacuee Property*, vol. II, 46.

43. *Topaz Times* 1, no. 18 (November 19, 1942).

44. 9_Matsuyama_001, Morrish Collection.

45. 18_Rikimaru_007, Morrish Collection.

46. 24_Yamada_029, April 17, 1943, Morrish Collection.

47. 24_Yamada_30, 31, and 32, Morrish Collection.

48. 24_Yamada _054, Dec. 6, 1943, Morrish Collection.

49. 11_Mori_003, May 4, 1942, Morrish Collection.

50. 11_Mori_004, Morrish Collection.

51. 14_Nakano_021, Morrish Collection.

52. 14_Nakano_022, Nov. 25, 1943, Morrish Collection.

53. As noted by Mike Burton in an email message to Kevin Kaatz, January 19, 2016.

54. 24_Yamada_040, Morrish Collection.

55. 05_Kashima_027, Morrish Collection.

56. 05_Kashima_028, Oct. 27, 1943, Morrish Collection.

57. 05_Kashima_029, Nov. 1, 1943, Morrish Collection.

58. 05_Kashima_031, Morrish Collection.

59. 05_Kashima_032, Morrish Collection.

60. 05_Kashima_033, Morrish Collection.

61. 14_Nakano_020, Morrish Collection.

62. 14_Nakano_023, Morrish Collection. See also 08_Kitayama_018, Morrish Collection.

63. 10_Mayeda_036, Dec. 8, 1943; 11_Mori_009, Dec. 8, 1943; 01_Adachi_072, Dec. 8, 1943; and 05_Kashima_031—all Morrish Collection.

64. 11_Mori_009, Dec. 8, 1943, Morrish Collection.

65. 01_Adachi_072, Dec. 8, 1943, Morrish Collection.

66. 02_Enomoto_009, Morrish Collection.

67. 15_Nakano_014, Feb. 18, 1944, Morrish Collection.

68. 24_Yamada_041, Morrish Collection.

69. 24_Yamada_042, Sept. 10, 1943, Morrish Collection.

70. 24_Yamada_048, Oct. 5, 1943, Morrish Collection.

71. 21_Tsukagawa_001, May 7, 1943, Morrish Collection.

72. 21_Tsukagawa_003, June 7, 1943, Morrish Collection.

73. *Tanforan Totalizer* 1, no. 5 (June 13, 1942): 3.

74. 24_Yamada_065, Feb. 20, 1944, Morrish Collection.

75. 24_Yamada_071, March 17, 1944, Morrish Collection.

76. *The Wartime Handling of Evacuee Property*, 3–4.

CHAPTER FOUR

The Move to Tanforan

The best-laid plans of conducting the internment "as a democracy should" began to go astray in the first phase of the internment, in early 1942. In the minds of military leadership, time was of the essence in safeguarding Americans against the potential threat of espionage. The menacing murmurs of an antsy public with a deep history of anti-Asian sentiment also propelled the process forward, under the reasoning of "protecting" those of Japanese descent. The rushed timing of this early phase demonstrated that the guarantees of citizenship were flexible at best in a nation at war, and in a nation in fear. The monstrous question faced by the architects of the internment was where to send the evacuees—especially in a short time frame. Thus, the accommodations of phase one were not particularly ideal.

Many of the writers found in the Morrish Collection were housed temporarily at the Tanforan Racetrack in San Bruno, California, at the beginning of the relocation process. There were 7,816 people there, with 891 of the residents coming from San Mateo County.[1] Tanforan's racetrack facilities contained horse-stalls, which became home to many of the internees who were kept there until they were removed to more permanent camps. The other assembly centers were also placed in racetracks or fairgrounds, mostly because of their size and because they were already built. The Tanforan Assembly Center was opened in late April and closed in September 1942, with the last people leaving on October 13, 1942.[2]

The planning for these assembly centers and relocations centers had to be done quickly. On March 28, General DeWitt informed Rex L. Nicholson, the Regional Works Projects Administration (WPA) Supervisor, that the WPA was now in charge of "direction and management of such assembly points and reception centers as may be assigned in connection with the program of evacuation of German, Italian, and Japanese enemy aliens and persons of Japanese ancestry from restricted zones. . . ."[3] The WPA, originally created in 1935 to generate employment in public works throughout the country during the Great Depression, took its job of building/managing the assembly centers and relocation centers seriously. During most of 1942 it spent more than any other government agency working on the evacuation—nearly $4.5 million.[4]

The initial plan of execution called for evacuees to be sent to the assembly centers within six or seven days, with day one being the posting of the Exclusion Order within a specified area, and day six or seven being when the internees would be moved out.[5] There were exceptions, especially when the registration process (days two and three) involved more than 1,500 people. Another exception was made in the case of an individual or family who could not settle their financial affairs in this short period. But in general, this was all that they were given—one week to register their families, make plans, and move. Thus, they had very little time to prepare for being "evacuated." As mentioned above, it was only in late March 1942 when plans were made to actually build or find the assembly centers (temporary housing areas) while the actual internment camps were being built. The U.S. government had made the decision earlier that it needed to house the internees in areas close to where they had been living until permanent camps could be established. As a result, many of these temporary holding camps were built on fairgrounds or racetracks, close to electricity and water.[6] The government had established a few goals for the evacuation. Of importance to the Morrish Collection, one of the goals was not to split up families. Another was not to split up communities. Finally, the evacuation should be accomplished with the minimum amount of financial loss to those being moved.[7] In San Francisco in the dock areas, the Exclusion Order was posted on April 1, 1942, and those of Japanese descent (Americans and aliens) were given until April 7 to get out. Other exclusion orders were issued for different geographical areas, but it was clear to people of Japanese ancestry that they were about to be physically moved from their residences.[8]

A month later, on May 3, 1942, the Western Defense Command and Fourth Army Wartime Civil Control Administration, located in the Presidio, issued Civilian Exclusion Order 35 that was directed at "all persons of

Japanese ancestry" living in San Mateo County. The wording for this particular exclusion order was similar to that of other orders. It stated that "all persons of Japanese ancestry, both alien and non-alien, will be evacuated from the above area by 12 o'clock noon, P.W.T., Saturday May 9th," and that the Civil Control Station (which in this case was the Masonic Temple Building in San Mateo, California) would help the evacuees in a number of different ways. It read:

1. Give advice and instructions on the evacuation.
2. Provide services with respect to the management, leasing, sale, storage or other disposition of most kinds of property, such as real estate, business and professional equipment, household goods, boats, automobiles and livestock.
3. Provide temporary residence elsewhere for all Japanese in family groups.
4. Transport persons and a limited amount of clothing and equipment to their new residence.[9]

One person from each family was to show up on Monday, May 4, or Tuesday, May 5, to receive their instructions. The order also stated what evacuees could and could not take with them to the assembly center. For example, each family needed to take bedding (but no mattresses), cutlery, and toiletry articles with them. All materials needed to be crated and labeled. It also stated that they were not allowed to bring any pets and that "no personal items and no household goods will be shipped to the Assembly Center." It did say that the government (at the owners' risk) would store large household items like washers and other crated household items. Finally, the order said that it would provide transportation to the assembly center, or groups of evacuees could travel in their own vehicles, but they needed to be supervised. It was signed by General DeWitt.

Once those people represented in the Morrish Collection (and the rest of the population of Japanese ancestry from San Mateo County) actually presented themselves to the authorities, they were shunted through the control station. It was here that the evacuees were told about the process, were asked about their businesses, properties, and personal affairs, and were offered services through the Farm Security Administration (FSA) and the Federal Reserve Bank (in the case of personal affairs and the storage of personal property). Money was given to them if they needed help with purchasing things they would need at the assembly centers, with the crating of their personal goods, and with housing until they were moved. They were examined for disease and general health and given a tag telling them when to show up for the trip to the assembly center.[10] One internee found in the Morrish Collection, Tomiko Nakano Honda, said that the bus to take them to Tanforan picked them up at Horgan Ranch, where many had rented land to grow their flowers. They could take only what they could carry, and that included bedding and utensils. There was an armed guard also stationed outside the bus.[11]

Considering they had less than a week to pack up and leave, it is no surprise that a few of the people in the Morrish Collection talk about how disorganized it all was for them. For example, Morrish had sent a letter to George Nakano asking for the keys to his safety-deposit box. Nakano could not find them and wasn't quite sure where they were. He wrote:

> In regard to my safe deposit box keys, I have looked in every conceivable places [sic] to find them but with no success. Ever since evacuation I have had no occasion to open the box and I can't think of any place where I have left it. Perhaps in my haste of leaving home I might have left it in my desk. That is the only logical conclusion I can draw.[12]

In the end, Nakano could not find his key, so Morrish had to have the lock on the security box drilled to get access. Another evacuee, K. Yamada, had Morrish sell her car, and when it was sold it was discovered that the radio had been removed. She told Morrish that it might have been in one storeroom, but Morrish could not find it. She then wrote:

> . . . the car radio might have been left in the room some place if not with the cloth. He [her husband] was in a hurry when he bought [sic] those things back and so it could be stored in the back room. Would you please look in there.

Incidentally, Morrish wrote in his own hand on this letter, "Could never find radio."[13]

The final example of the confusion is the Honda family. Masaji Honda sent a letter to Morrish, dated March 31, 1942. He wrote about the rush and confusion that occurred as they were leaving. This family had left before the exclusion orders were issued and were probably taking advantage of the invitation that the government sent out to get people to leave before they were forced to. Honda wrote: "I am awfully sorry that I had to leave in such a hurry that I didn't have time to explain everything." He then told Morrish that he left a caretaker for his house (a Mr. Hernandez) but wasn't able to do the same for his nursery:

> I was in such a hurry that I didn't have time to think right that I just left everything up to Mr. Hernandez. I hope you can smooth thing [sic] out as I didn't know what I was doing all the time. I will write again in few day [sic] just as

soon as I settle down. Thanking you for all the thing you done for me [sic] and I hope you can help me out in this situation. Sincerely yours, Masaji Honda. [In a postscript]: I am very sorry that I can't write so you can understand better but I am so worry about the whole thing I can even think right [sic].[14]

While those represented in the Morrish Collection did not always discuss their feelings and actions in the time after the exclusion order was issued and when they were taken to Tanforan, it is clear that it was a confusing period for those going through the process of removal. There are, however, other sources that can help us piece together what happened to them at Tanforan. Like many of the assembly camps, Tanforan's internees published their own newspaper, the *Tanforan Totalizer*. These newspapers are incredibly important for understanding what happened in Tanforan (and the other camps, since almost all had their own newspapers). *The WRA Relocation Guide* stated, "Like all other newspapers in the United States, relocation center papers will enjoy full freedom of editorial expression. The Project Director, however, may suspend publication of the newspaper at any time if this seems necessary in the interest of public peace and community security."[15] The editors of the *Totalizer* had a different understanding of what the WRA had written—the newspapers were actually censored, so as a historical source, great care must be taken when using what the assembly center newspapers printed.[16] Some internees certainly knew the paper was being censored. Bennie Nobori drew a cartoon for the last page of some of the issues of the *Topaz Times*. In the very first issue of the paper, he drew a cartoon of a small boy talking to someone in the military. In the cartoon, a newspaper editor tells him to "write it up!" and he writes eight pages. The last part of the cartoon shows the little boy looking at the *Topaz Times* and seeing his article reduced (presumably by the editor) to a few lines.[17] The newspapers were used primarily to "teach" the internees about American life, which was ironic, since most were American citizens, and to act as the mouthpiece of the Wartime Civil Control Association (WCCA). Historian Mizuno discussed the main forms of censorship that occurred with these newspapers:

1. The printing in Japanese of the news sheet or bulletin is prohibited.
2. The Public Relations representative of [each camp] is to edit and approve all copy of a proposed assembly center newspaper prior to its being mimeographed and released. This approved copy will be turned over to the center manager.
3. A check by the center manager, or his representative, is to be made of approved copy with the stencil, prior to mimeographing. Final check by the

assembly center manager, or his representative, is to be made of the approved copy and the issue prior to its distribution.[18]

Despite the censorship, the newspapers are still a vital source of information about what went on in the various assembly centers, particularly Tanforan. The very first issue of the *Tanforan Totalizer* was published on May 15, 1942, not too long after the center was opened. The headlines of the first paper read, "Assembly Center Head Greets Residents." The assembly manager was William R. Lawson, and his statement called the internees "residents" and made it clear to them that he wanted the assembly center to be self-governed and that it was the responsibility of each resident to do his or her part. As pointed out, the assembly centers (and the camps themselves) were designed to have the internees do a large part of the work to keep them going. The very first article in volume one of the newspaper states: "The Tanforan Totalizer is intended to be this center's paper in every way. Its interests are those of all the residents here"; and the article continues to say that it will not be an arm of any political party.

Although the *Totalizer* gave a rosy picture of Tanforan, conditions were bad when the first evacuees began to arrive, chiefly because the site was not fully prepared. The size of the "apartments" (really horse stalls) at Tanforan and the other assembly centers was 10 feet by 20 feet for a couple; these could be larger if the family size was larger. In an undated letter from Tanforan, George Nakano wrote about the conditions he found soon after arriving:

> Dear Mister Morrish: Arrived here in this center last Friday and we are settled comfortably in our new abode. The situation here is very well organized, a certain credit to the democratic American way of doing things. The facilities as yet are not quite complete but after a few weeks of work and construction, everything will be clean and well organized. I wish to take this opportunity to thank you for all the trouble you have gone to to take care of us. I know our property and our business will be taken care [of] in the best of fashion. If anything come [sic] up please do not hesitate to consult me and even visiting hours are established between 8 and 4 daily.[19]

Part of the "not quite complete" mentioned by Nakano was that functioning toilets were found only in the grandstand area, and the internees, for the most part, were in charge of cooking their own food, even though many of them had no experience cooking for large crowds.[20] The food itself, at least in the beginning, was limited in terms of variety and was not enough to feed all of the internees. Historian Sandra C. Taylor noted that "for the first ten days they were served lima beans, cold tea, canned food, stale bread, and sometimes Jell-O."[21] The budget set aside for feeding the internees was 50 cents/day, which was the same as that for soldiers. Some of the internees were put to work in the kitchens. Michiko Nishida Nakata wrote to Morrish in August 1942, telling him, "We are getting along as best we can. . . . My husband is still cook at our mess hall—he claims he's getting his practice for the hot climate we're going to, very soon."[22] The "apartments," according to K. Nakano, contained unfinished walls, and the ceilings were seven feet tall but open to other apartments. His brother Jim Nakano said that there were cobwebs all over and horse manure still under the floors, which could be lifted up.[23]

The unfinished conditions and bad food at Tanforan mirrored those of the other assembly centers. As Smith noted, Ted Nakashima published an article in the *New Republic* in which he complained bitterly about what he experienced in Portland's Livestock Exposition, the assembly center for that area:

> The food and sanitation problems are the worst. We have had absolutely no fresh meat, vegetables or butter since we came here. Mealtime queues extend for blocks; standing in rain-swept line, feet in the mud, waiting for the scant portions of canned wieners and boiled potatoes, hash for breakfast or canned wieners and beans for dinner. Milk only for the kids. Coffee or tea dosed with saltpeter or stale bread are the adults' staples. Dirty, unwiped dishes, greasy silver, a starchy diet, no butter, no milk, bawling kids, mud, wet mud that stinks when it dries, no vegetables—a sad thing for people who raised them in such abundance. . . . Can this be the same America we left a few weeks ago?[24]

There must have been some grumbling in Tanforan as well since the *Tanforan Totalizer* stated that John E. Fogarty, the chief steward of the commissary, had a meeting with the house managers and the mess hall managers to assure them that he was doing everything he could to stabilize the food supply. He told them that the food was ordered a month in advance and that he had to ask for emergency rations, but that "has not been always possible." The article also stated that people were appreciative of the workers and that many had donated their own household goods to the kitchens.[25] By the end of June 1942 it appears that the food problems at Tanforan had stabilized. The *Tanforan Totalizer* printed the weekly food ration.[26] It listed (among other things): 6,000 pounds of cabbages, 4,000 pounds of carrots, 160 sacks of potatoes, 100 pounds of bananas, 22,000 pounds of beef carcasses, and 18,900 pounds of rice. There were special diets for infants and those with medical issues. At this point, almost 8,000 people were being held at Tanforan.

"Can this be the same America we left a few weeks ago?"—a grim question revealing how quickly the promises of freedom can be taken away. Indeed, Tanforan has been described as a "prison city,"[27] and the visitation policy highlights this description. The internees were not allowed to leave, nor were visitors allowed to just show up and go in. As Yoshio "Yo" Kasia wrote in his autobiography, visitors were allowed as long as they received a pass to enter and a pass to leave.[28] Morrish was one such visitor. Many times in his letters he mentioned going to Tanforan to see the various internees. For example, he wrote to S. Adachi:

> It is possible that I will be able to get up tomorrow as I wanted to see Ham Honda. I also understand that some of the folks may be moved and I would like to see them before they leave; so should you see any of the Redwood City folks thereabouts in the morning, will you please ask them to be some-where around the Pavilion around ten thirty.[29]

Two days later, Morrish sent a letter to Nakata to tell her that he had been at Tanforan the day before but had missed her because the letter he sent telling them he would be there had never arrived. He wanted to say goodbye "and wish you every success in your new location."[30] He did not mention in his letters, however, that all visitors had to be searched by the guards before being allowed into a "special meeting room at the grand-stand to chat across tables with internees. Armed guards patrolled the area the whole time."[31] It is possible that he felt there was no reason to burden these people with his own problems. Morrish certainly was not the only visitor to the internees. The *Tanforan Totalizer* mentioned that between May 14 and May 24, 1942, the internees had 1,135 individual visitors, plus 654 people who came in groups. On the Sunday of Morrish's visit there were nearly 400 people who came to visit. There were so many that it was necessary to remind the internees of the rules for visiting: those who were expecting visitors should be in the grandstand to wait. The *Tanforan Totalizer* stated that this was necessary since "only a limited number of messenger boys are available."[32]

Another indication of the center's prison-like quality is that people were literally *counted* twice a day. There was a curfew, even though it was rarely kept. The assembly center was also searched. The *Tanforan Totalizer* stated that in June 1942, the barracks were fully searched because baggage that internees had brought in with them when they first arrived had not been examined. The newspaper reported that dangerous tools and Japanese lit-erature were taken away and would be disposed of by Frank E. Davis, the center manager. Religious texts were not confiscated.[33] This issue of the paper also reported that all incoming packages would now be inspected and that the director of education, Frank E. Kilpatrick, had announced in a packed town hall that community-wide meetings must be conducted in English. The newspaper also reported that all signs in Japanese had been removed from the assembly center "pursuant to Army orders."[34]

Very few of the people in the Morrish Collection complained of the conditions in Tanforan, despite what was happening to them. This isn't to say that they were happy—far from it. The same S. Adachi wrote to Morrish on July 7, 1942: "We at Tanforan are fine and looking forward for brighter days. Deep in our hearts there is that deep appreciation for everything that you have been doing for us, but very hard to find the right words to express this thought."[35] She also wrote to Morrish toward the end of her stay at Tanforan that the WRA officials would not allow her to leave camp temporarily to obtain some financial records for the flower grower society from her safe. These papers would have allowed her to organize payment to her fellow growers. So she had to ask Morrish to help her with these records.[36] Another internee, T. Kitayama, wrote to Morrish at the end of August: "The life in here is just fine and hoping that it will be just as nice over there too. At the same time, I'm hoping that this whole thing will be over real soon so that we may all be back to normal life again."[37]

Although the Morrish letters do not detail harsh living conditions in Tanforan, there is a section of the *Tanforan Totalizer* titled "Out of the Horse's Mouth," no doubt referring to the fact that the apartments at the center were really horse stalls. It began:

This stall is reserved for the incidental whinnyings [sic] of the paper's staff. But what comes out of the horse's mouth will depend a good deal on what goes into its ear. So, residents, it is your column as well as ours—give us the provender[38] and we will neigh to your taste. . . . HEY, CAREFUL THERE! When putting up those shelves, closets, etc., make sure of two things: (1) that your neighbor is not blissfully leaning against the wall on the other side, and (2) that nail length and wall thickness are proportionate. We know of one person who almost got an involuntary inoculation in the back from the energetic party in the next stall.

The column right beside this was titled "Home Sweet Stall" and reported: "Those still far from an earthly paradise, Tanforan has come a long way since the first week when residents were whinnying to one another, 'Is it my imagination, or is my face really getting longer?' With the addition of curtains and hand-made furniture, most apartments have lost the appearance of horse stalls." The article further stated that many of the internees had ordered things like curtains and chairs from the outside to spruce things up.[39] And at the end of July the evacuees produced their own play titled "Horse's Stall and That Ain't All," which also included an 11-piece orchestra. The play consisted of "a series of sketches on Center life, several audience gags and song numbers, offerings from the orchestra and the antics of the 'Cossacks.'"[40]

In the assembly centers and especially the camps, internees needed to make do with whatever they could find in terms of building materials. They employed cartoons to get the point across that stealing wood was not acceptable. One drawing showed a character running with a load of lumber on his back while being chased by someone with a club. The headline read, "You can't take lumber!" Wood was in short supply, and since the government did not supply wood for bookshelves, night stands, and so on, people regularly pilfered what they could find. Another section of the first printed newspaper stated that there were two Montgomery Ward catalogs for anyone who wanted to order things for their "apartments" instead of getting things from the neighboring cities.[41] By the end of May 1942, the *Tanforan Totalizer* noted that the post office at Tanforan had received 125 Montgomery Ward catalogs and was overflowing in packages, keeping nine people busy delivering all of the mail.[42]

By all accounts, the internees at Tanforan tried to make their lives as normal as possible. There were weddings and Boy Scout troop meetings; kids decorated the recreation hall with red, white, and blue; and babies were born. On August 5, 1942, Morrish wrote to George Nakano specifically to congratulation his family on the birth of their baby: "Congratulations to you and Mrs. Nakano on the new arrival. I heard of the big event and I am very glad for you both. Sincerely hope they are both getting along fine."[43] George Nakano wrote back to Morrish to thank him for the note about the baby and to say that they were all fine. Morrish then wrote to George Nakano again at the end of August to say that he was hoping to see him before he left (for Utah) and that he was happy to hear that the baby and his wife were still doing well.[44]

Some evacuees, not knowing how long they would be staying at Tanforan, even planted Victory Gardens.[45] These were gardens planted so that people could grow their own food, thus helping save the food grown on industrial farms for the war effort. Charles Kikuchi, an internee who was first transferred to Tanforan, mentioned such a garden in his diary.[46] Many times the *Tanforan Totalizer* mentioned these gardens.[47] There was even a large one (35 by 50 feet) put between part of the hospital and the maternity ward. It was planted with flowers that were to be sent to those in the hospital.[48]

As indicated before, the evacuees also had access to the mail. According to the *Final Report*, a post office was set up in every assembly center and camp. By all accounts the post office in Tanforan was a very busy place. In May 1942 (the month that Tanforan opened), the post office handled 6,000 pieces of mail, with equal numbers going in and being sent out. It was called "one of the busiest places in the center." It was also busy selling and cashing money orders.[49] By early June the evacuees in Tanforan were sending out more than $1,000 per day in money orders through the mail, presumably from their pre-war savings.[50]

The post office also reminded the evacuees that despite their incarcerated status, in some ways the life of a U.S. citizen carried on as usual: "The second installment of income taxes are due June 15, even if you are now at Tanforan." The paying of taxes was one of the main jobs that Morrish had during the war. He did this for almost every single family he dealt with, especially once they were removed to Topaz. It was clearly a concern to the evacuees since taxes had to be paid, even though they were removed from their properties and their sources of income. In the July 25, 1942, edition, the *Tanforan Totalizer* reported that Toby Ogawa, who was the chairman of the Tanforan Legislative Council, had written a letter to the Federal Reserve "in regard to taxes on evacuees' property," but unfortunately nothing else is mentioned about why he was writing.[51] A guess would be that the evacuees were stripped of the right to earn of living, at least temporarily, and yet they were still responsible for paying their taxes on time and, according to Morrish, were subject to fines if they were late. The WRA also told the evacuees that they must pay their taxes, both to the federal government and even to the states that they would be relocated to. Their income would include anything coming from outside the relocation centers as well as their wage earnings from within the centers.[52]

When the evacuation planning had first begun, one of the discussions centered on the idea that the internees should be employed to run the camps. There was a concern that they would cause trouble if they were left without anything to do. Since they would be employed by the WRA, they needed to be paid. The *Tanforan Totalizer*, published on May 23, 1942, stated that there were 7,796 people in Tanforan, and it listed all of the jobs and their pay based on whether they were categorized as "unskilled" ($8/month), "skilled" ($12/month), or "professional and technical" ($16/month). This was the pay for all of the assembly centers and would carry over into the relocation centers. Many people started to volunteer for the various paid positions, but at the end of May the *Tanforan Totalizer* reported that people would no longer need to apply for jobs in person. They would be put into jobs based on "their induction records according to USES ratings."[53] These United States Employment Service induction records were collected for each individual when they were transferred to Tanforan. The *Final Report* stated that while internees were not required to work, if they volunteered to do so, it was expected that they show up. Once they started working, they averaged nearly 48 hours per week.[54]

There were some issues that came up that only Morrish could help with. The evacuees had access to a bank in Tanforan and some of the amenities associated with banking. However, one internee, Noaye Mayeda, needed to write Morrish because she wasn't able to cash a check. Instead, she enclosed it in a letter to Morrish and asked him to deposit it for her. She wrote:

> Dear Mr. Morrish, Thank you for your recent letter. It was very nice of you to write to us. We received a check for $3.52 today and we can't cash it here. Could you deposit it in my brother's or my account for us? My brother drives a truck around all day and is never home so I had to sign it. Mr. Hassler cashed one for me that way too.[55]

The check must have been a personal check, and these could not be cashed at Tanforan.

It also appears that, even though the internees were being held against their will and under the care of the government, they still needed to pay their various insurances. Morrish wrote to many of them to remind them that they had to keep up with their premiums. The WRA was also concerned about who had insurance. The WCCA took a survey of life insurance policies with the intention of storing the information in San Francisco. The internees were assured that the information was not going to be used to cancel the policies but had been collected to preserve the policies. An article in the newspaper ended by saying that the information would be sent to the life insurance companies.[56] This is verified by Hajime Nakano, who wrote to Morrish on July 1:

> Dear Mr. Morrish, Local officials are requiring the information regarding the various insurance policies in force among the residents of Tanforan. I, in my haste in evacuating from Redwood City on May 8, misplaced the book I had copied down the policy numbers and I cannot find it here with me. Will you please let me know the following information regarding the various policies left with you:
>
> 1-policy number
> 2-Name of the company
> 3-policy holders name and the beneficiary

4-amount of premium due annually

5-maturity date.

Thanking you for the past favors rendered and kind regards.[57]

Morrish wrote the very next day to tell Nakano that he was sending off the requested information.

Another more serious problem for Mrs. Nakata was that her mother had some money deposited into the Yokohama Specie Bank and that the bank was "in the hands of the Superintendent of Banks as Conservator." She was having trouble getting her money out and had asked Morrish to look into this. On March 26, 1942 (before the Nakata family was taken to Tanforan), Morrish had received a letter from the State Banking Department of California to inform him that it was too early to contact people about the certificates of deposit. Morrish must also have written to the bank a bit earlier because George Knox (from the State Banking Department) continued: "We believe that sometime in the past we wrote you regarding a similar matter and suggest that you might save yourself a great deal of trouble by returning these instruments to the parties and telling them to await notice as to when to file claims."[58] The Yokohama Specie Bank was about the only bank available to Japanese immigrants, starting from 1911. It did not lend money but only took deposits.[59] Morrish tried again in February 1943 but decided to send the deposit certificates back to Topaz so that the family could hang on to them.[60] The next time (that we know of) that Morrish wrote to the bank was in August 1945, but it wasn't until August 1948 that the family finally received 80 percent of their deposited money.[61]

In addition to financial concerns, the internees also had to pay attention to the education of their children, despite being housed in a horse stall. The *Final Report* noted that since the assembly centers were designed to be temporary, schooling had not been part of the original plan. Once it became clear that many people would be held longer than anticipated, it was decided that temporary schools should be set up.[62] This happened very quickly at Tanforan—the school system was set up and started in two weeks.[63] Classes were then held, with attendance being voluntary.[64] According to the *Tanforan Totalizer,* school first met on Tuesday, May 26, for up to 300 children in first, second, and third grade. There were only four teachers for all of these students.[65] On June 6, 1942, it was reported that the fourth, fifth, and sixth grade classes were opened up with about 350 kids, with a staff of eight.[66] By the end of June 1942, there were nearly 700 high school students enrolled at Tanforan.[67] School helped not only the children but also the parents, especially considering the cramped living quarters at Tanforan. Nishida Nakata had written to Morrish on August

10, 1942, and told him that "her older boy (2 yrs 10 mt) has started nursery school, so we have some quiet from 9 to 11."[68] Clearly, she was relieved to get a bit of a break considering they were living in a horse stall with no internal room dividers.

Those at Tanforan also had to make their own toys and play structures for the kids. This was challenging because of the lack of wood, but the internees still managed to do it. The *Final Report*, making things sound better than they actually were, contained a picture of children playing on homemade wooden toys. Along with the photo was a caption that read: "A play scene at Tanforan (California) Assembly Center, with home-made rocking horses, teeter-totters, and swings. Playfields with rustic equipment made of scrap material and other installations stimulated recreational and outdoor play activities which many young evacuees had never before enjoyed."[69] Access to recreation was certainly a welcome part of the experience, although many studies have since commented on the impact of this suspended reality on family dynamics within the Japanese and Japanese American community.[70]

Once many of the Japanese Americans and Japanese aliens were at Tanforan, as early as June 1942 the WRA began looking for volunteers to leave the assembly center and work in the sugar beet fields in Oregon, Idaho, and Montana. The internees were told that they would be given paid passage (by the farms); paid in cash; and given food, housing, and medical care, all provided by the employers. As an added attraction, Thomas Holland, the WRA employment division head, told the internees, "There will be no federal troops or barbed wire confinement in work camps. The degree and type of protection will depend entirely on the locality."[71] The *Tanforan Totalizer* also ran reports on those who had left to work. It was reported in the June 13 edition that (only) 13 people had signed up to work in Idaho and that more were needed.[72] At the end of that month an unnamed beet worker wrote to the paper about the working conditions in Idaho:

> Families with employable members are welcome. Curfew from 8 pm to 6 am. And the sun sets at 9 pm! Movie in Rupert about a mile away. Beet thinning for two more weeks, followed by hoeing. After which come hay work and pea picking. Pay at end of job. Jobs seem to be plentiful and the consensus is that we'll be making money. All the officials here go out of their way to be kind and considerate. Lots of Nisei coming from interior assembly centers.[73]

If anything, the *Tanforan Totalizer* underestimated how many more people were actually needed to work in the beet fields. At the beginning of the war the entire country was put on sugar rationing. This was partly because the main areas where the United States obtained its sugar (the Philippines and Java) were under Japanese occupation. Another reason, related to the war, was that many of the available farm workers were leaving to fight in the war instead of staying on their farms or working for growers (if they were given the option: many of those who did not volunteer were drafted).[74] America's sugar beet farmers needed the labor, and they were (mostly) happy using the evacuees.

Phase one was indeed only temporary, and by summer the long-term "relocation camps" began to open, in various states of assembly. Many people held in Tanforan (including a large majority of those represented in the Morrish Collection) were sent to Topaz, Utah, including 722 from San Mateo County.[75] News of the move had been released to the evacuees in early June 1942, although they were not told of the details. All they were told was that there were three new relocation zones. This was reported in the newspaper:

> He [Edwin Ferguson, the regional attorney for the WRA] painted no rosy picture of the relocation areas, but he indicated their potentiality for development. "Each relocation area," he stated, "will be about what you choose to make it. The standards of living, the quality of community life, your own happiness will largely depend on your own initiative, resourcefulness and skill." He pointed out that the task would not be easy, but added, "I am confident that you possess the qualities that will make you come out on top." Ferguson announced 3 new relocation zones, in southeast Colorado, in southeast Arkansas and in Wyoming. All evacuees will be out of the Military Areas 1 and 2 before fall, he reported. Moderator was Henry Tani. Ferguson was accompanied by his assistant, R.R. Throckmorton.[76]

The majority of the evacuees at Tanforan were not sent to these three areas, but by the end of August, many were guessing that they were going to Utah. The September 12, 1942, issue of the *Tanforan Totalizer* was the final issue, and it reported that the main evacuation to Utah would start on the 15th, while a few days before that a contingent of 400 evacuees had left in order to prepare the camp for the rest of the evacuees. Michiko N. Nakata sent a postcard to Morrish from Tanforan regarding the first group to leave. She wrote:

> The first group of volunteers start tomorrow (Wed. Sept. 9) night for Delta, Utah—about 300 people—mostly young men, to get the place started. First group to move, families and all, is on the 15th. Our turn will probably come on the 20th. We move by mess halls—each mess halls [*sic*] contain from

600 to 700. That is my understanding. Of course, nothing is official except the volunteers and the date of the first move.[77]

The last issue of the *Tanforan Totalizer* also contained a long and detailed account of how the WRA wanted the evacuees to proceed to Utah. They were organized by mess hall numbers, and checking stations were set up to process their removal. Family units were to meet near the baggage-checking tables, and all hand luggage would be taken and inspected. They were then to be organized into groups for the train ride. When that was done, they were to pick up their inspected hand luggage and go directly to the trains. The paper also listed the "basic provisions" that the WRA would provide to the evacuees:

> Subsistence needs, food, shelter, medical care, elementary and high school education shall be provided by the WRA. Cash wage advances and clothing allowances, as distinct from subsistence provisioning, shall be treated as compensation for work and be paid only to those who work. In addition to the above provisions, relief care shall be given to needy individuals and families.

Many people from the Morrish Collection wrote to Morrish just as they were preparing to leave Tanforan. George Nakano, who had recently had a baby, wrote to Morrish on August 28, 1942:

> It seems that our days in Tanforan are numbered since visitors are not permitted after Sept. 11 and notices are out that we will be going on a trip to destinations unknown (probably Abraham, Utah). Our life here was quite nice considering that the nation is at war and I hope it will be the same.

He put a note at the bottom: "Our date of leaving here is between the dates of Sept. 15–30."[78] Just a few days after this, T. Kitayama wrote to Morrish:

> It seems that we will be moved to inland in the near future. The life in here is just fine and hoping that it will be just as nice over there too. At the same time, I'm hoping that this whole thing will be over real soon so that we may all be back to normal life again.[79]

Adachi, a flower grower from Redwood City, was one of the early evacuees to be moved to Utah, and she was able to send Morrish a letter on the very day she was leaving (September 15, 1942). She wrote:

> I am leaving for Utah tonight on a train that will leave between 5:00 and 8:00 o'clock. . . . Since this is my last letter from Tanforan, I want to thank

you for everything you have done for me. Because I am leaving California, I will have to depend so much more on you. Do take care of yourself and the best health always.[80]

N. Mayeda sent a similar letter to Morrish toward the end of the evacuation of Tanforan: "Just a few lines to say goodbye to you from Tanforan. We will leave on the 27th and that's pretty close. We want to thank you for everything you've done for us while we were here."[81]

Tanforan was officially shut down on October 13, 1942, when the last of the evacuees were sent out. Afterward the assembly center was converted back to a racetrack, functioning as such until it burned down in the middle of 1961. A shopping mall now stands where the assembly center was.

Notes

1. Gayle K. Yamada, Dianne Fukami, and Dianne Yen-Mei Wong, eds., *Building a Community: The Story of Japanese Americans in San Mateo County* (San Mateo, CA: AACP, Inc., 2003), 69.

2. Ibid., 107.

3. General DeWitt to Rex L. Nicholson, WPA Supervisor, Whitcomb Hotel, San Francisco, March 28, 1942, as found in J. L. DeWitt, *Final Report: Japanese Evacuation from the West Coast, 1942* (Washington, D.C.: United States Government Printing Office, 1943), 47.

4. Jason Scott Smith, "New Deal Public Works at War: The WPA and Japanese American Internment," *Pacific Historical Review* 72, no. 1 (February 2003): 71.

5. DeWitt, *Final Report*, 92.

6. Brian Masaru Hayashi, *Democratizing the Enemy: The Japanese American Internment* (Princeton, NJ: Princeton University Press, 2004), 88.

7. DeWitt, *Final Report*, 77–78.

8. Konrad Linke, "Dominance, Resistance, and Cooperation in the Tanforan Assembly Center," *Amerikastudien/American Studies* 54, no. 4 (2009): 627.

9. *1872–1942: A Community Story* (San Mateo, CA: The San Mateo Chapter JACL, 1981), 74–75.

10. DeWitt, *Final Report*, 118–126.

11. Video interview, Nakano Family, August 27, 2003.

12. 15_Nakano_014, Feb. 18, 1944, Morrish Collection.

13. 24_Yamada_082, May 11, 1944, Morrish Collection.

14. 4_Honda_002, March 31, 1942, Morrish Collection.

15. U.S. War Relocation Authority, U.S. Department of the Interior, *The Relocation Program: A Guidebook for the Residents of Relocation Centers* vol. 6 (Washington D.C.: War Relocation Authority, May 1943), 10.

16. Sandra C. Taylor, *Jewel of the Desert: Japanese American Internment at Topaz* (Berkeley: University of California Press, 1993), 79. See also Takeya Mizuno,

"Journalism under Military Guards and Searchlights: Newspaper Censorship at Japanese American Assembly Camps during World War II," *Journalism History* 29.3 (2003): 98–106, which is specifically about the *Tanforan Totalizer* and the *Santa Anita Pacemaker*; and Hayashi, *Democratizing the Enemy*, xv–xvi.

17. *Topaz Times* 1, no. 1 (October 27, 1942): 4.

18. Mizuno, "Journalism under Military Guards," 100.

19. 14_Nakano_038, undated, Morrish Collection.

20. Yamada, *Building a Community*, 78–80.

21. Taylor, *Jewel of the Desert*, 64.

22. 16_Nakata_003, Aug. 10, 1942; 16_Nakata_056, undated—both Morrish Collection.

23. Video interview, Nakano family, August 27, 2003.

24. Smith, "New Deal Public Works at War," 74.

25. *Tanforan Totalizer* 1 (May 30, 1942): 4.

26. Ibid. 1, no. 7 (June 27, 1942): 6.

27. Taylor, *Jewel of the Desert*, 67.

28. As told in Yamada, *Building a Community*, 83.

29. 01_Adachi_036, Sept. 10, 1942, Morrish Collection.

30. 16_Nakata_006, Sept. 12, 1942, Morrish Collection.

31. Yamada, *Building a Community*, 97–98.

32. *Tanforan Totalizer* 1, no. 3 (May 30, 1942): 1.

33. Ibid., 1, no. 7 (June 27, 1942): 1.

34. Ibid., 1 no 9 (July 1942): 2.

35. 01_Adachi_012, July 7, 1942, Morrish Collection.

36. 01_Adachi_037, Sept. 15, 1942, Morrish Collection.

37. 08_Kitayama_003, August 30, 1942, Morrish Collection.

38. Animal fodder.

39. *Tanforan Totalizer* 1, no. 1 (May 15, 1942): 2.

40. Ibid., 1, no. 12 (July 25, 1942): 4.

41. Ibid., 1, no.1 (May 15, 1942): 3.

42. Ibid., 1, no. 3 (May 30, 1942): 2.

43. 14_Nakano_013, Aug. 5, 1942, Morrish Collection.

44. 15_Nakano_002, Aug. 29, 1942, and 15 Nakano_003, Aug. 28, 1942—both Morrish Collection.

45. Victory gardens were planted at the home front both as a way to ensure food supply during the war and as a show of patriotism. It is especially interesting to consider these gardens under the circumstances of internment. See Cecilia Gowdy-Wygant, *Cultivating Victory: The Women's Land Army and the Victory Garden Movement* (Pittsburgh, PA: University of Pittsburgh, 2013).

46. Charles Kikuchi, *The Kikuchi Diary: The Chronicle of an American Concentration Camp. The Tanforan Journals of Charles Kikuchi*, ed. John Modell (Urbana: University of Illinois Press, 1973). See the entries for May 3, 1942, and May 4, 1942.

47. *Tanforan Totalizer* 1, no. 5 (June 13, 1942): 4–5.

48. Ibid., 1, no. 12 (July 25, 1942): 3.

49. Ibid., 1, no.1 (May 15, 1942).

50. Ibid., 1, no. 4 (June 6, 1942): 2.

51. Ibid., 12 (July 25, 1942): 2.

52. WRA, *The Relocation Program: A Guidebook*, 16.

53. The records can be found here: http://www.archives.gov/research/japanese
-americans/wra.html, accessed April 21, 2016.

54. DeWitt, *Final Report*, 205.

55. 10_Mayeda_005, May 29, 1942, Morrish Collection.

56. *Tanforan Totalizer* 1, no. 8 (July 4, 1942): 2.

57. 14_Nakano_011, July 1, 1942 from Tanforan, Morrish Collection.

58. 16_Nakata_001, March 26, 1942, Morrish Collection.

59. Yuji Ichioka, "Japanese Immigrant Response to the 1920 California Alien
Land Law," *Agricultural History* 58, no. 2 (April 1984): 161.

60. 16_Nakata_011, Feb. 24, 1943, Morrish Collection.

61. 16_Nakata_059, Aug. 14, 1948, Morrish Collection.

62. DeWitt, *Final Report*, 207.

63. Ibid., 208.

64. Taylor, *Jewel of the Desert*, 81.

65. *Tanforan Totalizer* 1, no. 3 (May 30, 1942): 3.

66. Ibid., 1, no. 4 (June 6, 1942): 3.

67. Ibid., 1, no. 7 (June 27, 1942): 4.

68. 16_Nakata_003, Aug. 10, 1942, Morrish Collection.

69. DeWitt, *Final Report*, fig. 73, 469.

70. Thomas Y. Fujita-Rony, "Remaking the 'Home Front' in World War II:
Japanese American Women's Work and the Colorado River Relocation Center,"
Southern California Quarterly 88, no. 2 (Summer 2006): 161–204.

71. *Tanforan Totalizer* 1, no. 4 (June 6, 1942): 2.

72. Ibid., 1, no. 5 (June 13, 1942): 3.

73. Ibid., 1, no. 7 (June 27, 1942): 5.

74. Louis Fiset, "Thinning, Topping, and Loading: Japanese Americans and
Beet Sugar in World War II," *The Pacific Northwest Quarterly* 90, no. 3 (Summer
1999): 123.

75. Yamada, *Building a Community*, 111.

76. *Tanforan Totalizer* 1, no. 5 (June 13, 1942): 3.

77. 16_Nakata_005, Sept. 8, 1942, Morrish Collection.

78. 15_Nakano_003, Aug. 28, 1942, Morrish Collection.

79. 08_Kitayama_003, Aug. 30, 1942, Morrish Collection.

80. 01_Adachi_037, Sept. 15, 1942, Morrish Collection.

81. 10_Mayeda_016 Sept. 22, 1942, Morrish Collection.

CHAPTER FIVE

The Move to Topaz

The organization of the relocation camps (as they are called in U.S. government documents) was a massive undertaking that took place in a relatively quick period of time, much like the organization of the assembly centers. It was a herculean effort to set up places for more than 100,000 people to be housed and fed, and for an undetermined amount of time. There were actually three different types of relocation camps: the relocation centers, run by the War Relocation Authority (WRA); the internment camps, run by the Department of Justice; and the citizen isolation camps.[1] The U.S. government, when it was trying to find places for these relocation centers, ran into difficulties with some state governors. Many people in the proposed areas were totally against having the Japanese Americans and Japanese aliens moved to their states. For example, the governor of Idaho, Chase Clark, stated:

> The Japs live like rats, breed like rats, and act like rats. We don't want them buying or leasing land and becoming permanently located in our state. I have always been willing to help the army in every way possible with the evacuation of Japanese from the coast, but I don't want them coming to Idaho, and I don't want them taking seats in our university at Moscow vacated by our young men who have gone to war against Japan.[2]

Idaho's attorney general called for a more extreme measure—put all the evacuees in concentration camps and not allow them to work at all.[3] It appears that urban centers were taken out of the equation, and as a result, the camps were located in isolated areas. This reduced the chances of anyone's escaping into the general population of a city, and it made the process of building a relocation center easier for the government. In April 1942 the WRA held a conference in Salt Lake City about the possibility of creating work camps throughout the country and about what the internees could do in terms of helping local communities, but state government officials rejected this suggestion and demanded that the evacuees be interned in camps.[4]

In these early planning stages, it becomes clear that the concept of flexible citizenship was not solely a Californian phenomenon and was fueled by the international political dynamic as well as a legacy of discrimination. As a general rule, the WRA promoted the concept of assimilation as a way to "blend in," and as the most peaceful route for Japanese to come across as loyal to otherwise suspicious Americans.[5] Using the term "100% Americanism," progressives in the United States had long pushed an agenda for assimilation of language and culture as the key to a peaceful and unified multicultural nation. The WRA adopted this language, and it was generally accepted by those who felt that internment was a show of loyalty to the United States.

This idea of becoming more "American" or displaying your "Americaness" to prove your identity or worthiness as a citizen or resident is a tricky concept winding its way through the history of the Internment. It speaks to a controversial notion of how white liberal allies, in supporting the interned, were to some degree also supporting internment itself, and allowing it to function. By encouraging assimilation, the WRA at once promoted complacency in the face of unconstitutional action and ignored the prevalent national sentiments of xenophobia and racism—in some sense, setting the internees up to fail. The camps were both an outcome of this preference for separation and a tool that furthered the divide within a diverse American population. The camps were ghettos, in effect, pushing so-called undesirables out of sight and cementing cultural divisions already in place. The relocation program reaffirmed an unspoken notion that the rights of citizenship were not uniform across lines of color or nationality, nor were they unassailable.

Construction of the various relocation centers began in earnest in the summer of 1942. The WRA pledged to continue its efforts to proceed as a model for the treatment of enemy aliens in democratic nations at war. Eventually, the WRA did develop work-furlough programs, opportunities for educational visas outside of the camps, and the opportunity to enlist in the armed forces. But for the duration of the war, most evacuees remained in the camps.

Many of those people represented in the Morrish Collection who had been held at Tanforan were transferred to Topaz, a relocation camp in Utah. The construction of Topaz began in July 1942 and finished in January 1943. *TREK*, a newspaper printed in Topaz, stated that the first thing done in July was the drilling of the water wells, followed by construction of a building for the U.S. Army Corps of Engineers, and that more than 800 men were working on the camp to get it ready.[6] Everything had to be rushed, and it wasn't until September 15, 1942, that the U.S. government received the title to the land and water use.[7] The living quarters themselves ranged in size from 16 by 20 feet to 20 by 25 feet.[8] The first evacuees arrived on September 17, 1942, and the last came in the middle of October, which meant that many people who were detained there arrived even before the detention center was finished.[9] The total cost to build it was close to $5 million.[10] It was the fifth largest city in Utah and cost $5 million per year to run.[11] Unlike a few other camps that caused quite a bit of friction between the owners/neighbors of the land (like Poston, built on a Native American reservation in Arizona and Manzanar, where locals were worried that the camp constituted a land-grab by the government), Topaz was chosen because it was fairly isolated. However, the choice was not a random one. The U.S. Army Corps of Engineers had planned a large irrigation project that the internees would build and develop. The land at Topaz, at least according to the WRA, was claimed to be 100 percent agricultural land, meaning that all 19,900 acres were totally suited to growing food.[12] Nothing could have been further from the truth. However, it was hoped that when the war was over, the internees would leave and people of non-Japanese ancestry would benefit from the improved land. Many local farmers accepted the building of the camp with the promise of this land after the war.[13] However, the U.S. government did not keep that promise, and in the end the residents in and around Delta, Utah, received nothing when the war was over and the camp shut down.[14]

According to Tomiko Nakano Honda, the train ride from Tanforan to Topaz took two nights and three days.[15] She also stated that the cars were packed and that an armed guard was at each car. The shades had to be pulled down. While the Wartime Civil Control Administration (WCCA) set up some of the camp in a rush before the internees arrived, many of the early arrivals had to actually build much the camp (as Nakata noted earlier). Jim Nakano, age 16, was one such person. In an interview in 2003 he said that he worked "dawn to dusk loading trucks with supplies." He was also driving these supplies (beds, bedding, food supplies) into the camp. In an undated letter, N. Mayeda wrote to Morrish (this must have been toward the beginning of their arrival at Topaz) to say that "people are coming in here in bunches of 500. I'll bet there isn't another city in Utah which grew so rapidly in population as Topaz. I guess living condition [sic] at home is getting rather difficult with all their (?) rationing. I wish this war would blow away and blow quickly."[16] As Nakata stated, people began to be moved out of Tanforan and forced to go (mostly) to Topaz. K. K. Yamane described the camp itself soon after his arrival. He wrote to Morrish:

> We have all arrived safely here and are now fixing up our apartment into more of a home-like place. Topaz is right in the middle of a sage brush desert. The building proper is 1 mile sq. with 42 blocks of buildings beside the residence section there are about 20,000 acres of farming land. Right now the area is covered with sage brush but after it is cleared up it will be quite a land for farming but we all wish that we do soon return to California where everything is much more favorable.[17]

George Nakano wrote to Morrish in early October 1942, soon after arriving, about the conditions in the new camp. Even three weeks after arriving, the camp was not prepared:

> Dear Mr. Morrish: This is our third week here in Topaz, Utah center and we are all fine and happy. The camp life here is more normal and we do not feel like the dangerous saboteurs the newspapers have us classified and the freedom (comparatively speaking with Tanforan) we have is just grand. The camp director and the whole personel [sic] are very capable leaders and we all feel like cooperating with their efforts making this a livable camp. The camp at present is far from complete and the construction work is progressing fairly well but not rapid enough as our apartments are all single walled and unfinished. If they don't speed up their work we'll all probably be in for a spell of freezing weather with inadequate houses.[18]

We are fortunate that there is other material written by those at Topaz who were not part of the Morrish Collection of letters. This includes a diary and a set of notes on various aspects of Topaz by Fred Hoshiyama (kept in the University of California, Berkeley, collection[19]). In his section titled *Community Activities Reception Activities*, he stated that the first group of people (the work group) arrived at Topaz on September 11, 1942, followed by the first set of internees on September 17 (which corresponds to Nakata's letter, above). Hoshiyama said that new arrivals would be met by the Community Activities with a drum and bugle fanfare, and the 500 people who began entering on the 17th would also meet with Mr. Ernst, the director, and some of his staff and their families. The audience would say the Pledge of Allegiance, then sing "God Bless America." Reverend Goto would then greet the internees, after which Ernst would talk about the basic setup of Topaz and explain that Topaz would be self-governed by the detainees themselves.[20]

The first issue of the *Topaz Times*, the relocation also newspaper, confirmed what Hoshiyama had written. Ernst greeted people, and the reverend gave a speech. In it he stated that:

> Topaz is more than just an engineering marvel. It is more than just an iso-lated settlement for evacuees. It is the sum total of dreams, deep think-ing, courage, and faith—it is a living personality. Topaz is born of the great Mother America. We are again the pioneers, blazing the road into the wil-derness of our social frontiers. Not that we alone march but that we follow the ever guiding pillar of the divine wisdom and light—it is our strength. When the first contingent arrived here after the long journey from the west-ern shore, we were welcomed personally by Mr. and Mrs. Ernst, the project director and his wife. We knew then that we were in a big, warm, family. Let us do our uttermost in making this Center a bit of His Kingdom on earth.[21]

It is worth noting that the implied patriotism of "pioneers, blazing the road into the wilderness" is an attempt to at least intellectually ameliorate the condition of internment.

Despite the welcome party's description of an "engineering marvel," some internees found the physical conditions less than desirable. Hoshi-yama wrote in his diary that people were being dropped off at Topaz after the long train ride in, only to find that the places where they had to sleep had no roofs and they had to eat in unfinished dining halls (and these dining halls then had to be converted into sleeping areas until their hous-ing was completed).[22] The next day he mentioned that the lights were dimming and the toilets and the showers had no water (October 4). This happened again on October 6, 1942, and lasted for two days. He also men-tioned a condemned well that had been dug for drinking water and related that people were now starting to complain to the engineers. According to the *Topaz Times*, the dimming of the lights was due to inadequate trans-formers.[23] Finally, Hoshiyama mentioned an "incident" that occurred on October 11, 1942:

> A group of ired [sic] men picked up crowbars, sticks and hammers and went after Mr. Art Eaton, head of Housing Section for not providing them with finished rooms and minimum necessities, stoves, etc.[24]

He didn't describe the outcome.

The *Topaz Times* chronicled the structural issues as the camp slowly ground into functioning mode. The paper detailed housing issues, especially with families who had children, and noted that it was particularly difficult to provide shelter and bedding for the new arrivals.[25] It was also not until the end of October that the toilet seats were installed, individual mirrors put up, and internees finally had a good supply of hot water since the coal shipment had begun to arrive. Steady coal supplies did not occur until the middle of November, after the relocation camp experienced its second snowfall.[26] The hot water, though, was reserved for hot showers and was not for doing laundry since there wasn't enough coal for both. At the same time, the supply of food was unreliable; as Fred Hoshiyama wrote, there was a food shortage and one night all they had to eat were turnips.[27] Dorothy Hayashi described her first view of Topaz in her diary—there were no stoves, no inner walls in the apartments, and no closets. Like Hoshiyama, she wrote that the new arrivals had to sleep in roofless houses and that one of her friends complained about the camp and said she was "rather disgusted with the place, as everyone else is. . . ."[28] And when the Nakano family arrived in September, there were no outer walls—just tar paper—and no stoves. Once the stoves were put in, internees had to go out to the coal pile and bring it in every couple of days.[29] Jim Mori, another member of the Morrish Collection, said that six of them had to fit into these "apartments" and that they built bunk beds and tried to separate the kids' section with blankets.[30]

The fact that the camp was located in the middle of the desert certainly did not help matters. Dust was mentioned as a constant problem for the internees, mostly because of the dust storms and the fact that their housing was inadequate. In an excerpt of a note, Henry Ebihara (not in the Morrish Collection), writing to a girl outside of camp, complained, "Dust, dust, dust————that's what we've been having since yesterday. It's really a hell-hole. After trees and shrubbery are planted and roads paved, things should improve considerably."[31] A few members of the Morrish Collection also wrote about the dust. S. Adachi sent a letter to Morrish on October 7, 1942, just a few weeks after her arrival:

Dear Mr. Morrish: A new state, a new camp, a new climate is Topaz, the future jewel of the desert. I have been very busy re-establishing myself and so I find that I have delayed writing to you. Amidst my confusion and organization, I have meant to write but I am very sorry that the days have gone by and I am just writing today. . . . Topaz is located about 15 miles from Delta, Utah and at present I must declare that the dust is one thing that bother us most. I must say that everyone is working very hard and the moral [sic] is so much higher than I know that it is only a matter of time. . . .[32]

On October 14, 1942, Morrish wrote back to Adachi and said he hoped that when the rains came it would make the dust settle and that "it will be a very interesting experience there I am sure for all of you after you get the gardens growing and the camp in order. . . ."[33]

Michiko Nakata sent Morrish a long hand-written letter (undated, but she said they had been at Topaz for only three weeks) about her early impressions of the camp.

> Dear Mr. Morrish, After being here over three weeks, we still can't get used to the climate and the surroundings. We're so far away from the busy every-day life we used to lead. The soil here is just like flour and when the wind blows—whew! We run for cover, close all the windows, and put wet cloths over our nose and mouth. Thank goodness that doesn't happen daily. No trees or greens in sight, nothing but sagebrush and greasewood for tens and tens of miles—off to the western horizon there are a few hill[s]—one is called Topaz Hill—therefore the name of our camp—Topaz City. The visions that the administration have for this camp is wonderful—if it ever comes true. . . . As usual I'm busy looking after the children and trying to keep house in a 25 by 20 apartment with no inside walls as yet. No matter how often I mop in a day, the dust seems to seep thru the walls and windows. And we have that dusty smell in the air constantly. On cold mornings the coal smoke from the mess halls, laundry boilers, and individual apts [sic] make the sky black. Enough of all of this—as you probably heard from other people. . . . We often think of what we left behind and long for those times— I miss the flowers and vegetables and decent climate and good water.[34]

George Nakano (in the same letter mentioned above) also wrote about the problems with the dust:

> We are mile (nearly 4,600 + feet) high and the atmosphere is dry and the nites [sic] are cold and days warm. It seems to be a healthful country but the only trouble with this place is the dust that sometimes chokes our throat, smarts our eyes and makes living here highly uncomfortable. This happens about once a week (usually lasts 2 to 3 days). One can hardly see 25 feet in front and dust just simmers thru the cracks in the floor and other apertures into the room. Makes housekeeping a constant drudge.[35]

K. Nakano, in a video interview in 2003, still remembered the dust covering him while he lay sick in the family "apartment" and said that he could not see 25 feet away when a storm came through.[36] Some internees were still mentioning the dust in December 1942. In the first volume of *TREK*, in an article titled "The State of the City," Taro Katayama wrote:

Asked what the infant city was like, those first residents might have, with
some justice, summed it up with one word—dust. For dust was the prin-
cipal, most ubiquitous, ingredient of community existence at the beginning. It pervaded and accompanied every activity from sleeping and eating
and breathing on through all the multitude of other pursuits necessary to
maintain and prepare the city for those yet to come. It lay on every exposed
surface inside the buildings and out and it rose in clouds underfoot and
overhead on every bit of exposed ground wherever construction work had
loosened the hold of greasewood roots on the talcum-fine alkali earth. It
obscured almost every other consideration of communal life just as, when a
wind rose, it almost obscured the physical fact of the city itself.[37]

The government was well aware of this problem, and the WRA tried
to reduce the dust by planting nearly 18,000 plants, including 75 large
trees.[38] A pre-issue of the *Topaz Times* mapped out what the greenery of
Topaz was going to look like. It stated that each block would have its own
"miniature park" that would include plants of the evacuees' choosing.[39]
The streets running north and south were also named primarily after trees
and plants: "Tule, Cactus, Ponderosa, Greasewood, Cottonwood, Elm,
Sage, Tamarisk, Juniper, Poplar, Willow and Locust."[40] *TREK*, in the very
first issue, contained a drawing of a new tree, still in its container, being
moved.[41] On page four was another drawing showing a row of trees, still
in their containers, standing in front of various buildings. These draw-
ings were created by the famed Japanese American artist Mine Okubo.
By December 1942 there were 4,800 willow trees and a number of larger
trees, along with shrubs. The WRA had hoped that the shade would help
with the high heat and would help to eliminate the dust. The local nurseries even donated some of these trees. One resident, Toyo Suyamoto,
penned a poem titled "Gain," on the hope and futility that the planting of
Topaz brought:

> I sought to see the barren earth
> And make wild beauty take
> Firm root, but how could I have known
> The wailing long would shake
> Me inwardly, until I dared
> Not say what would be gain
> From such untimely planting, or
> What flower worth the pain?[42]

The harsh landscape was too much for the new plants, and most of them
died. Jim Mori remembered that there was no shade; his friends would

play outside constantly in the sun and would have chapped faces. Eventually, their skin would split and bleed.[43]

   The soil was also not in the best condition for agriculture, as mentioned by some of the internees. George Nakano sent a letter to Morrish, stating that he was working for the Agricultural Department at Topaz and doing a soil survey. He told Morrish that the soil didn't look good since it was "heavy and high in alkali, but we will endeavor to grow somethings next year and we will try out best."[44] The bad soil did not stop the attempt at agriculture. By December 1942, nearly 2,000 acres were in some form of preparation for crops or had already been planted. *TREK* noted that 150 acres had already been planted with barley and clover, with more being prepared for seed. Besides that, there were already "165 head of cattle, 111 hogs, and several sows and litters," as well as the buildings to house them. There were still a number of items not yet built, but the plan was to have them completed by the WRA. These included "high school and elementary school buildings, administration dwellings, community church, slaughter house, meat packing plant, bakery, engineers' and agricultural buildings, garage and repair shops, chicken brooders, permanent hog pens, and others."[45]

   At least one of the Morrish Collection internees had planted her own garden, probably with hopes of diversifying the diet for her family. But as mentioned above, the agricultural conditions were not good for gardening. In one of the more chatty series of letters to Morrish, Nakata had written on July 8, 1943, that her garden wasn't doing very well (we don't have this letter in the collection). Morrish responded: "I was very interested in hearing about your garden. It is too bad things don't do a little better as it is rather discouraging to do all that work without results." He went on to describe the success of his own garden.[46] Later in August, Nakata sent Morrish a letter describing some more of the problems she was having with her garden:

> The nights are getting cold again. Still hot during the days tho [sic]! I can feel the autumn in the air. The one tree on our block is turning yellow now. I have a few hills of melons planted—not even one melon on it. They get about marble-size, then turn yellow and fall off. Must be the soil and intense heat. The radishes grow, but they're tough and the flavor is hot and nippy, not juicy and sweet like the Calif. variety. Too hot and dry, I suppose. How is Calif. now? Harvesting season in full swing, I suppose.[47]

Despite being prisoners and not knowing when they would be released, the internees made the best of a bad situation. They tried to make life as normal as possible, much as they had in Tanforan. The nearly 2,000 children went to school; they had concerts, community gardens, adult classes; and internees could also take classes such as sewing, bonsai, and jewelry making.[48] Many of the teachers were themselves internees. They were even able to create a large library with donations from universities, public libraries, and private donations.[49] Many people (40 percent total, or 3,679 people, as of December 1942) worked within the camp itself, although the pay was so much less than what they would have been making outside. The pay ranged from $12 to $19 per month.[50] But it was work, and it kept them busy.

FEMALE INTERNEES

When evaluating the many effects of the Japanese and Japanese American internment, the concept of female empowerment does not easily spring to mind. While many American women on the West Coast famously joined the workforce for the first time during World War II, embodied by the enduring figure of "Rosie the Riveter," their Japanese American counterparts remained isolated in high-fenced camps, often in remote desert regions. However, the Morrish Collection sheds a new light on the important role of young interned women who managed their families' property holdings back home. Similar to the women who moved into traditionally male positions after so many men entered the armed forces, the cultural promotion of women internees was born out of necessity, but many women thrived in their new roles.

In reading the correspondence in the Morrish Collection, a noticeable trend appears in that many of the letters are signed by names like Miss Sumiye Adachi, Miss Kay Yamada, Miss Famiko Takagi, Miss Naoye Mayeda, and so on. The reason for this is rarely explicitly stated, although the most logical assumption is that these American-born *Nisei* daughters maintained a better grasp of writing in English than their Japanese-born *Issei* fathers. The sons and brothers in interned families often made use of their farming skills by taking jobs outside the camps to earn extra money, as was the case with Ryuji Adachi[1] and Satoru Yamada.[2] Other instances see young women managing property in correspondence with Morrish because their husbands had joined the military, as with Kuni Yatabe, whose husband, Takeshi, volunteered for the highly decorated all–Japanese American 442 Regiment of the Army.[3]

In the early months of internment, Morrish repeatedly addressed his letters to the father in each family, even if most replies came from a person with the title of "Miss." Rather than assuming Morrish harbored a sexist refusal for recognizing female capabilities, the banker may have assumed the daughters were reading the letters to their fathers and then wrote dictated responses. Additionally, having maintained relationships with many Japanese American families for years prior to the war, Morrish was likely aware that the first generation *Issei* immigrated from a society even more patriarchal than that of the early-20th-century United States, and sought to approach the matter with a degree of delicacy. Nevertheless, within the first year of internment, Morrish corrected his headings to correspond with the actual letter writer of each family.

Morrish's confusion can be further excused by the fact that the first year of the internment remained a morass as various family members wrote letters on overlapping business interests from ever-shifting locations. For example, while most Redwood City internees were first placed in the Tanforan Assembly Center in San Bruno before being resettled in Topaz, Utah, the Yamada family were assigned to the Turlock Assembly Center before permanent internment in Gila, Arizona. Once there, members of the Yamada family regularly left the camp for work or medical leaves that took them to Colorado, Illinois, and New York. To blur matters further, both Ko (father) and Kazuko (daughter) signed letters as "K. Yamada" and, initially, used pronouns referring to the whole family—"we" and "our"—as in "If it's possible to rent out the whole property, excluding the Barn, we will very much like to do so."[4]

However, it was Kazuko who eventually emerged as the dominant letter writer and made matters clear by signing with her Americanized name, "Kay Yamada." Upon taking up the mantle of family business, Miss Kay made a noticeable shift in her use of pronouns, telling Morrish, "I am not interested at all in selling any of my acreage, but will not object to leasing the land."[5] Morrish never questioned Kay's authority, but strikingly, when the banker relayed her wishes to outside parties, he maintained the pretense that Kay's father was still making the decisions. To Anton Mosunic, the person interested in buying the Yamada ranch, Morrish wrote, "Today I heard from Mr. Yamada, who owns the property on Woodside Road just back of your lot, advising that he would not be interested in selling any part of his property at present. Later on if he shows an interest in selling, we would be very glad to contact you."[6] By this time, March 1944, Mr. Ko Yamada had not written a letter to Morrish in almost two years, and over a year had passed since Kay Yamada mentioned consulting with any of her male family members concerning the management of property back home. In that time, Kay had advised Morrish on the sale of farm equipment, nursery materials, and the family cars. Additionally, although there was little she could do from an internment camp in Arizona, she continuously corresponded with Morrish regarding a series of difficult tenets who sought to take advantage of the owners' imprisonment and Morrish's busy schedule by avoiding the payment of rent.

The only hint that Miss Yamada recognized the peculiarities of her position comes from an undated, hand-drawn map of the Yamada property at 925 Woodside Road, at the bottom of which she wrote the words, "Kazuko Yamada (a simple woman)."[7] By referring to herself as "a simple woman," was Kay displaying sincere modesty? Was she attempting to maintain Morrish's fiction for the public that her father still headed the family finances? Or was this some sort of wink, an ironic hint, that Kay knew herself to be anything but "a simple woman"? Any answer is sheer speculation, undoubtedly colored for the modern reader by the seven decades of feminist progression, but the fact remains that she did not *need* to write those words and thus meant to add *some* statement about herself and her position to the map.

At some point, the property was legally transferred to Kay's name, as her brother, Satoru, mentioned in a letter in January 1945.[8] It is possible the deed was in her name prior to the war, but it is more likely that the transfer away from the elder Yamada occurred during, or just before, internment due to the complex restrictions regarding the ownership of property by Japanese-born citizens. Satoru spent little time in the actual camp, instead taking jobs at nurseries on the East Coast and sending much needed revenue back to his family in Gila. This letter was Satoru's first to Morrish, but he wrote that though the property was in his sister's name, "being the eldest son I deem it my responsibility to re-establish the family." Soon after, Kay wrote to confirm that her brother would return to Redwood City soon and asked Morrish to prepare the small house on the property for him (only a month prior, the tenant of the main Yamada house re-signed a lease for the next year). She further expressed hope to join her brother soon after.[9] At this point the letters end, but the lack of further correspondence with Morrish implies that the siblings' return was successful and that they proceeded to manage the property from their home.

Miss Sumiye Adachi likewise took on the management of her family's interests in Redwood City while interned in Topaz, Utah, as well as the additional role of being the treasurer of the California

Chrysanthemum Growers Association. While the CCGA officially dissolved just prior to the internment and signed over power of attorney to Morrish,[10] the group left behind a warehouse that required regular upkeep, thousands of dollars' worth of materials that would rot if left unused, and a number of open cases of litigation filed on behalf of various members prior to evacuation. All of the CCGA's property was co-owned by a number of families who were now scattered and interned in camps across the country; thus how to allocate funds and responsibilities proved no easy task. According to the power of attorney, the CCGA's president was George Nankano, but it was the treasurer, Sumiye Adachi, who provided the most assistance to Morrish.

Whereas Morrish sought to help temporarily protected all other properties owned by the interned Redwood City families, his stewardship over the CCGA property saw him seeking to liquidate all the holdings as quickly as possible and distribute the funds to the correct people.[11] In this effort, Adachi worked tirelessly during 1942 and 1943 to track down who owned which crops, tools, and materials left behind at the CCGA warehouse, whether that meant writing on behalf of her fellow internees in Topaz, or writing letters to her former neighbors interned in other camps. It was also Adachi who authorized the release of money from the CCGA account to members who fell behind on payments to cover their personal property expenses. By early 1944, all holdings of the former CCGA had been sold and the account emptied. Despite the association's termination, Santa Clara County still considered the CCGA responsible for maintaining Woodside Road, and one of the last acts of the CCGA was Adachi's approval for Morrish to use the funds to pay for the repair and graveling of a road none of the members had the luxury of using for almost two years.[12]

On top of her CCGA responsibilities, Adachi managed her family's personal farm via letters with Morrish. However, whereas Kay Yamada incrementally took over the family finances, Adachi moved away from her managerial role over time. Before the evacuation, the Adachi family had made a deal with their new tenant farmer, Walter Gillo, to give them half the money made from the sweet pea crop they had already planted. Adachi immediately took control of the family's finances, even meeting with Gillo in person several times while at the Tanforan Assembly Center in San Bruno.[13] When Gillo fell behind on his rent and made only partial payment for profits from the harvest, she hounded the man with letters demanding repayment.[14] From the tone of the letters, she seemed as annoyed by the man's lack of organizational skills as she was with his lack of payment.[15] Over the years Gillo did eventually pay all that he owed to the Adachis and remained a good tenant, but Adachi wrote letters with less frequency, and her early energy and optimism appeared to drain from her when she did write. The day she left Tanforan, she wrote to Morrish to update him on current CCGA business and expressed worry that she would be out of contact for a few days.[16] Upon arriving in Utah, she wrote straight away, mentioning that morale was high and that though she was bothered by the amount of dust, she said that Topaz would be "the future jewel of the desert."[17] At this point, Adachi's letters, which had once gone out to Morrish almost daily, began to appear months apart. She expressed frustration with all the "red tape" involved with her request to leave the camp to become a student in the Midwest[18] and referred to how terrible she felt constantly being forced to ask Morrish for favors.[19] By late 1943, Sumiye no longer wrote to Morrish, and her brother, Ryuji, took control of the family affairs. Her mother died in Topaz in November 1943,[20] and in a letter to Mr. Yamane, Morrish mentioned that he knew how the elder woman's prolonged illness greatly distracted Sumiye.[21] In a letter to Kay Yamada, Morrish revealed that by January 1945, Sumiye had moved back to Redwood City with her siblings and that her brother, Ryuji, had taken a job teaching Japanese at Stanford.[22]

Sometimes the written record can only leave us guessing about gender roles and what those involved were really experiencing. One odd story emerges from the collection when Morrish reacted to a rumor that Sumiye had married in Topaz. In a letter from June 1944 he wrote, "I have heard somewhere that you have married, but hardly believe that is true because you haven't written to me to ask if it was alright."[23] Sumiye never responded, and the rumor appears untrue, as others still referred to her as "Miss" and she moved in with her siblings once back in California. But the question remains, why would the banker believe he should be consulted on a decision so personal as the young woman's marriage? Was it a tongue-in-cheek reference to Morrish's having acted as a fatherly figure? Nowhere else in the collection did Morrish adopt this type of paternalistic attitude toward the young women with whom he corresponded, so we can only guess his interest was somehow financial, or perhaps he felt hurt by not being informed of such a major life decision. Ours is to wonder.

The dynamics of gender in the camps, as they emerge from the Morrish Collection, are the ongoing subject of much scholarship. Within the context of lost citizenship rights, it seems that perhaps traditional family dynamics were disrupted enough to bring about some unexpected, and perhaps empowering, repercussions.

Notes

1. 01_Adachi_057, July 7, 1943, Morrish Collection.
2. 24_Yamada_070, March 14, 1944, Morrish Collection.
3. 26_Yatabe_013, April 2, 1943; 26_Yatabe_030, November 13, 1944—both Morrish Collection.
4. 24_Yamada_007, November 16, 1942, Morrish Collection.
5. 24_Yamada_065, February 20, 1944, Morrish Collection.
6. 24 Yamada_067, March 7, 1944, Morrish Collection.
7. 24_Yamada_099, undated, Morrish Collection.
8. 24_Yamada_090, January 6, 1945, Morrish Collection.
9. 24_Yamada_094, January 21, 1945, Morrish Collection.
10. 28_CA_Chrysanthemum_Growers_087, March 28, 1942, Morrish Collection.
11. 01_Adachi_052, March 23, 1943, Morrish Collection.
12. 01_Adachi_065, October 18, 1943; 01_Adachi_066, November 3, 1943—both Morrish Collection.
13. 01_Adachi_018, July 17, 1942, Morrish Collection.
14. 01_Adachi_041, November 5, 1942; 01_Adachi_044, December 11, 1942; 01_Adachi_047, February 8, 1943—all Morrish Collection.
15. 01_Adachi_044, December 11, 1942, Morrish Collection.
16. 01_Adachi_037, September 15, 1942, Morrish Collection.
17. 01_Adachi_039, October 7, 1942, Morrish Collection.
18. 01_Adachi_047, February 8, 1943, Morrish Collection.
19. 01_Adachi_052, March 23, 1943, Morrish Collection.
20. 01_Adachi_069, November 18, 1943, Morrish Collection.
21. 25_Yamane_023, December 30, 1943, Morrish Collection.
22. 27_Yamada_042, January 19, 1945, Morrish Collection.
23. 01_Adachi_076, January 17, 1945, Morrish Collection.

Leaving the Camp for Outside Work

Besides working in the camp, the evacuees could also eventually work outside of the camp and even permanently relocate under specific conditions. A pre-issue of the *Topaz Times*, published September 26, 1942, notified residents of the opportunities they had of getting outside work, mostly in agriculture (although there were some white-collar and domestic positions available).[51] Some internees were also able to leave temporarily, even if it was only for a day. For example, children were able to go off to neighboring areas for summer camps. Working outside of the camp doing field work, especially in nearby Delta, occurred as early as October 1942, but the process to get people to consider this type of work had begun in June.[52] Hoshiyama had written in his diary in early October 1942 that many inexperienced 18-to-24 year olds were signing up to work on the beet farms. He wrote a few days later that some people were working in Delta at night and would come back to the camp at 6 a.m.[53]

Once they did leave to work in the fields, they became useful in the war effort, but their safety needed to be guaranteed. Milton Eisenhower, the first director of the WRA, realized that the Japanese American workers would be in danger from the public and early on decided that they would not be allowed to work outside of the camps. As the war went on, however, farmers began to feel the sting of a shrunken labor market, and many began to entertain the idea of hiring, if not put the pressure on the government to allow, evacuees to work in the fields. The WRA altered its policy and allowed those in the camps to work for private companies and individuals outside of the relocation centers.[54] One industry that benefitted from this policy was the sugar industry. The December 1942 *TREK* noted that about 400 people who were brought to Topaz were working outside of the camp, and a large proportion of them (300) were working in agriculture, either near Delta or elsewhere throughout the country. In particular, working in the sugar beet fields was mentioned. It is thought that they (and nearly 33,000 others) helped produce nearly 300 million pounds of sugar during the war.[55]

The local paper *The Deseret News* had two articles on Japanese American labor in its September 2, 1942 issue. The first article was an appeal by Utah's governor, Herbert B. Maw, for the War Department to "draft Japanese-American citizens and assign them to farm work at army wages if they do not feel justified in putting them into active service." Some farmers had been complaining about the "great influx of Japanese" who were taking work away from other farmers. The governor told the farmers that the state had no control over what the federal government would do but that there was a real labor shortage and this plan would help.[56] News of this "draft" certainly found its way into Topaz. Dorothy Hayashi, who detailed part of her life in the camp, recorded in her diary on October 31, 1942, that someone wanted to count all the young men, and she wrote, "I think they are going to draft sugar beet workers, won't that be terrible!"[57]

Another article featured a photo of a Japanese American family helping with the tomato harvest, and the accompanying text stated that the tomato and beet harvest was in trouble because there wasn't enough labor to handle it, and that the "civilian population is going to go without" if the farmers couldn't get all the crops in. The article proposed using the Japanese Americans. Selvov J. Boyer, of the Utah State Labor Committee, stated that the Japanese Americans were industrious and that the government would see that they were all registered and fingerprinted. H. C. McShane, the secretary of the U.S. Employment Service, stated:

If we will treat these evacuees like citizens and friendly aliens and not like enemy slaves, we will be able to get the work done. Many of them live in fear of reprisals and also are afraid that they will be regimented in the fields. Should we do that our work will not get done.[58]

To affirm the value of the Japanese American labor pool, the American Crystal Sugar Company, in the *San Francisco Chronicle* (October 12, 1942), credited the internees with saving the sugar beet crop. After this, many states were "clamoring" for more Japanese American workers to help with agriculture.[59] A few members of the Morrish Collection also indicated that they were leaving to work in sugar beets or that they had family members who were going to do this. Adachi had written to Morrish soon after arriving in Topaz. She mentioned the problem with the dust (see previous pages) and that her brother and many of the young men in the camp were leaving for work in the sugar beet fields in Idaho.[60] Many chose to go to Idaho primarily because it was one of the earliest states to call for Japanese American labor (despite what the state's governor had to say). This happened in May 1942 while many of the internees were still being held in the assembly camps. It was also in May 1942 that the nation as a whole began to ration sugar, as organized by the Office of Price Administration, and this certainly accounts for the panic over this necessity.[61] Once news spread that there were internees leaving the camps and safely working, many others volunteered to go.[62] When Morrish wrote back to Adachi, he told her that it was a good thing to get out and work in the sugar beets.[63] Another evacuee, N. Mayeda, had written to Morrish sometime in July 1943 and mentioned that she was working on a farm and that her brother was working on a sugar beet farm in Delta:

> At the present moment I'm working on a farm in Provo. My brother, Shozo, is working on a farm (sugar beet) in Delta. We are trying to save and earn all we can so that we may be able to carry on after the war is over but it's a tough pull at the moment.[64]

By the end of October 1942 there were nearly 700 people working outside of Topaz, with most of them in agriculture.[65] The February 1943 issue of *TREK* also mentioned the evacuees who were leaving to work outside of the camp for agricultural work.[66] The WRA actively encouraged people to leave the camps and go east, as long as they passed FBI security checks and had some type of proof that they could support themselves at their destination. Technically, the internee who left could apply for financial help if he or she did not have the cash to provide for moving and food costs, but those members of the Morrish Collection either did not know about this program or did not take advantage of it. For example, according to the WRA's *The Relocation Program: A Guidebook*, internees could apply for travel costs of a railway ticket and could get up to $3 per day per person for the cost of food. Internees could also apply for something called "family subsistence" after arriving at their destination, and this was calculated at $50 for a single person, $75 for an applicant with one dependent, and $100 for multiple dependents.[67] To prepare the public, movies were shown to describe how loyal the Japanese Americans were, and the internees were shown movies showing how welcoming people were to those with Japanese ancestry.[68] The WRA then set up field offices in a number of large cities, from Salt Lake City eastward, to help the internees move to another part of the country.

But in reality, this was not enough money. In fact, one of the internees left to look for work, but the money was not enough to survive on, so he went back to the camp and decided to stay there until the war was over. T. Kitayama, who had left Topaz to look for work in Chicago, had written to Morrish on November 12, 1942:

> I've been to Chicago for about a month looking for a prospect for a relocation but didn't have much luck. There's no use in getting job because my earnings can't support my family. Yet, I can't invest in any business as I'm uncertain of everything. Therefore, I think its [sic] best that we stay in the camp until the war is over.[69]

Although Kitayama did not say where his family was, it is a good guess that they were still in camp. The WRA charged people a monthly fee for commuting to work outside the camp. This charge was $20 per month, and in addition, the worker had to pay $16 per dependent still in the camp. As Dorothy Hayashi noted in her diary, it was hardly worth getting employment outside of the camp if someone had a large family to support.[70]

Other internees in the Morrish Collection also informed Morrish that they were searching for work outside of the camp. However, they could not just leave—they needed a letter of recommendation on their character. For example, in February 1943 George Nakano sent a letter to Morrish to tell him, "Last few days we have been signing up for possible outside employment and my brother (H. Nakano) and I have given your name as our character references. We hope we will not inconvenience you in any way."[71] Morrish wrote quite a few of these letters of reference for the internees. This process will be discussed later in the book, but what would normally happen was that internees would have to ask permission of the military to leave the camp, and part of the process to let him or her out would be to get a letter from a Caucasian stating that the internee was a good American. We can see this in a form letter sent by Dillon S. Myer, who ran the WRA for most of the war, to Morrish, asking about Ryuji Adachi who was applying to leave Topaz. Myer wrote:

> Dear Sir: Ryuji Adachi has given your name as a reference in connection with an application to leave a relocation center of this Authority for employment, education, or residence elsewhere. We would appreciate it if you would give us your opinion of this individual with respect to such matters as the extent of Americanization through education and upbringing, general standing and reputation in the community, and occupational abilities. If you have ever employed the applicant, a statement concerning the quality of the work performed for you would be helpful.[72]

Morrish would always respond to these requests. He wrote to the WRA on February 8, 1943, telling them that:

> Ryuji Adachi has been known to me for several years. I believe that he is thoroughly honest and reliable and have no reason to believe that he is other than a good citizen. He went to the local high school here and seems to have a good reputation in the community.[73]

This response, and many others like it, allowed many internees to leave Topaz to try to make their lives better, and they could even get WRA assistance to do so.

But as mentioned above, the internees in the Morrish Collection did not take advantage of the WRA program to financially assist those who wanted to relocate outside of the camp. Part of the reason for this is that it wasn't until May 3, 1943, that the WRA distributed a pamphlet to the internees titled "The Relocation Program: A Guidebook for the Residents of Relocation Centers."[74] In his introduction, Director Myer stated that he had wanted to get the information out earlier but that "the swift pace of events and the lack of any previous governmental experience with large-scale wartime relocation have made this a virtual impossibility."[75] He noted that because things were moving so quickly it was impossible to even know what they were planning to do from week to week. He then made it very clear that the U.S. government had tried to do its best at making things easy for the internees, including making it possible for them to leave the camps. This was stressed a number of times, both in the introduction and in the document. In fact, the very first paragraph stated that the WRA's

fundamental objectives included "to help as many of the evacuees as possible in effecting a personal relocation outside of the evacuated area. . . ."[76]
People could leave temporarily for agricultural or industrial work (called
"seasonal leave"); they could move east of the Western Defense Command
(called "indefinite leave"); or they could leave for personal business (called
"short-term leave"). These three types of leave were first published at the
end of September 1942 in the Federal Register, but the main information
was not made available to the internees until the middle of 1943.[77]

Problems While at Topaz

The WRA also produced the pamphlet "Policies Governing the Opera-
tion of Relocation Centers."[78] Again, this was published almost too late
for many of the internees, but it was still useful in that it described the
role of the U.S. government in internment and what it was doing to
protect those in the relocation centers. The duties of the governmental bodies included the provision of nutritious food; housing; medical
coverage; paid employment; clothing allowances; a way for the internees to partially govern themselves; education, preschool through high
school and, in some cases, adult education courses, though education
proved to be very difficult for the WRA to provide, especially when it
came to personnel and materials. The government also facilitated the for-
mation of an evacuee police force, civil-service organizations, stores, self-
published newspapers, and legal-aid services, plus access to public assistance grants, recreation, places for religious practices, and, in case of
death, burial services.[79] *The Relocation Program: A Guidebook* mentioned
the property-assistance program, which covered everything from helping
internees to lease their property while they were interned to helping with
claims in case of damage. It also listed items that the internees could not
have in the camps, including radio transmitting sets, short-wave radios,
and cameras (among other things). People who were not American citizens could request to be taken back to Japan, and American citizens
could be expatriated to Japan as well. Finally, the guidebook stated that
some internees still had the right to vote by absentee ballot and that all
internees, despite being taken away from their communities, were still
liable to pay their federal income taxes, "the same as all other residents of
the United States."[80]

Despite the efforts of the U.S. government to treat these citizens and
aliens carefully, it was not enough to keep them healthy (both mentally
and physically) while they were held in the camps. Nor did it do much to
help with all of the problems they were having with their businesses and

properties back home. Those members of the Morrish Collection encountered numerous issues while they were at Topaz, and many of these problems could have been successfully dealt with if the internees had not been removed or if the U.S. government had been more organized. The following section will discuss four concerns the Japanese Americans had while they were at Topaz: despondency, sickness, troublemakers in the camps, and rental problems with their houses back home.

Despondency

One of the primary themes that emerges from the Morrish letter-writers is how they were despondent about their position and their uncertainty about if and when they would ever be allowed to go back home. One visitor from the Plymouth Congregational Church in Oakland noted "that a consistent fear of the future was marring the rich potentialities of the American Japanese."[81] The conditions listed above reveal the roots of despondency: the camp was unfinished when they arrived; there was not enough food, and certainly not the variety they were used to; while they were allowed to work outside of the camp, the WRA made it fairly difficult for people to leave the camp, and once they were allowed to, they then had to deal with a skeptical and, in many cases, racist populous. Some of them left and then had to return when they could not find work or could not make enough money to support themselves and their families. The weather was also terrible, and the housing, when finished, was not weatherproof. If anything, it is surprising that more people did not become depressed as a result of their situation.

T. Kitayama wrote a number of letters to Morrish to relay his feelings about being in the camp for so long, missing California and its weather, and hoping to return home. In one letter he wrote:

> We are experiencing a very cold weather for the past weeks. We already had 3 snow falls and the ground is frozen stiff. We certainly miss the good California weather, and hoping that we may return there real soon.[82]

T. Kitayama's mood darkened as time went by and there still was no news of when they could go home. He wrote to Morrish in November 1943:

> It looks as though we are going to spend another Christmas and many more in the camp. It sure is a very dull life but I guess it's one of those things that couldn't be helped. How are you Mr. Morrish? I suppose the town looks as same as ever. We certainly like to take a look at the town at this time.[83]

He was also depressed that he had traveled to Chicago but had not been able to make enough money and had returned to Topaz (described below). He sent another letter to Morrish a year later: "It has been almost two years since we left our homes in California and still at this time no sign or hope for returning to our homes."

Others who were not members of the Morrish Collection also referred to their plight while at Topaz. In one of the more moving statements, Taro Katayama wrote an article for *TREK* titled "Digressions," on the celebration (or noncelebration) of their first Christmas in captivity, which includes the following passage:

> We have been in a mild quandary the last few days. With the war's second Christmas near at hand, we find ourself a little disquieted at its sudden appearance on the pathway of our consciousness. Frankly, we don't quite know how to greet the approaching holiday. It is as if an unexpected guest were at the front gate, and both ourself and the house wholly unprepared to receive him. . . . For one thing, we are divorced for the first time in our life from most of the familiar external concomitants of the season—the shopping and the crowds, the street corner Santa Clauses. . . . Even our remembered reactions to that first Noel after Pearl Harbor, though in themselves decidedly a departure from normality, offer no behavior pattern suitable to our current need. At that time, the personal collective calamity of December 7 had left us in a state of mind and spirit which combined anger, awareness of a seemingly irremediable hurt and premonitions of still other woes to come. As for greeting the annual holiday, to mouth its traditional merriness would be, we felt, a painful mockery both of our plight and of our actual feelings.[84]

He continued by stating that they would not be sending out Christmas cards, would have no trees to trim, and would not be doing their normal shopping. He was glad, however, that the little children would be able to get some cheer and that there would be Christmas carols and a hope for snow on Christmas Eve. His article, more than anything written from Topaz, shows the lack of hope and the depression that many of the internees felt at being held in the relocation camps.

One internee, Henry Ebihara, left a record of his experiences when he first arrived at Topaz.[85] He stated that when the internees got off the train, they usually had to run to get a job, whether they were able to do the job or not. He thought this was unfair, especially to the people who were coming later. It is clear that there was general confusion for those first arriving at Topaz. He also described the arrival of one group on October 1, 1942:

What a dusty reception for the poor, incoming people from Tanforan tonite! On top of that, the acute housing situation. Some of them wandered aimlessly about the camp trying to find a place to sleep—even laundry rooms afforded a welcome shelter. Little wonder, many persons downheartedly shook their heads, "this is too much."[86]

Fred Hoshiyama wrote in his diary that petty thievery was increasing and that people were getting desperate because they were running out of money.[87] And, of course, another reason why people held at Topaz were despondent was that Topaz itself was, in effect, a prison. It was no secret that their mail was censored. In the middle of February 1943 the *Topaz Times* reported on the censorship of internee mail, relating that all letters must go to New York, with "Prisoner of War Mail—Free" because a letter didn't need a stamp to go there.[88] The degree to which this happened consistently is unclear, but the appearance of it in the camp newspaper shows how it was part of the culture of the camps.

There was a barbed-wire fence surrounding the whole camp, with security guards and guard towers located at various points. If the evacuees got too close to the fence, the security guards would yell at them to get back. On one occasion, likely the most infamous event to take place at Topaz, an evacuee was shot and killed by military police. This happened on Sunday, April 11, 1943, when James Wakasa (63 years old) was shot by the west fence. There are conflicting views about what happened to Wakasa, but it appears that he was within the fence and was shot as he faced the military policeman. The policeman thought that he was trying to escape, but that doesn't appear to be the case. The camp itself was put under a general alert after the shooting because the administration was worried about how the evacuees would handle the news that one of their own had been shot and killed. Of course, this event added to the stress of their lives. Many internees feared the military police and wondered why Wakasa had not been given a warning shot before he was killed.[89]

Sickness

As noted, the government assumed responsibility for providing health care for those interned. All of the relocation centers had a medical unit. *The Relocation Program: A Guidebook* stated that the health of the internees was of utmost priority and that the government would do everything in its power to make sure that diseases did not spread and that the internees received medical care. The guidebook also warned that there might be shortcomings in this area because of the war.[90]

The government had planned to build state-of-the-art hospitals in each of the relocation camps. According to the *Final Report*, these would include X-ray machines, operating theaters, and morgues. The buildings associated with the hospital, along with the hospital itself, would be heated by steam.[91] The facility would also be equipped with a mess hall and all medications and associated equipment that a normal, outside hospital would have.[92] Despite all of the plans listed in the *Final Report*, the reality of medical care at Topaz was very different, and indeed was different for all the relocation centers.[93]

The *Topaz Times* happily reported that the hospital was up and running with the first contingent of evacuees, with five people being treated on the first day.[94] While Topaz did have a hospital, it took quite a while for it to become usable. In fact, there wasn't much there, even two months after the opening of the camp. In November 1942 the authorities in the camp received a letter from the medical staff complaining that although they had been promised a hospital, what they had actually received was "a pile of lumber"—making basic surgery impossible. In addition, only half of the promised beds had arrived, and there was a severe shortage of medicines.[95]

The hospital, at least in the beginning, could not treat the severely ill or injured. These people were usually sent to local hospitals to be treated, at government expense. The medical unit in Topaz was usually staffed by Japanese Americans or Japanese aliens who were either doctors or nurses or had some type of medical background, along with Caucasian doctors and nurses who would also treat the internees within the camps. The mixing of the two caused some problems. There were squabbles between the Caucasian and the Japanese American doctors over who should be giving orders, and the conflicts did not really improve later in the war. This seemed to be a common problem in other camps as well. Historian Gwenn Jensen noted the same issues at Heart Mountain, Gila, Tule Lake, and Poston.[96] The fact that the Caucasian doctors were getting paid much more than the Japanese American doctors ($21 per month) may have contributed to the tensions. Another problem was that there was a shortage of doctors and, in particular, nurses and nurse's aides, which made it difficult to get treatment, or to get it in a reasonable amount of time. This shortage of medical staff put more pressure on those who were working in the hospital, and as a result, many doctors were working themselves too hard.

A few internees wrote about the health conditions in the camps. Many times Dorothy Hayashi discussed health issues in her diary. She said that on the train trip from Tanforan, quite a few people were sick, including many of the elderly. She also wrote that once she reached the camp, ". . .

everyone seems to have diahherea [*sic*], heat exhaustion, colds and all sorts of sicknesses. I think the change of altitude and climate, and the salty water is bad. Hope all this will change soon."[97] Tomiko Nakano Honda also stated that many people were sick on the trip.[98] Finally, the second pre-issue of the *Topaz Times* reported that there was a "widespread attack of the intestinal flu" soon after the evacuees began to arrive.[99] Some of the evacuees were blaming the food for all of the illnesses. The camp administration announced in the *Topaz Times* that the food was not causing people to be sick because "this condition was prevalent among construction workers and administrative officials even before the City's dining halls were opened."[100]

One internee in the Morrish Collection specifically mentioned all of the illnesses and medical issues her family was having, both while at Topaz and again when the family was transferred to Tule Lake. Nakata sent a letter to Morrish from Topaz in late March, probably 1943. In it she said that all of her kids were sick and that there was a shortage of doctors in the camp:

> Both of my children have had colds and fever and last week I had to take them up to the hospital to get them examined. Due to the shortage of doctors (1 surgeon and 3 internees who just became doctors—for nearly 9000 people), we have to go to the hospital to have the doctor see us. Even for heart attacks, the patient is carried by ambulance to the hospital. Doctors are too busy to make calls. My older boy, Bruce, has bronchial cold and must stay in the house—otherwise it might turn into pneumonia—so the doctor says. It's so cold outside, small children can't get used to it. We're so congested in one spot, that if one person catches cold, it spreads like an epidemic. We thought mumps was gone, but just now the little girl in the next apartment has it. I guess we're the next in line—altho' [*sic*] we're trying very hard not to expose them to the other children. I figure that the older they get, the more resistance they have to contagious diseases.[101]

In August 1943 she wrote another letter to Morrish, telling him that the nights were getting cold and the days were still hot. She asked Morrish about the weather in California and then stated that with the onset of the cold weather, she expected "lots of colds to the camp."[102] She and her family were transferred to Tule Lake, which she realized was a mistake once they arrived. She explained her complaint in a series of letters that spanned November 1944 to August 1945. She wrote to Morrish on November 22, 1944, and told him that her entire family had intestinal flu and that her husband had to be taken to the hospital for an infection in his finger and his nose. He was operated on and was taking double doses of sulfa tablets. She specifically mentioned that his surgeon was Japanese (Dr. Hashiba).[103] In July 1945 she said that she was still having trouble with her sinuses, and she was afraid to relocate from the camp because she has "2 weak children and an old mother."[104] In one of her last letters to Morrish, she told him that her two kids had enlarged tonsils, but that the doctors were too busy to take them out.[105] Issues with medical care (or the lack thereof) continued almost until the end of the internees' residence in the camp.[106]

Troublemakers in the Camps

Relocation camp life was not particularly comfortable for the evacuees. They had been taken away from normal society, put into relatively small areas in large numbers, and forced to interact in ways that they were not used to. It is not surprising that some of the evacuees behaved differently in the camps. Sometimes this behavior was intended to cause trouble, not only between the internees themselves but also for the camp administration in their interactions with the internees. Some members of the Morrish Collection only hinted at problems that were happening in Topaz. When Nakata was at Topaz, she told Morrish that she and her family had been in the camp for three weeks, so this would put the letter sometime in October 1942. She told him that there were "lazy ones and ones who want to lord over everybody else, etc. so it's hard." She then wrote that that her husband was put to work in the mess hall within hours of arriving at Topaz and had been working there ever since.[107] Her family was eventually moved to Tule Lake, and it was there that she encountered more problems with some internees. Another was Fumiko Tagaki, whose family had originally been interned at Tule Lake and then was transferred to Topaz when Tule Lake became the site for "disloyal" Japanese.

A population diverse in age, background, and politics (if not race) was forced to live in close quarters, and thus there emerged issues between the evacuees. Myriad issues sparked conflict. As discussed previously, getting jobs at Topaz was nearly a crapshoot, and this certainly would have added some stress to the new arrivals. The "lazy ones" that Nakata referred to were probably the people who decided that they would not take part in the relocation "experiment" and that since they had been taken away from their homes and businesses, there was no point in doing anything beyond securing just basic survival. Those that wanted to "lord over everybody else" are also hard to pinpoint. Many evacuees outside of the Morrish Collection discussed the superior positions the Caucasians had in the camps, and this was certainly the case in the mess hall where Nakata's husband worked. Nearly every job in Topaz (and this was also the case for the other relocation camps) had Caucasian supervisors; some were good, while others were not.

Fred Hoshiyama mentioned that there were tensions between those internees that had internal jobs (and were making no more than $16 per month if they were skilled) and those internees who found an external employer and who also did work on the camp. Hoshiyama worked on the water systems in camp for a private company and was very excited to be making $0.85 per hour (about $134 per month), which eventually increased to $1.25 per hour ($200 per month). He noted that many people in the camp were upset about this pay difference between those who were working for the camp and those who were working in the camp but with private contractors. There were calls for those who were employed privately to set up a fund for those who were not. Hoshiyama also noted in his diary that there were also divisions "bet. [sic] Nissei-Issei over agriculture." It was just a short note, given without details.[108] Finally, as mentioned earlier, Hoshiyama remarked on the rise of petty thievery, which was also an issue for many held at Tanforan.[109] Many of things being stolen were clothes off the drying line and wood, which was in high demand since the government did not supply wood for building furniture. The lumber shortage was certainly an issue from the very first day that Topaz opened. The *Topaz Times* printed an article titled "Scrap Lumber" which stated that there would be plenty of scrap lumber but that the residents needed to allow the carpenters to work. A committee was set up to distribute the leftovers.[110]

More significant divisions arose when the very questions of citizenship and loyalty were brought into camp. Perhaps in anticipation of complacency, the WRA addressed the issue of how to determine whether an internee was a possible security threat. The government wanted to organize people for release and to create a pool of men who would be inducted into an all Japanese American combat unit. In early 1943 the War Department and the WRA asked all of the evacuees over the age of 17 to take a questionnaire, titled the Leave Clearance form. This questionnaire seemed pretty innocuous, and it was originally designed to find out who wanted to be resettled. After that it was decided that it would be a good way to test for loyalty to the United States.[111] It asked about education (in the United States and in Japan), employment, religion, sports, and hobbies. The internees at Topaz were also given the letter that President Roosevelt had written when he approved of this combat unit. Part of his statement read:

No loyal citizens of the United States should be denied the democratic right to exercise the responsibilities of his citizenship, regardless of his ancestry. The principle on which this country was founded and by which it has always been governed is that Americanism is a matter of the mind and heart; Americanism is not, and never was, a matter of race or ancestry. A good American is one who is loyal to this country and to our creed of liberty and democracy.[112]

The irony of being interned just because of their race and ancestry could not have been lost on the people held at Topaz. The newspaper stated that government officials would explain the program that evening (February 8, 1943). Two particular questions caused some trouble for many of the internees, and not just at Topaz. These were Questions 27 and 28:

"Are you willing to serve in the armed forces of the United States on combat duty, wherever ordered?" And "Will you swear unqualified allegiance to the United States of America and faithfully defend the United States from any and all attack by foreign or domestic forces, and foreswear any form of allegiance to the Japanese Emperor or any other foreign government, power, or organization?"[113]

On February 9, 1943, the *Topaz Times* printed both a regular paper and a special edition to report on what government officials had had to say, especially since the questionnaire would be handed out on the morning of Thursday, February 11 (this was later postponed until Saturday, February 13).[114] The regular edition discussed how the registration for this all-Japanese-ancestry combat unit would be established, and it also contained questions that the Topaz community had for government officials. These questions circled around the actual need for a separate all-Japanese-ancestry unit. The special edition was about the questionnaire. According to Lt. William L. Tracey, the government official sent to Topaz to explain the process, the goal of giving the questionnaire was to return the evacuees to a normal life. He stated that the success of it depended on "the voluntary acts of free American citizens." Tracey continued:

You may object that this—your life here—is not freedom. The circumstances were not of your own choosing, though it is true that the majority of you and of your families accepted the restrictions placed upon your life with little complaint and without deviating from loyalty to the United States. In any time of crisis, however, when national survival presents itself as the all-important issue, the best interests of the few must sometimes be temporarily sacrificed or disregarded for what seems the good of many. The proof of a nation's good faith is to be found in whether it moves to restore full privileges at the earliest opportunity.[115]

Tracey told the listeners that the burdens of those in the camps differed from the burdens of those on the outside, and in essence, the rest of his speech was on the reasons why the evacuation had to be done—because there were disloyal people living in the United States, both citizen and noncitizen. He also told the internees that the government needed Japanese Americans in combat. The questionnaire would be able to separate the loyal from the nonloyal in terms of who would fight for the government, and those who were loyal would show Americans on the outside that their prejudice against Japanese Americans was unfounded. The community was allowed to gather written questions; a committee of internees randomly picked questions, and they were answered by Lt. Tracey or other officials. The *Topaz Times* reported that the community was full of worry and concern about the questionnaire. It was also made clear that filling out the form was compulsory for everyone, male and female, 17 years and older (unless there was a request for repatriation to Japan).[116]

The residents at Topaz directly addressed the absurdity of the questionnaire. On February 15, 1943, a committee was put together of representatives from all of the blocks in Topaz. This committee then chose members for a subcommittee whose job was to create a resolution, directed to Secretary of War Henry L. Stimson and WRA Director Myer. The resolution reminded those in the government that the internees were loyal people who were primarily citizens. It asked that their rights be restored with assistance from the president, and requested that the Office of the President help create a friendly atmosphere for those of Japanese ancestry who would be returning home. They also demanded immediate answers to all of their questions.[117] Myer sent a wire the very next morning and stated that Secretary of War Stimson would not be answering any of the questions in the resolution. Myer stated that the answers would have to be given by the residents themselves, and he ended his wire, "It is my hope and my belief that they will not fail this crucial test."[118] On February 19, the *Topaz Times* reported that the committee put forth another statement and decided that it would accept the registration as a good-faith effort of the government. The daily paper was filled with accounts of the numbers of people filling out the form swamping the buildings where registration was taking place (they were not allowed to fill the form out at home because of all the errors that were being made in filling it out). The *Topaz Times* reported on February 26, 1943, that 100 percent of the internees had filled out the forms.

The government sorted through tens of thousands of forms, only to find out that some internees had put "No" and "No" down for questions 27 and 28. Of course, this did not necessarily indicate disloyalty; in fact, many of these respondents were taking a stand against the inequity in citizenship rights they were facing, and against the absurdity of the language in those two potentially damning questions. People could change their answers, usually after getting a lawyer and filling out the paperwork again. The final day to change the answers was July 15, 1943.[119] But some refused to change their answers since, after all, many had already registered for the draft and wondered why they were again being asked if they would serve in the military. Others questioned the implication that they had any connection with Japan or its emperor. And still others replied "No" to both questions in sheer protest, refusing to offer their lives for a country that had unfairly deprived them of property and freedom. After the fallout, nearly 550 people in Topaz and 1,000 from other camps who had answered "No" to both questions were transferred from their camps to Tule Lake, a relocation camp in northern California that was converted to hold "trouble makers."[120]

While there is no direct mention of the infamous questionnaire in the Morrish Collection, a few correspondents do mention the problems that came from it. One is Fumiko Takagi. She sent a letter to Morrish on July 17, 1943, from Tule Lake. This was just two days after the final date to change answers on the questionnaire. She wrote:

> Much to our disgust, segregation of loyal and disloyal Japanese has become a reality. Of course, we will be put in the loyal section when segregated, but it is the idea of moving again. We will let you know as soon as we are segregated and conditions as they exist. I am presuming that you have received a letter from Mr. Dillon S. Myer for recommendation of my loyalty and qualifications for leave clearance. As this camp is no place for us, we have finally decided to relocate. I don't think that my folks will ever relocate, as they still have hopes and ambitions of returning to our home in Los Altos. They aren't particularly anxious to relocate as they have heard of many bad incidents in Chicago and thereabouts against the Japanese who have already relocated. Perhaps after I relocate and find conditions better, I will relocate them for the duration also. But at the present time, they will remain in camp.[121]

Tule Lake was also the camp that had the most internal problems, with inmates going on strike and engaging in skirmishes with the camp employees. And as Tagaki mentioned, many of the older people decided that they would stay in Tule Lake because they did not want to be moved again.[122]

She wrote to Morrish again at the end of July 1943, saying that Tule Lake "has officially been claimed as the camp for the disloyal Japanese, so we will probably be moving into another center about November." She hoped to go to Philadelphia and asked Morrish if he knew of anyone there who had a secretarial job.[123] She wrote again in the middle of August to tell Morrish that they were being transferred to Topaz.[124] Her family must have answered "Yes" to both questions 27 and 28, as that was the condition families had for leaving Tule Lake.[125] Her family was transferred out toward the end of September 1943. Then on November 22, 1943, Fumiko sent a letter to Morrish in which she mentioned the "Tule Lake incident" and added her hope that the "rioteers [sic]" would be removed from the camp.[126]

She was referring to a riot that occurred in the middle of October 1943, after an underage driver of an agricultural truck flipped over, killing one person. Blame was put on the camp administration, and this led to a strike; within a few days, the strikers surrounded the camp administration building. Consequently, the army went into the camp with tanks and took full control. Eventually, the riot was put down, and many of the ringleaders were put in the stockade. Topaz did not experience anything like what had happened at Tule Lake.

One family, the Nakatas, were moved from Topaz *into* Tule Lake, just after the camp was designated for those who were disloyal (although it isn't clear if this is why the family was moved there). According to a WRA Train Route List for September 23, 1943, which names the families that were transferred from Topaz to Tule Lake, the Nakata family (Arthur, 31; Michiko, 32; and their two sons, Tadashi Bruce, 4, and Satoru Kent, 3) were moved, along with 485 other people.[127] Morrish noted the change of address in his December 24, 1943, letter to Nakata.[128] He said that he was sorry to hear that they had had to move and that he thought Topaz might have been a bit more comfortable than Tule Lake, but that he hoped they would ultimately make it home. Nakata never mentioned why they made the move to Tule Lake, except to say later that it was a mistake to go there. Families could ask for a transfer between camps, especially to be reunited with other family members. Mrs. Nakata had mentioned her husband in previous letters, but nothing she said was out of the ordinary. Both of them were U.S. citizens and had never been to Japan. Unfortunately, there is nearly a year break in the Morrish Collection between December 1943 and November 1944, when Nakata sent Morrish a letter from Tule Lake, dated November 22, 1944. She was not very happy with the conditions in the camp. After she told Morrish about all the medical problems her family was having, she wrote:

We're so disgusted with the camp, and more & more I realize this is no place for us to stay, that we've applied for a leave clearance to another camp. After all, we're both Nisei & we've been brought up in the American system of education and thinking, & I just can't swallow the trouble makers way of thought and living. If Japan is like this camp, I certainly don't want to go. We regret ever coming to this camp, but we've learned our lesson & I think we could be better citizens for having had a taste of this camp. We certainly realize our mistake in coming here. Arthur's father & his sisters & brothers are in Gila—altho' one sister & a brother & their families have relocated. His youngest brother, Tom, volunteers & is fighting in France I think. All my relatives are in Poston, & three of my cousins are in the army. One, a volunteer, was wounded in action last month in France. My aunt writes all of the time, & everybody is so glad we've made the decision to leave here. So far we have 6 relatives in the army, & more coming up. In our application papers, we had to give 5 Caucasian references. We gave your name as one, so if you should get a letter asking about us, will you tell them about our characters? I hope it was all right. It takes quite a long time for the O.K. to come from Washington. . . .[129]

Morrish wrote back a few days later expressing his wish that they would be able to move and that he would write a letter for them when the request arrived.[130]

But despite her desire to move, the family would not be able to relocate. Nakata wrote to Morrish in the middle of January 1945 to tell him that there were no transfer requests granted between the relocation centers, but that the WRA would be opening a relocation office at Tule Lake.[131] The WRA offices were set up to help people plan to relocate when they were able to, and especially to help them plan for what would happen when the war finished. She wrote again at the end of May 1945, asking Morrish if he could write a recommendation for her husband as he was going up before the Army Hearing Board. She said that his status was "exclude" and that all men at Tule Lake were in that category, while her status was "free."[132] Morrish wrote the letter for him and sent Nakata a note saying he had sent it to the board.

She wrote a long letter on July 2, 1945, to say that her husband was waiting for the army to let him know its decision:

He won't know the answer yet—they will let him know something this month. (Californians who are so afraid that people are being released from Tule Lake willy-nilly are very much wrong. In fact, the Army has its say with all residents released from all the relocation centers. There are many who are in the "exclude" list in other centers too.) In the meantime trouble-makers in this camp are being sent to alien enemy internment camps. About a week ago about 400 went, and today I heard that around 100 were sent. I'm not curious enough to see who goes, so I get all these news second hand.[133]

As the WRA once again relocated families, in most cases without clear evidence of wrongdoing, the process once again ignored the rights of legal residents. The status of "trouble maker"—a phrase found in the letters—could have been assigned for a number of reasons, including questionable alliances before the war to unacceptable answers on the questionnaire. In any case, life in the camps perpetually reminded those internees that their legal status was in flux.

Rent Not Being Paid

As noted before, money was a continual problem for many members of the Morrish Collection. They could work in the camp (for measly sums that were not enough to even pay their insurance premiums), or some would work outside of the camp, but many remained inside and so were dependent on money coming in from their businesses (if they still existed) and from rent on their homes that they had had to leave so quickly. If they were lucky, they might also have had savings to draw on. Morrish was called upon many times to help the internees deal with rent issues, which included collecting rent from tenants or trying to get money from the tenants. In one case, squatters moved in, and Morrish could not get them to leave. For the internees, if the money was not deposited in their accounts, then cash flow became a serious problem.

The first example is the Mayeda family. The very first letter in the Mayeda file (dated May 1, 1942) is a note from the Los Angeles Probate Office, directed to N. and S. Mayeda (sister and brother), in care of Morrish at the bank in Redwood City. Morrish had written to the Probate Office in late April 1942, requesting information on a remittance that was due to the Mayedas from a Mr. Carlson. The Probate Office responded that Carlson was no longer on probation and it was unlikely that the Mayedas would be getting any further money from him. Morrish responded by asking for the address of Carlson so that he could pursue the matter. Carlson owed them some money, but unfortunately the later letters make no mention of possible collection. Their money problems continued from here.

When the Mayedas left for the Tanforan Assembly Center, they rented out their place to a Mr. Hasler for $37.50 per month. He made the first rent payment on May 15, 1942.[134] The Mayedas were also collecting rent on a sign put on their property by a firm named Foster and Kleisner. The representatives stopped by the bank and paid $10 for the period between June 1942 and December 1942.[135] But in late June 1942, an agent for Foster and Kleisner told Morrish that they were reducing the number of signs they were using and that they were no longer going to pay rent on the signs that remained, including the one on the Mayeda property. They told Morrish they were going to reduce the amount by one-third. Morrish refused this but signed a new sign lease for $15, starting in December 1942. He said his choice was to either have them remove the sign and not get $15, or keep it and collect the rent.[136]

It wasn't until the beginning of September 1942 that Morrish told the Mayedas that Hasler, their tenant, was six months behind on his rent. Hasler thought he would be able to pay the balance within the next 30 to 60 days. Morrish told the Mayedas that Hasler was doing a good job but was short of money until he harvested the chrysanthemums.[137] Morrish wrote again at the end of November 1942, saying that he had been out to their ranch and had noticed that many of the flowers were unpicked. Hasler told him he was having trouble with finding labor (a common complaint during this period). Hasler also said that he was disappointed by the amount of money he made. Morrish told the Mayedas that he was still six months behind and was hoping to have the money in the next two weeks.[138] Morrish continued to correspond with the Mayedas about Hasler's not paying rent. In March 1943, Morrish told the Mayedas that Hasler was now nine months behind but had found someone to help him with the planting:

> Today I went out to the ranch to see if I could get some rent from Mr. Hasler, but he is not in a position to make any payment just at this time, however, I believe that directly after the first of next month he can make part payment of his delinquent rent. I believe it is nine months now that he is behind, but feel that he will be in a position to do better the coming year as apparently he has made a fairly good connection with a group of Chinese, so his labor will not be the problem it was last year. This morning he was discing [sic] the front piece to plant cauliflower. They had spinach planted there but had to disc about half the crop under on account of the continual rains as it turned all yellow. I believe that he is a good hard worker and a very well-meaning chap, and think that probably during this year the matter will work out all right. It is very much better to have someone there taking care of the place and I feel he is doing a very good job.[139]

Morrish wrote again in April 1943 to say that Hasler still had not paid rent but believed he could pay fully in the next 60 days; it wasn't until July 1943 that Hasler gave up the property. Morrish wrote the Mayedas a long letter about this. Hasler claimed to be totally broke and could not pay any of the back rent. He also had taken advantage of a governmental loan program for people to take over farms, and he couldn't repay that money either. The only upside for the Mayedas was that one of the Chinese workers (Quan) contacted Morrish to see if he could take over the property, although he wasn't willing to pay more than $250 for the year ($20.83 per month). Morrish wanted him to pay this money up front, and Quan was willing to do this. Morrish thought that while the rent was greatly reduced, it was better than keeping the place vacant. He ended his letter by including a deposit slip for $7.50 for the sign rental.[140] N. Mayeda wrote back to Morrish and told him that she was working on a farm in Provo and agreed that $250 was better than nothing. She told him, "We appreciate your letter to us and your interest in our ranch, at a time like this when we are so helpless in taking care of our property ourselves." She also told Morrish that Hasler had been in contact and had agreed to return all the equipment he had borrowed and that he and her brother had made out a list a week before evacuation. Another problem was that the Mayedas had sold a truck to Hasler for $300, and N. Mayeda asked Morrish to see if he could get it back in lieu of rent. She was worried that she would have to buy another one after the war if she didn't get it back. Finally, she asked Morrish to check a locked room in her house where all of their belongings were kept. She was clearly worried that the room had been emptied out.[141]

Unfortunately for the Mayedas, problems with their property continued under the new tenants. As mentioned, Hasler had taken out a governmental loan to help pay for growing crops. In August 1943, Quan's lawyer sent Morrish a note stating that Hassler had recorded a chattel mortgage on the Mayeda property on June 22, 1943 (just ten days before he told Morrish he could not pay the back rent and would be giving up the property). The mortgage applied to crops grown under the current lease but could be extended to cover crops grown later. Quan's lawyer was concerned that the government could take the crops Quan would grow, and he wanted Morrish to contact the U.S. Department of Agriculture, Office of the Soliciter, in the Phelan Building (San Francisco) about this to secure written assurance that this would not happen. Otherwise, Quan would not be leasing the land.[142] It isn't clear if Morrish wrote this letter, but in October 1943 Morrish sent a note to N. Mayeda to tell her that the government had sued Quan and "tied up the crop that was on the land until after harvest." Quan had not paid for the lease, and Morrish was going to give him two to three weeks to do so before trying to find someone else. By now the Mayedas had received only $37.50 for their land in the past fourteen months.[143] Morrish then wrote (on October 21, 1943) to the Department of Agriculture to ask if the new tenant was clear to grow his crops. The next day (October 22, 1943) the Department of Agriculture said it had received his letter from the day before and that the government "will have no interest whatsoever in any future crops to be grown by your new tenant." The letter stated that the county Farm Security Association supervisor (T. Goethe) would be sent to find out how much of Hassler's crop had already been harvested and what remained.[144] A few days later Morrish received a letter stating that there were no other crops and the tenant was free to start growing his own. Soon after this, Morrish wrote to N. Mayeda to tell her that he had found tenants who would pay $350 per year, with half down and half due in six months.

Another family in the Morrish Collection had similar problems to that of the Mayedas. The Yamadas had rented out their property and had issues with their first tenant. They had rented their house to a Mr. Miller, and in January 1943, a Mr. Panetta, the real estate agent acting for the Yamadas, sent a letter to Miller, stating that they were kicking him out of the house because "they have been very destructive to the property burning the fence posts for fire word, using attached garage for horses and feed and have also taken possession of a garage across the street from their residence and are using it to stable horses. Removing sliding doors and defacing property."[145] It wasn't until the end of March 1943 that they were able to remove him. However, he did not pay the last month of rent. Morrish arranged to have the whole place cleaned up.[146] At the end of April 1943, Morrish was able to find someone to rent the property for $200, but the lessee did not want to rent the house.

In June 1943, Morrish was certain he had found a tenant for the house, a M. Spinella, for $27.50 per month. Morrish had sent a letter to the Office of Price Administration to tell them the amount he wanted for rent, and further: "We are holding the money to get your approval before paying it to the owner of the property. We are not sure if you are interested in the occupancy of a house on ranch property. If so, will you please let us have your advice, and if not, advise us if we should check with any department before accepting the above amount."[147] The Office of Price Administration, created in 1941, was set up to take care of rationing and to control the prices of various goods and services.[148] For some, this office was the most intrusive governmental office to operate during the war, and as indicated by Morrish's letter, it also regulated rent. According to historian Meg Jacobs, the Office of Price Administration "issued regulations controlling 8 million prices, stabilizing rents in 14 million dwellings occupied by 45 million tenants, and rationing food to 30 million shoppers."[149] This office replied to Morrish that the house was not registered and that they would need more information. Unfortunately, there isn't anything else in the collection regarding the outcome of this question, and there are no other letters about this particular office. We do know, however, that Mrs. Spinella was not an actual tenant. Morrish wrote to Yamada in August 1943 to explain how Spinella gained occupancy:

> Sometime ago I had a good many inquiries on your house and one particular family, M. Spinella, tramped on my trail for quite a while. Perhaps you know them. The husband and wife had some difficulty and the wife wanted a place to live and she knew of your house, so one day while I was out of town she came into the bank and left $27.00 with one of the boys for the first month's rent. She had asked me about it several times and I told her we had planned to rent it to the Chinese boy who was leasing the land. Apparently she spoke to him and found that he was not going to take the house so she moved in. She has four children and I do not want to have the same problem that we had before, getting rid of the last family there. Another problem is the ceiling of the rent. I told her so as to discourage her that the rent would be $27.00 or $30.00 but apparently that did not discourage her. Since she moved in I have never been able to find her to collect the next month's rent. The family tells me, though, that she is in in the evenings and that she works all day, so I will endeavor to see her some evening soon and ask her to move.[150]

Mrs. Yamada soon wrote back and asked Morrish to get rid of the Spinellas. Morrish responded by telling her that Spinella had paid the rent and would try to leave as soon as she could find another place.

At some point the Spinellas moved since Morrish sent a letter to the Yamadas in December 1943, talking about more tenant issues. These new "tenants," like the Spinellas, had moved in illegally. Morrish threatened to call the sheriff and the Board of Health on them. The family living there consisted of a mother and her six children (Morrish thought there might have been more). The mother told Morrish that she would be out by the end of the year.[151] At the end of January 1944 this particular family had moved out, but there was yet another group living in the house. And to add insult to injury, those people now living there illegally were paying rent to the woman with six kids. The new illegal occupants told Morrish they would be out by February 1, and that was good since Morrish had lined up a real tenant who wanted to be in by that date.[152] He managed to collect $15 for rent from the illegal tenants and got a promise they would be out by March 1. That date came and went, and toward the middle of March 1944, Morrish was giving up on trying to get them out of the house. He told the Yamadas that their house was in bad condition and that the people were still occupying it, but that it was now up to the man who was leasing their land to get the people out.[153] This problem continued through the beginning of January 1945, when the Yamada family wrote to Morrish to ask about the conditions for coming home. He told them that there was still a family living in their house and that he could not get them out.[154] It wasn't until December 1945, that Morrish addressed a letter to the Yamadas with a Redwood City, California, address.

These were two of the extreme cases mentioned in the correspondence in the Morrish Collection. There were other, more minor examples. But as mentioned, the lack of income from these properties put these families in a serious bind. They still had to pay their taxes on their property, and they had to pay for insurance and upkeep, even though they were nearly powerless to help themselves. They had to rely on Morrish totally to handle these tenants, to gather the rent, and to make deposits into the internees' accounts (that is, when the tenants paid the rent). The lack of rent payment, along with the low rents of between $12 and $19 per month when they were able to collect, put the internees in extreme hardship and really forced them to sell much of their personal property just to pay their bills and taxes.

Notes

1. Wendy Ng, *Japanese American Internment during World War II: A History and Reference Guide* (Westport, CT: Greenwood Press, 2002), xiii.

2. Carey McWilliams, *Japanese Evacuation: Interim Report* (New York, NY: American Council Institute of Pacific Relations, 1942), 19.

3. Louis Fisit, "Thinning, Topping, and Loading: Japanese Americans and Beet Sugar in World War II," *The Pacific Northwest Quarterly* 90, no. 3 (Summer 1999): 126.

4. Leonard J. Arrington, *The Price of Prejudice: The Japanese-American Relocation Center in Utah during World War II* (Logan: The Faculty Association, Utah State University, 1962), 17.

5. Myer reaffirmed his policy on, and belief in, assimilation as the pathway to social peace in his subsequent work with the Bureau of Indian Affairs and the Relocation Programs of the post-WWII era in the United States. See Richard Drinnon, *Keeper of Concentration Camps: Dillon S. Myer and American Racism* (Berkeley: University of California Press, 1987), 1987.

6. *TREK* (December 1942): 3.

7. *Deseret News* (September 15, 1942): 1.

8. Sandra C. Taylor, *Jewel of the Desert: Japanese American Internment at Topaz* (Berkeley: University of California Press, 1993), 94.

9. Ibid., 90.

10. Arrington, *The Price of Prejudice*, 17, 23.

11. Gayle K. Yamada, Dianne Fukami, and Dianne Yen-Mei Wong, eds., *Building a Community: The Story of Japanese Americans in San Mateo County* (San Mateo, CA: AACP, Inc., 2003), 120.

12. Carey McWillians, *Japanese Evacuation: Interim Report* (New York, NY: American Council Institute of Pacific Relations, 1942), 20.

13. Brian Masaru Hayashi, *Democratizing the Enemy: The Japanese American Internment* (Princeton, NJ: Princeton University Press, 2004), 89.

14. Ibid., 207–208.

15. Video interview, Aug., 2003. She also gave extensive interviews in 2010. See http://archive.densho.org/main.aspx

16. 10_Mayeda_083, undated, Morrish Collection.

17. 25_Yamane_044, undated, but probably sometime in Oct. 1942, Morrish Collection.

18. 14_Nakano_014, Oct. 5, 1942, Morrish Collection.

19. Fred Hoshiyama, Diary, http://digitalassets.lib.berkeley.edu/jarda/ucb/text/cubanc6714_b095h09_0004.pdf, accessed May 1, 2016. *Topaz Administration,* http://digitalassets.lib.berkeley.edu/jarda/ucb/text/cubanc6714_b095h09_0006.pdf, accessed May 1, 2016.

20. Fred Hoshiyama, *Topaz Administration*, 33–35 http://digitalassets.lib.berkeley.edu/jarda/ucb/text/cubanc6714_b095h09_0006.pdf.

21. *Topaz Times* (Sept. 17, 1942): 1.

22. Hoshiyama, Diary, October 2, 1942, 5; and October 3, 1942, 9.

23. *Topaz Times* 1, no. 3 (October 29, 1942).

24. Hoshiyama, Diary, October 11, 1942, 31.

25. *Topaz Times* pre-issue no. 6 (October 10, 1942), 2.

26. Ibid., 1, no. 16 (November 17, 1942).

27. Hoshiyama, Diary, October 26, 1942, 53.

28. Dorothy Hayashi, Diary, October 3 and 4, 1942.

29. Video interview, Nakano family, August 27, 2003.

30. Oral interview, March, 2003.

31. Henry A. Ebihara, Notes and Observations, September 29, 1942, 1. http://digitalassets.lib.berkeley.edu/jarda/ucb/text/cubanc6714_b095h09_0001.pdf, accessed May 1, 2016.

32. 01_adachi_039, Oct. 7, 1942, Morrish Collection.

33. 01_adachi_038, Oct. 3, 1942 (this letter was out of order in the collection), Morrish Collection.

34. 16_Nakata_056, undated, Morrish Collection. The underlining is hers.

35. 14_Nakano_014, Oct. 5, 1942, Morrish Collection.

36. Video interview, Nakano family, August 27, 2003.

37. *TREK* (December 1942): 3.

38. Taylor, *Jewel of the Desert*, 111–112.

39. *Topaz Times* third pre-issue (September 30, 1942): 3.

40. Ibid., 1, no. 13 (November 12, 1942): 1.

41. *TREK* (December 1942): 2.

42. Ibid., 6.

43. Oral history, March, 2003.

44. 14_Nakano_014, Oct. 5, 1942, Morrish Collection.

45. *TREK* (December 1942): 5.

46. 16_Nakata_015, July 10, 1943, Morrish Collection.

47. 16_Nakata_016, Aug. 27, 1943, Morrish Collection.

48. Yamada, *Building a Community*, 129; and *TREK* (December 1942): 9.

49. *TREK* (December 1942): 10.

50. Ibid., 7.

51. *Topaz Times* pre-issue (September 26, 1942): 1.

52. Fisit, "Thinning," 127; Taylor, *Jewel*, 113.

53. Hoshiyama, Diary, October 2, 1942, 7; and October 12, 1942, 33.

54. Fisit, "Thinning," 126.

55. Taylor, *Jewel of the Desert*, 115.

56. *Deseret News* (September 2, 1942): 8. https://news.google.com/newspapers?nid=Aul-kAQHnToC&dat=19420902&printsec=frontpage&hl=en, accessed April 28, 2016.

57. Hayashi, Diary, http://digitalassets.lib.berkeley.edu/jarda/ucb/text/cubanc6714_b095h09_0002_1.pdf, accessed February 20, 2016.

58. *Deseret News* (September 2, 1942): 1.

59. McWilliams, *Japanese Evacuation*, 29–30.

60. 01_Adachi_039, Oct. 7, 1942, Morrish Collection.

61. Fisit, "Thinning," 123.

62. Ibid., 129.

63. 01_Adachi_038, Oct 14, 1942, Morrish Collection.

64. 10_Mayeda_027, undated, but probably July 1943, Morrish Collection.

65. *Topaz Times* 1, no. 4 (October 30, 1942): 2.

66. *TREK* (February 1943): 6.

67. War Relocation Authority, *The Relocation Program: A Guidebook for the Residents of Relocation Centers*, vol. 6 (Washington, D.C.: U.S. Government Printing Office, 1943; reprinted New York, NY: AMS Press, 1975), 3.

68. Yamada, *Building a Community*, 138.

69. 08_Kitayama_016, Nov. 12, 1942, Morrish Collection.

70. Hayashi, Diary, October 20, 1942, 32.

71. 14_Nakano_017, Feb. 22, 1943, Morrish Collection.

72. 01_Adachi_086, undated, Morrish Collection.

73. 01_Adachi_048, Feb. 8, 1943, Morrish Collection.

74. WRA, *Relocation Program: A Guidebook*, 25.

75. Ibid., iii.

76. Ibid., 1.

77. McWillians, *Japanese Evacuation*, 9.

78. WRA, *Relocation Program: A Guidebook*, 4–16

79. McWillians, *Japanese Evacuation*, 25.

80. WRA, *Relocation Program: A Guidebook*, 16.

81. *Topaz Times* 1, no. 20 (November 21, 1942): 1.

82. 8_Kiayama_009, Dec. 2, 1942, Morrish Collection.

83. 08_Kitayama_016, Nov. 12, 1943, Morrish Collection.

84. *TREK* (December 1942): 28.

85. Ebihara, Notes and Observations, September 29, 1942, http://digitalassets .lib.berkeley.edu/jarda/ucb/text/cubanc6714_b095h09_0001.pdf, accessed May 1, 2016.

86. Ibid.

87. Hoshiyama, Diary, November 18, 1942, 87.

88. *Topaz Times* (February 12, 1943): 2.

89. See Taylor, *Jewel of the Desert*, 136–46 for a fuller account.

90. WRA, *Relocation Program: A Guidebook*, 4.

91. Ibid., 265.

92. Ibid., 274–275.

93. Gwenn M. Jensen, "System Failure: Health-Care Deficiencies in the World War II Japanese American Detention Centers," *Bulletin of the History of Medicine* 73, no. 4 (Winter 1999): 606 ff.

94. *Topaz Times* (September 17, 1942): 2.

95. Taylor, *Jewel of the Desert*, 162. See http://archive.densho.org/Core /ArchiveItem.aspx?i=denshopd-i37-00561 for an image of the hospital dedication.

96. Jensen, "*System Failure*," 623–626.

97. Hayashi, Diary, October 3, 1942, 7.

98. Video interview, August 27, 2003.

99. *Topaz Times* second pre-issue (September 26, 1942).

100. Ibid. third pre-issue (September 30, 1942): 2.

101. 16_Nakata_013, March 22, no year given, Morrish Collection.

102. 16_Nakata_016, Aug. 27, 1943, Morrish Collection.

103. 16_Nakata_023, Nov. 22 1944, Morrish Collection.

104. 16_Nakata_030, July 2, 1945, Morrish Collection.

105. 16_Nakata_032, Aug 3, 1945, Morrish Collection.

106. Taylor, *Jewel of the Desert*, 178–180.

107. 16_Nakata_056, undated, but probably written sometime in October 1942, Morrish Collection.

108. Hoshiyama, Diary, October 29, 1942, 58.

109. Ibid., November 18, 1942, 87.

110. *Topaz Times* (September 17, 1942): 3.

111. Taylor, *Jewel of the Desert*, 148.

112. Given February 1, 1943, and printed in the *Topaz Times* 2, no. 38 (February 8, 1943): 1.

113. Yamada, *Building a Community*, 138n58.

114. *Topaz Times* 2, no. 35 (February 11, 1943): 1.

115. Ibid., special edition (February 9, 1943): 1–3.

116. Ibid., (February 12, 1943): 1.

117. Ibid., 2, no. 38 (February 15, 1943): 1–2.

118. Ibid., 2, no. 39 (February 16, 1943): 1.

119. Taylor, *Jewel of the Desert*, 152.

120. Yamada, *Building a Community*, 139; Taylor, *Jewel of the Desert*, 152.

121. 20_Tagaki_143, July 17, 1943, Morrish Collection.

122. Taylor, *Jewel of the Desert*, 154.

123. 20_Tagaki_145, July 30, 1943, Morrish Collection.

124. 20_Tagaki_146, August 16, 1943, Morrish Collection.

125. Taylor, *Jewel of the Desert*, 154.

126. 20_Tagaki_159, Nov. 22, 1943, Morrish Collection.

127. War Relocation Authority, Train Route List from Topaz to Tule Lake, September, 1943, 22, http://digitalassets.lib.berkeley.edu/jarda/ucb/text/cubanc6714
_b051e06_0051.pdf, accessed September 14, 2016.

128. 16_Nakata_021, Dec. 24, 1943, Morrish Collection.

129. 16_Nakata_023, Nov. 22, 1944, Morrish Collection.

130. 16_Nakata_024, Nov. 28, 1944, Morrish Collection.

131. 16_Nakata_026, Jan 14, 1945, Morrish Collection.

132. 16_Nakata_027, May 31, 1945, Morrish Collection.

133. 16_Nakata_030, July 2, 1945, Morrish Collection.

134. 10_Mayeda_004, May 15, 1942, Morrish Collection.

135. 10_Mayeda_007, June 19, 1942, Morrish Collection.

136. 10_Mayeda_009, June 25, 1942, Morrish Collection.

137. 10_Mayeda_015, Sept 1, 1942, Morrish Collection.

138. 10_Mayeda_019, Nov. 23, 1942, Morrish Collection.

139. 10_Mayeda_024, March 23, 1943, Morrish Collection.

140. 10_Mayeda_026, July 2, 1943, Morrish Collection.

141. 10_Mayeda_027, no date, but probably early/middle July, 1943, Morrish Collection.

142. 10_Mayeda_028, Aug. 13, 1943, Morrish Collection.

143. 10_Mayeda_029, Oct. 16, 1943, Morrish Collection.

144. 10_Mayeda_031, Oct. 22, 1943, Morrish Collection.

145. 24_Yamada_020, Jan 26, 1943, Morrish Collection.

146. 24_Yamada_024, March 23, 1943, Morrish Collection.

147. 24_Yamada_035, June 10, 1943, Morrish Collection.

148. Meg Jacobs, "'How About Some Meat?': The Office of Price Administration, Consumption Politics, and State Building from the Bottom Up, 1941–1946," *The Journal of American History* 84, no. 3 (December 1997): 910–941.

149. Ibid., 918.

150. 24_Yamada_037, August 4, 1943, Morrish Collection.

151. 24_Yamada_057, Dec. 16, 1943, Morrish Collection.

152. 24_Yamada_061, Jan 24, 1944, Morrish Collection.

153. 24_Yamada_071, March 17, 1944, Morrish Collection.

154. 24_Yamada_093, Jan 17, 1945, Morrish Collection.

CHAPTER SIX

Citizenship Restored? Joining the Army, Going Home

The July 4, 1942, edition of the *Tanforan Totalizer* contained a front-page editorial that recognized the problems of being kept in an assembly center while celebrating the ideas of freedom that July Fourth commemorates. It stated:

> To some, both here and on the outside, our observance of America's Independence Day in this Center will undoubtedly seem to partake of the nature of a paradox. The surface irony of our situation is apparent enough. But to let the mind dwell on this single facet of the matter would not only be fruitless; it would be prejudicial to all our hopes of returning eventually to the main stream of American life as useful citizens.[1]

The editorial ended with a plea not to dwell on the "special constraints and hardships—and, in many cases, the seeming injustices"—but to think about the future and the end of the war. Ironically enough, right next to this article was another on the Selective Service and the requirement that all 18–20-year-olds needed to register, including all aliens in this age group. Japanese Americans had been allowed to serve in the U.S. military before World War II. With the Japanese bombing of Pearl Harbor, however, that changed. Many were discharged for the same reason that

Japanese Americans were forced out of their homes and into internment camps—their race and the belief that some of them would be loyal to Japan simply due to their Japanese ancestry. And just as those interned still had to pay their taxes and maintain their property, while at the same time they were denied their livelihoods, so too did the men still have to register for the Selective Service from within the confines of the camps. And on January 20, 1944, the U.S. government announced that the internees could be conscripted to fight in the war.[2]

Many of the Japanese Americans and Japanese aliens being held in the camps wanted to be able to fight in the war, despite being held behind barbed wire. One alien evacuee from Topaz, Henry Ebihara, had written a letter to Secretary of War Stimson to request that the U.S. government allow him to serve in the military. He said that although he was an alien and born in Japan, he had lived the United States since he was two years old and was "American in thought, American in act, as American as any other citizen." He told Stimson that some of his friends had been injured in the "treacherous attack" at Pearl Harbor and that many of his friends were volunteering. He ended his letter by stating that he was sending a copy of it to President Roosevelt.[3]

Many second-generation U.S. citizens also voluntarily enlisted. Some internees in the Morrish Collection mentioned family members who were in the military. Mrs. Nakata wrote that her brother-in-law was fighting in France, three of her cousins were in the army, and one of these had been wounded in action in France. In total, she had six family members fighting in the military.[4] Mr. and Mrs. Yatabe, in particular, kept Morrish up to date with news about Yatabe's induction into the military and what happened in the fighting, right through the end of the war. On April 8, 1943, Yatabe wrote a letter to Morrish and told him, "Last month I volunteered for the newly created Japanese-American Combat Unit of the U.S. Army. I have already passed the first medical examination and am anxiously awaiting induction which I understand will take place very shortly."[5] The combat unit he is referring to is the famed 442nd, which was the all—Japanese American combat unit that would be sent to Europe to fight against the Germans (they were not allowed to fight in the Pacific theater). Morrish wrote back a few days later, wishing him good luck and advising that if his wife needed anything, to please have her contact him.[6] Later, on July 18, 1943, Yatabe told Morrish that he was finally about to be inducted the following Thursday at Fort Douglas and that his wife (who then began writing to Morrish) would be staying at Topaz while he was away on training. He also stated that he had friends in training and that it sounded very exhausting, so he probably wouldn't be writing for a while.[7] Toward the end of January 1944, Morrish had written to Mrs. Yatabe about some other matters and asked how her husband was doing. She replied on January 26, 1944, telling him that his first furlough was coming up and that he would be spending it in Topaz. She stated: "He finds army life very hard as they are preparing for active combat duty. In fact I doubt if actual battle conditions would be as difficult as the ordeals they go through in practice. However, he reports he is well and I can ask no more than that."[8]

What followed from Yatabe was a series of letters about her husband's getting injured numerous times while fighting in Europe. She wrote to Morrish on August 1, 1944, telling him that her husband had been wounded in Italy and was in a base hospital. He had been sending her letters and was anxious to get back to the fighting. She finished her letter:

> So many of his company have been wounded or killed we in camp are continually receiving bad news. For the first time in months I feel relieved as I know exactly where he is and that he is safe for a while. I hope that you have been well. The summer here has been very trying in many ways and I remember with much longing our beautiful Redwood weather.[9]

Yatabe then went back into the fighting but was wounded once again by a shell fragment to the knee soon after returning to active duty. He also received the Purple Heart and an Oak Leaf cluster, but as she told Morrish, "I could do with less medals and fewer scars." Yatabe had written to her soon after arriving at the hospital, but she still wasn't sure of the extent of his injuries. Morrish wrote back to Yatabe (September 26, 1944) and said that he was sorry to hear of his injuries and that he "has certainly done his share and I am very glad to know that he has received the Purple Heart and the Oak Leaf Cluster."[10] Yatabe then wrote a long, handwritten letter to Morrish in November 1944, stating that her husband was once again wounded:

> This news is getting almost monotonous but I thought you might be interested to know my husband was wounded again. This time in France where the 442nd is fighting with the Seventh Army. You know the 442nd was the regiment that rescued the group that was trapped near Vosges I believe it was. I am very proud of him and all the citations his regiment has been receiving but I wonder how long his luck can hold out.[11]

In that same letter, Yatabe mentioned that she was invited to California by a Mrs. Frank Duveneck of the American Friends Committee, to stay at her house in Los Altos, California. She asked Morrish if he could write a letter of recommendation for her, addressed to General Bonesteel, the commander of the Western Defense Command. Morrish responded (on November 28) that he would be happy to do this for her and that he would write the letter on that day.

The last two letters we have from Yatabe (at least regarding her husband) were sent to Morrish in December 1944 and January 1945. In December she told Morrish that her husband was returning from overseas for a rotation:

> This is a very wonderful Christmas for my son and me and I wish we could share our happiness with everyone. Please extend my best wishes to our friends in Redwood City. I don't expect to be back for sometime but I hope some day I shall be able to see them all again.[12]

By January, Yatabe had arrived in Topaz to spend his 30-day furlough with his wife.[13]

A few members in the Morrish Collection mentioned being drafted into the army. By January 1944, military officials announced that Japanese Americans in the relocation camps would now be drafted into the war effort.[14] The draft itself was met with some opposition in other relocation camps. Some people in Poston were arrested for draft resistance.[15] There is no evidence of resistance in the Morrish Collection, but the draft was certainly part of the conversation among the internees at Topaz. The Topaz Community Council endorsed it.[16] At the same time, many wondered why they should be forced into the military after having their rights taken away from them. As historian Brian Hayashi noted, more than 1,100 women at Topaz sent a letter to government officials in March 1944, asking that their civil rights be restored before their sons were taken away from them.[17] This was not done, and the draft continued.

Two other drafted internees from the Morrish Collection were T. Kitayama and Tsukagawa. Kitayama had a long correspondence with Morrish while he was living at Topaz. In March 1944, as he was about to be drafted into the military, he directed Morrish to appoint trustees to his accounts in order to settle his financial affairs. He also sent Morrish his safe-deposit keys and asked him to cancel the rent on the boxes since he wouldn't be needing them.[18] Like Kitayama, Tsukagawa also wrote to Morrish in March 1944 to tell him that he was about to be drafted. Tsukagawa was there with his family and was worried about what would happen to them if he was killed in the war. The major issue for him was that his parents were not American citizens and, therefore, could not own property, nor could they inherit property because of the Alien Property

Act. He wanted to have a place to come home to if he survived the war, and he wanted his parents taken care of. But he knew the law and asked Morrish if he had any advice on how to protect them if he died. He didn't want the state to take his property. He also wondered how he could pay his mortgage and keep his house when he was in the military.[19] Morrish responded that he should have a will and make his parents the beneficiaries. He also told him that there was a law in place to protect those in the military from foreclosure. However, Morrish knew that leaving a will was not good enough to protect his parents since he ended his letter with a postscript: "If you prefer not to make a will and if anything should happen to you, the property would revert to your folks but being aliens they could not hold title to the property and would have to sell it immediately for distribution."[20]

It wasn't until July, when Tsukagawa had his pre-induction physical exam, that his letters made it clear he was very worried about his property. He had been having trouble paying his mortgage while he was being held in Topaz, and he was desperate to make sure he would still own it when he got out of the military. Again he asked Morrish about what would happen if he couldn't make the mortgage while in the army. He stated: "I am trying everything I can to hold on to the property, because that is the only thing I have to come back to and live for."[21] Finally, Tsukagawa wrote on January 21, 1945, telling Morrish that he was now working in the Tooele Ordnance Depot just south of Salt Lake City as an ammunition handler. He wrote, "Every day we are either loading or unloading all sorts of ammunition. I have become familiar with all kinds of shells, bombs, mines, and guns. The work is very interesting, and I am happy here." He told Morrish that even though he was able to return to California, he couldn't because of his work, and that he was lucky that he would have a home to return to when the war was over and the relocation camps were closed.[22]

Others in the Morrish Collection helped with the war effort and were able to leave the relocation center to do so. Suzukawa, for one example, had written in January 1945 to tell Morrish that he was now living in Wisconsin and working overtime at a war plant.[23]

The willingness and even desire to serve in the American armed forces during the war may seem nearly incredible. But for most of these inductees, it was the ultimate show of patriotism and of loyalty—regardless of the extenuating circumstances of internment and public opinion otherwise. It was certainly one way out of the camps. Moreover, it was a powerful showing of courage and affirmation of the belief of holding up one's duties as a citizen.

On Going Back Home

The evacuation order that had forced many Japanese American citizens and their extended families away from the West Coast was rescinded in December 1944. This allowed all of the evacuees to go back home, and the government started to plan for the shutdown of the camps. It was, however, not as simple as leaving the camps and going back to their previous lives. Many of those held at Topaz worried about the reception they would receive when they went home after the war finished. It must have been a stressful time, considering many of them were losing whatever they had managed to hang on to throughout their captivity. Added to that, if they still had a place to go home to, what would life be like? Many believed it would not be the same as it had been before the war. Many too believed (and they were correct) that they would have to start over, with a new life and new businesses, returning home with hardly anything left.

Letters reveal that internees were worried and nervous about the process of going home throughout their forced stay at Topaz. Many who were able to leave camp wrote about their outside experiences. One such person that mentioned harassment early on was Fred Hoshiyama. In October 1942 he mentioned that he had taken his car in for repair and that two of the workmen swore at him. The foreman of the shop then came out and said that he would do the repair work.[24] He also wrote of two other experiences he had in late 1942. One was with Lorne Bell, the assistant project director of Topaz. Bell was asked about some discrimination that was happening within the camp itself between the Caucasian and Japanese American inmates. His response was that the Japanese Americans should get used to it because the treatment there was like the treatment they would receive on the outside. Hoshiyama also wrote that there was a sign in the soldiers' canteen at Topaz that read "No Japs Allowed Here."[25]

The internees also consistently fretted about finances in their letters from Topaz. The Honda family had left California before the official exclusion order for the peninsula had been issued. They went to Nevada and had written many letters to Morrish, who was taking care of their business. Honda sent Morrish a letter on April 25, 1942, and told him that he would like him to try to find a renter for his nursery. He was very worried about money and was trying to share the cost of upkeep with a potential tenant. He wrote: "By the time the war ends it will make it hard for me to put up large sum [sic] of money to take over or pay the expense for what he invest [sic]. If you have anyone to take over the place please make a good understanding with him so that I do not have too much money."[26]

He wrote again at the end of May 1942, worried that he would not have enough money at the end of the war to start over.[27]

Others also wrote about the possibility of running out of money and not being able to start over when the war ended. Mayeda (probably writing in July 1943) told Morrish that she and her brother were both working outside of the camp and trying to save money. She said she had sold a truck to someone who hadn't made any payments and if Morrish could get the truck back and save it for them, that would just be one less thing she would have to worry about when they returned. She told him:

> You'll have to excuse me for thinking of money so much. To tell you the truth, we're getting somewhat desperate when we think we have to start all over again. . . . My bank account must be pretty low by now. If there isn't enough to cover the interest and taxes, will you let me know and I'll have my brother draw on his account.[28]

About the same time, Mrs. Nakata sent Morrish a long letter requesting bank statements and money transfers. She needed to transfer $200 from her personal savings account into her business account. Although she didn't state why she needed the money in her commercial account, it was almost certainly needed to pay the bills for the business, and it is clear that the business wasn't bringing in enough money. Right after requesting the transfer she told Morrish:

> I don't know where the money goes, but it certainly seems to disappear. When all this is over, we won't have anything. We'll all have to start from scratch. There's so much prejudice against us that I often wonder what will happen to all of us.[29]

The fears of prejudice and tight finances after the war were justified. In early 1943 there were many groups in California who were still calling for the deportation of all Japanese Americans, including the American Legion and many local governments.[30] Newspapers in 1943 were still printing anti-Japanese articles, and these sometimes found their way to politicians in Washington, D.C., who then gave scathing comments about the internees—and it didn't matter that they were American citizens as well.[31] It should, however, be pointed out that many of these very same groups refused to support ballot issues like creating a constitutional amendment to take away the citizenship of the *Nisei* and to force them to go to Japan.[32] Some of the internees who were working in agriculture were also having a difficult time. In Hamilton, Montana, (and other places) the internees noted that they were not served in cafés and that barbers would not cut their hair. The workers vowed not to return to work there the following year.[33]

Not all was bad news, however. While the worry was real and the actions of many groups of Caucasian citizens on the West Coast were threatening, an early indicator of the "on-the-ground" feeling toward Japanese Americans can be seen in a long article in *TREK*, in February 1943. It was titled "Beyond the Gate" and focused on what life would be like when people left the camp. Much of the article focused on people leaving Topaz to do agricultural work, and many who were working outside of the camp were asked to fill out a survey by the Project Reports Division at Topaz. In January 1943, questionnaires were sent out to 450 people who were permitted to leave the camp by February 1943 to work both in agriculture and other employment. They were specifically asked about the conditions for them outside the camp and how they were received. The main question was: "As you look back on your experience, what impressions remain strongest in your mind of your reception in the community and your association with your employer?" Of those surveyed, 165 people sent back the form, with 121 being agricultural workers. The results of the survey were probably not as bad as many were anticipating. Of those, a large majority (more than 80 percent) answered "Good" for the questions on community reception and employer-worker relations:

Agricultural Workers

	Good	Fair	Poor
Community reception	84%	11%	5%
Employer-worker Relations	80%	11%	9%

Non-Agricultural Workers

	Good	Fair	Poor
Community reception	83%	15%	2%
Employer-worker Relations[34]	89%	11%	0%

The article then reproduced some of the comments that the workers had sent back on their questionnaires, and by far they were positive. The article, however, pointed out that while the great majority of responses were positive, these couldn't be taken as indicators of what feelings would be like when the war was over or what the reception would be like for people in other jobs. Despite this surface good news, many still worried, both about what life was like outside for those of Japanese ancestry and about how they would be able to afford to start again when they were released.

The announcement that the internees could go back to the West Coast was made on December 17, 1944, and stated they could begin returning home starting on January 1, 1945. The U.S. government put into place a policy to help the evacuees get back home, which included getting any stored material out of government warehouses and giving assistance to the evacuees.[35] In the early period, after the announcement, very few moved back to California. There were a few reasons for this, one being the postwar economy. As historian Kevin Leonard noted only about 1,300 of the internees returned by April 1945, primarily because of the bad reception that others faced when going home.[36] There were certainly cases of violence, with 25 reported toward the returnees, between January and the beginning of March 1945.[37]

As the time came closer to when people were thinking about going home and actually leaving the relocating centers, there were still many newspapers that were printing anti-Japanese messages or local law-enforcement officials who were going easy on people who were harassing the returnees. For example, the *Sacramento Union*, on June 1, 1945, published an article about a Caucasian farmer from Parlier, California, who had fired his rifle four times into the home of a Japanese American family (Charles Iwasaki) who had just returned from the camps. The farmer believed that his nephew had been killed by the Japanese in the war (he was mistaken). He was sentenced to a six-month suspended sentence. Secretary of the Interior Harold L. Ickes was upset about the lax sentencing and was calling for the demotion of the justice of the peace. However, the justice who had sentenced the farmer claimed to have talked to local people and "98 per cent of the people of the community feel the War Relocation Authority was wrong in sending the Japanese back here at this time, and a jail sentence for Multanen [the farmer] would fan anger to the point where other violence would be likely." The justice of the peace further stated that Iwasaki did not complain about the sentence.[38] An article right next to this one was on a resolution by the Shasta-Trinity Pomona Grange calling for a constitutional amendment that would prevent people of Japanese ancestry from becoming U.S. citizens. It called for sending Japanese aliens back to Japan and encouraged Japanese Americans to move to Japan to help form a new democratic Japanese government. The *San Francisco Chronicle* also reported that California State Senator Irwin T. Quinn was unhappy that the Japanese Americans were allowed to return home. He stated, "As far as

I am concerned, Dillon Myer ought to be shipped off to Japan." There was also a call by State Senator Jack B. Tenney of Los Angeles for an investigation into every single Japanese American released by the WRA. Other state senators agreed.[39]

Starting in early 1944, Morrish began to receive letters from those who were returning for brief stints to the coast thanks to the issuing of short-term passes. In early February 1944, George Nakano wrote that he was hoping to come back to Redwood City for a brief visit ("under escort, if need be") to handle some financial issues he was having. He also mentioned the return of a few men who were taken from Redwood City by the FBI (Rikimaru, K. Inouye [returning soon], and Yamane). According to Nakano, their return meant that all those taken by the FBI were now with their families.[40] Nakano wrote in August, saying that Ruyji Adachi (brother to Sumiye Adachi) had been in Redwood City recently and had returned to Topaz, telling people that he "found the conditions there quite favorable." He told Morrish that he too was requesting a pass to visit. He was hoping to visit toward the beginning of September.[41] According to Morrish, Ruyji Adachi, George Nakano, and George Tsukagawa were all able to get ten-day passes.[42]

With the visitation and reporting back of those who had visited Redwood City becoming more common, some internees in Topaz began writing to Morrish about those reports, or to inform him where people were beginning to relocate. An example is Rikimaru, who at the very end of October 1944 sent instructions to pay his own taxes with money in his daughter's account and the CCGA's taxes from the association's funds. He said that he hoped to see George Nakano in a few days (Nakano, as stated above, had visited Redwood City), and he told Morrish that many people from Topaz were relocating east, including his three kids. He too wanted to relocate next year.[43] While he didn't ask about the conditions at home in this letter, he sent another letter to Morrish on December 31, 1944, stating that other internees would be arriving, and he asked that Morrish help them out as they readjusted.[44] He made the same request in early January 1945, when he told Morrish that a few in the community (Sumiye Adachi, her sister, and T. Tori) would be returning to Redwood City.[45]

With the news that people would be allowed to go back home, it is no surprise that many people wrote to Morrish to ask about the conditions for returning to Redwood City. For example, K. Yamada, writing from Gila River, wrote on December 12, 1944, requesting that Morrish visit her house and specifically the storeroom to make sure that things were still there. She also asked:

We also want to hear from you on this subject of returning to California. Please advise us on this situation. What are the people in Topaz planning to do? Would you kindly enlighten us on all the above inquires in your next letter? About a week ago we have sent you a gift so I hope you received and like them.[46]

Morrish wrote back three days later with a long response:

As far as I know there have been no plans by the people in Topaz for coming back. I have heard that there have been a few Japanese come back to the county; most of them, however, have come back to do domestic work and one berry grower in Santa Clara Country, I have been informed, has returned. There have been two or three of the boys come back on a ten-day leave during the last two or three months. They were George Tsukagawa, George Nakano, and young Adachi. They did not come together, but separately. One of them came to get a car. I noticed in the newspaper there was some difficulty with one of the boys with some of the Fillipinos [sic], but other than that, I believe their reception was all right.[47]

The one problem notwithstanding, Morrish seemed to believe that it would be fine for people to start returning.

Ms. Fumiko Tagaki also wrote to Morrish about the conditions back home. She mentioned "unfavorable reports" from California that some of the evacuees were receiving, and she wanted Morrish to send her any newspaper articles on what was going on.[48] However, his reponse to Tagaki on December 27, 1944, and many letters written by him in January 1945, tell a slightly different story than what he mentioned to Yamada. People must have been returning and finding that they had nowhere to go, or that they had to kick out the people who had been living in their houses while they were interned. He told Tagaki that many of the newspapers in San Francisco and on the peninsula were reporting the housing problem, mostly because those returning would have to displace those living in their houses.[49] He sent her a few articles to read on January 5, 1945.

Morrish also had written to Rikimaru in early January 1945, telling him that he had seen a few people from Redwood City and had heard of people returning to San Francisco and Los Angeles. He then stated: "The one thing I believe the folks should make sure of before returning is a place to stay. Housing seems to be a great problem at the present time and unless they arrange ahead of time for quarters, I am afraid that it will be a real problem for them."[50]

Kitayama sent Morrish a letter in the middle of January 1945, with the entire note being about returning. He wrote:

Now that the Exclusion Order is being lifted, many of us are thinking of returning to our homes. We too are very anxious to do so but we are too uncertain about the general feelings or atmosphere around the community. Frankly Mr. Morrish, you as a third person, can you give us your opinion? I heard number [sic] of "incidents" after few [sic] people returned in the early part. Will you please let me hear from you.[51]

He left a postscript asking Morrish to deposit a check into his commercial account. Like his response to Rikimaru, Morrish was worried about the housing situation. Sending a reply just three days later, Morrish wrote:

Your letter of January 14th enclosing a check for deposit was received and duplicate tag is enclosed. Several of the folks have been in recently, most of them on a visit and to look over their property. The only ones who have come back permanently are Sumiye Adachi and her sister, who are living on the place now and their brother and Haruke Inouye, who are living on the Stanford University campus and teaching Japanese at the university. Harumi Higaki was in last week for a few days but has gone back again. I think the feeling locally would be for most part all right; however there is a real problem on housing and any of the folks coming back should very definitely arrange their housing beforehand, as I think if it was necessary to move somebody, the action would not be so good. I believe, however, that wherever possible, it would be best to delay returning a few months until the general public got used to the idea of the return. Then it would be a more natural result by a few coming back at a time.[52]

The housing situation was certainly a serious one. Many people represented in the Morrish Collection had rented out their houses and farms, with legal leases, and now that the relocation centers were being closed down, those who were interned needed somewhere to go. It was natural that they wanted to go back to their own houses, but many of them would have to face the reality of coming back to no housing, and much of their saved money (if they had had any in the first place) was gone. The press reports did not make them feel any better. There were reports that people who were returning needed government assistance for not only food but also temporary housing. The *San Francisco Chronicle* reported on June 26, 1945, that 700 out of the 4,000 evacuees that had returned to California were on the state relief rolls.[53] In August 1945, the *Chronicle* also printed an article about some of the returning evacuees and the issues they were facing. Some of them were related to the fear of their reception back into their communities. For others, they had no housing, and hostels were set up, and representatives of the hostels would meet groups of the returnees at the train station.[54]

Some writers in the Morrish Collection asked about extending their leases as a possible path. Okamura inquired (by way of Rikimaru) whether he should sign a new two-year lease (running through 1947), stay with a one-year extension, or just sell. Okamura wanted to have a clause in the potential lease stating that he could come back at any point, with a two-month notice given to the tenant. He also needed a response as soon as possible since he would have no place to live once the relocation center closed.[55] Unfortunately we don't have the response from Morrish (if he indeed sent one).

There were others who were also renting out their houses and needed to vacate the renters so that they could move home. Ms. Fumilo Tagaki wrote to Morrish in March 1945, telling him that they had heard that Topaz would be closed by the end of the year and that her family would need to move back home. She wanted to know if the lease they had with the tenants could be changed to include a line that they could have the house back with a month's notice. She told Morrish that she understood it would be difficult for the tenants, and as a compromise, she suggested that the lessee rent out the land but not the house.[56] Morrish wrote back and said he had visited their ranch, and the lessees were having their own housing problems. Morrish suggested that the family stay in camp as long as possible.[57] He wrote again a few weeks later to tell her the exact same thing—to stay in the camp until the current lease was up. It wasn't until the end of July 1945 that Morrish told her that the lessees were planning to move out of the house when their lease was up, but this was not enough for her to get permission to go back home. She wrote to Morrish to tell him that despite his letter of recommendation, her application was turned down because, while she would have housing, she needed proof that she would have work.[58] Morrish wrote the letter for her.

In the meantime, Tagaki left her work in Detroit and took a train back to Topaz. She wrote to Morrish from there, reminding him that the lease on her house expired at the end of September, even though the lessee stated he and his family could not move out until the end of November. She wanted Morrish to make sure the house was ready for the family when they returned.[59] Despite this, the lessee told Tagaki, when she visited her ranch in the middle of September, that he would not be leaving until November 15. Morrish had written to Tagaki's father and told him that he should stay in camp until it officially closed, and in the end, he agreed that he would find alternative housing.[60] The Tagaki's were able to move back to their house, but there were still problems. Morrish sent a letter to the ex-lessee in December 1945, telling him that the Tagaki's noticed that many of their personal items were missing from their house. He sent a long list of these items, including a bed, pipes, kitchen chairs, encyclopedias, and a set of history books.[61] While they did get their house back, it is clear that they suffered an even greater financial loss with the property that was stolen when they were kept at Topaz.

The Mayedas, too, had some difficulties. N. Mayeda had written to Morrish in the middle of February 1945, telling Morrish that Topaz would be closing soon and that she didn't want Morrish to lease out her property again. Mayeda told Morrish that if it had been rented out, she would like the lessee to surrender the lease. If that was not possible, she would like Morrish to talk to the lessee and arrange to have her family live in a little room on the side of the barn until the lease was up.[62] S. Mayeda (the father of N. Mayeda) then wrote a few days later and told Morrish that they would be willing to keep a year lease on the house, but that he wanted to live in the room by the barn.[63] Morrish wrote back on February 20, 1945, stating that unfortunately the house had been leased, and the agreement was back-dated to November 1944, since that was when the lessee started using the property. He told Mayeda that they had done quite a bit of work on the property and that he would ask them about using the small room next to the barn.[64] A week later Morrish had talked to the lessee and was told that "they advise that they do not have sufficient room as it is on your place"; Morrish then stated, "I think the best thing for you to do when one of you folks come down is to go over the matter with them personally." Morrish thought that since all of their things were in the barn it shouldn't be a problem. He also mentioned that the lessee had done quite a bit of work getting the chrysanthemum beds ready for next year. Morrish told N. Mayeda that since it was an issue with the lease, the two of them would have to work out a solution.[65]

Mayeda's father must have made it back to California and more than likely was living in the room by the barn. However, he was having some difficulties. Mayeda sent a letter in May 1945, stating that her father was threatened with arrest by the inspector of San Mateo County. The inspector had looked at their property and decided that it wasn't clean enough. Her father did not speak English, and she asked Morrish if he could talk to the inspector.[66] As it turned out, her father was using an outhouse, and someone had complained about it. The city was building a new sewer line, and the Mayedas would have to arrange to have the house hooked up to it. In July 1945, Mrs. Fukuma (previously Ms. Mayeda) wrote to Morrish to tell him that the family was back in Palo Alto and that Mr. Mee, their lessee, was taking good care of the ranch. She also noted that they were now employees of Mee on their own ranch.[67]

The Yamada family had similar problems, although most of their issues centered on tenants who would not leave and should not have been there in the first place. S. Yamada wanted to move back to his home, and Morrish told him (January 5, 1945) that before he moved back to make sure the house would be available. He reminded him that the property (but not the house) was leased for the year.[68] A few days later Yamada wrote back to Morrish to tell him that there was a clause in the lease that stated it could be dissolved when they returned, as long as they gave notice. He told Morrish that he was probably going into the army, and when he temporarily returned to Redwood City, he would arrange to stay in their other house, which contained all of their furnishings. Rikimaru, to whom Morrish had written about the same time, had recommended to Yamada and others to remain in the camp. He wrote that they should stay because of the "many problems and handicaps of starting over again and has advised them to stay in camp. The reason for this is because he knows our financial status is not favorable and that we sold most of our equipment. It hurts my pride to see my folks left behind there in camp so I wish to return to get into some defense job and prepare for my family's return as soon as proper arrangements can be made. If we can make a deal with the party leasing our place to move into the other house and share our land till the lease expires, so much the better. I hope to return around the 1st of February or later."[69]

Morrish wrote back to Yamada, reminding him that there was still a family in their house and that they could not get them out. The current tenants were there illegally and had been a source of problems for Morrish, starting back in 1943. People had moved in who did not pay rent, and when he finally got them out, another family just moved in. In December 1943 Morrish even threatened to call the police to get them to move out.[70] However, the family (as stated earlier) had promised to pay rent after the new year, so Morrish let them stay. This family was still there in January 1945, and Morrish still could not get them out. The Yamada family was back in their home by December 1945.[71]

The last example we can look at is Mrs. Nakata. She kept up a lively correspondence with Morrish through most of the war, updating him on what her family was doing. Starting in January 1945, she told Morrish that her family wanted to go back to Tracy, California, where her husband's family was from.[72] In July 1945 she wrote about the troublemakers at Tule Lake and also related that her children were doing well. She told him that her husband wanted to relocate east, but she said she has two "weak children and an old mother" and was worried about the cold winters. She also wrote: "But at the relocation office—we notice more attractive offers in the

East than on the Pacific Coast. He has always wanted to go into farming or dairying—we're afraid to return to our home on the Bayshore Highway— it's too public." She told him about all the other places her family members had relocated and ended her letter by asking Morrish about employment prospects in the area since she had met someone who had just visited San Francisco and said that everyone was very friendly to him.[73] Morrish responded:

> If you folks really want to come back to your place on the highway, I can see no reason why you shouldn't do so. I have heard of no trouble whatsoever locally and a good many of the folks are back in their homes and a number of younger girls I know are out doing housework and seem to be getting along fine.[74]

He mentioned other housekeeping jobs. Finally, he wrote to her on August 8, 1945, telling her that many from the community were back, and he thought that by Thanksgiving most of them would be back.[75] The Nakata family had relocated back to the area by December 1945, although they were not in the Bayshore property because they could not get their tenants out.[76] It wasn't until February 1946 that Nakata wrote to Morrish from their Bayshore address, telling him that her husband was working five days a week and she was busy planting seedlings. She hoped to sell plants and bedding material.[77]

Those families who came back home to Redwood City generally did not experience much conflict, according to the correspondence. The Nakano family, who went back home in March 1945, was one of them. The family received $25 per person from the WRA and train tickets, and they were then on their own. Jim Nakano stated that "they went through every store and bought things" with ration cards and had no problems with the community receiving them back. The family also said that they were lucky to have a place to come back to as many did not. They were also fortunate that their lessee, Harry Lee, gave back the business to them. Their family even hosted a family from Tule Lake who were considering going back to Japan when they had no place to go.[78] Jim Mori, in an interview, stated that his family too had no problem with moving back to Redwood City, other than one issue with a cashier at the local Safeway grocery store.[79]

The return "home" after internment remains relatively underresearched. Whether internees returned to their previous hometowns or relocated to points east, the adjustment and resettlement after the war was likely as jarring as the relocation to the camps in the first place, although in a different sense. The destabilization of security as either a citizen or a legal resident of the United States left an indelible signature on those who had been interned. It also left an indelible signature of the democratic government of the United States. It remains an American legacy that structures of government, the military, and individual citizens functioned together to support the stripping of the constitutional rights of one population, characterized by their nationality and by their race, and that something like the internment could be architected so quickly, with relatively little widespread destabilization, except against those upon whom the act was perpetrated. In the aftermath, the status of citizenship remains unsecured.

Notes

1. *Tanforan Totalizer* 1, no. 8 (July 4, 1942): 1.
2. Brian Masaru Hayashi, *Democratizing the Enemy: The Japanese American Internment* (Princeton, NJ: Princeton University Press, 2004), 181.
3. *TREK* (February 1943): 12.
4. 16_Nakata_023, Nov. 22, 1944, Morrish Collection.
5. 26_Yatabe_012, April 8, 1943, Morrish Collection.
6. 26_Yatabe_013, April 12, 1943, Morrish Collection.
7. 26_Yatabe_015, July 18, 1943, Morrish Collection.
8. 26_Yatabe_022, Jan. 26, 1944, Morrish Collection.
9. 26_Yatabe_026, Aug. 1, 1944, Morrish Collection.
10. 26_Yatabe_029, Sept. 26, 1944, Morrish Collection.
11. 26_Yatabe_030, Nov. 13, 1944, Morrish Collection.
12. 26_Yatabe_032, Dec. 22, 1944, Morrish Collection.
13. 26_Yatabe_033, Jan. 29, 1945, Morrish Collection.
14. Hayashi, *Democratizing the Enemy*, 180.
15. Ibid., 181. Hayashi also notes that there was some resistance at Manzanar, 185.
16. Ibid., 181.
17. Ibid., 183.
18. 08_Kitayama_019, March 2, 1944, Morrish Collection.
19. 21_Tsukagawa_030, March 26, 1944, Morrish Collection.
20. 21_Tsukagawa_031, March 31, 1944, Morrish Collection.
21. 21_Tsukagawa_036, July 14, 1944, Morrish Collection.
22. 21_Tsukagawa_042, Jan. 21, 1945, Morrish Collection.
23. 19_Suzukawa_015, Jan. 12, 1945, Morrish Collection.
24. Fred Hoshiyama, Diary, October 19, 1942, 46, http://digitalassets.lib.berkeley.edu/jarda/ucb/text/cubanc6714_b095h09_0004.pdf, accessed May 1, 2016.
25. Ibid., November 8, 1942, 72; and November 13, 1942, 78.
26. 04_Honda_32, April 25, 1942, Morrish Collection.
27. 04_Honda_053, May 30, 1942, Morrish Collection.
28. 10_Mayeda_027, probably July 1943, Morrish Collection.

29. 16_Nakata_016, Aug. 27, 1943, Morrish Collection.

30. K. A. Leonard, "'Is That What We Fought for?' Japanese Americans and Racism in California, The Impact of World War II," *The Western Historical Quarterly* 21, no. 4 (November 1990): 465.

31. Ibid., 466.

32. Carey McWillians, *Japanese Evacuation: Interim Report* (New York, NY: American Council Institute of Pacific Relations, 1942), 36.

33. Louis Fisit, "Thinning, Topping, and Loading: Japanese Americans and Beet Sugar in World War II," *The Pacific Northwest Quarterly* 90, no. 3 (Summer 1999): 131.

34. Table reproduced from *TREK* (February 1943): 6.

35. U.S. War Relocation Authority, U.S. Department of the Interior, *The Wartime Handling of Evacuee Property*, vol. II (Washington, D.C.: U.S. Government Printing Office, n.d.; reprinted in New York, NY: AMS Press, 1975), 84.

36. Leonard, "Is That What We Fought for?" 468.

37. Sandra C. Taylor, *Jewel of the Desert: Japanese American Internment at Topaz* (Berkeley: University of California Press, 1993), 212.

38. *Sacramento Union* (June 1, 1945), http://digitalassets.lib.berkeley.edu/jarda /ucb/text/cubanc6714_b326w02_0054_2.pdf#page=27, accessed May 18, 2016.

39. *San Francisco Chronicle* (June 7, 1945), http://digitalassets.lib.berkeley.edu /jarda/ucb/text/cubanc6714_b326w02_0054_2.pdf#page=27, accessed May 18, 2016.

40. 15_Nakano_014, Feb. 18, 1944, Morrish Collection.

41. 14_Nakano_026, Aug. 16, 1944, Morrish Collection.

42. 24_Yamada_089, Dec. 15, 1944, Morrish Collection.

43. 18_Rikimaru_029, Oct. 31, 1944, Morrish Collection.

44. 18_Rikimaru_034, Dec. 31, 1944, Morrish Collection.

45. 18_Rikimaru_036, Jan. 6, 1945, Morrish Collection.

46. 24_Yamada_087, Dec. 12, 1944, Morrish Collection.

47. 24_Yamada_089, Dec. 15, 1944, Morrish Collection.

48. 20_Tagaki_183, Dec. 17, 1944, Morrish Collection.

49. 20_Tagaki_184, Dec. 27, 1944, Morrish Collection.

50. 18_Rikimaru_035, Jan. 5, 1945, Morrish Collection.

51. 08_Kitayama_040, Jan. 14, 1945, Morrish Collection.

52. 08_Kitayama_041, Jan. 17, 1945, Morrish Collection.

53. *San Francisco Chronicle* (June 26, 1945).

54. Ibid. (Aug. 2, 1945).

55. 18_Rikimaru_039, Feb. 6, 1945, Morrish Collection.

56. 20_Tagaki_190, March 5, 1945, Morrish Collection.

57. 20_Tagaki_191, March 19, 1945, Morrish Collection.

58. 20_Tagaki_200, Aug. 5, 1945, Morrish Collection.

59. 20_Tagaki_204, Aug. 29, 1945, Morrish Collection.

60. 20_Tagaki_205, Sept. 14, 1945; 20_Tagaki_206, Sept. 20, 1945—both Morrish Collection.

61. 20_Tagaki_208, Dec. 14, 1945, Morrish Collection.

62. 10_Mayeda_055, Feb. 16, 1945, Morrish Collection.

63. 10_Mayeda_056, Feb. 19, 1945, Morrish Collection.

64. 10_Mayeda_057, Feb. 20, 1945, Morrish Collection.

65. 10_Mayeda_058, Feb. 28, 1945, Morrish Collection.

66. 10_Mayeda_065, May 4, 1945, Morrish Collection.

67. 10_Mayeda_071, July 1, 1945, Morrish Collection.

68. 24_Yamada_091, Jan. 10, 1945, Morrish Collection.

69. 24_Yamada_092, Jan. 15, 1945, Morrish Collection.

70. 24_Yamada_057, Dec. 16, 1943, Morrish Collection.

71. It might have been earlier, but the first letter we have from the family with their home address was December.

72. 16_Nakata_026, Jan. 14, 1945, Morrish Collection.

73. 16_Nakata_030, July 2, 1945, Morrish Collection.

74. 16_Nakata_030, July 2, 1945, Morrish Collection.

75. 16_Nakata_033, Aug. 8, 1945, Morrish Collection.

76. 16_Nakata_046, Dec. 11, 1945, Morrish Collection.

77. 16_Nakata_048, Feb. 15, 1946, Morrish Collection.

78. Video interview, Aug. 27, 2003.

79. Oral Interview, March 2003.

PART 2

The Banker and His Documents

CHAPTER SEVEN

What Morrish Was Doing during This Period (Transcribed Letters)

There is one theme of the Morrish Collection that permeates almost all of the correspondence: gratitude. However we may choose to analyze his role in supporting the interned, and thus in some sense the internment itself, any criticism by no means undermines the efforts he took on behalf of his clients. Morrish was the vice president of the First National Bank in Redwood City during the war. While it isn't clear how exactly he became involved in the direct affairs of Japanese American citizens and residents during this period, it is clear that he spent a huge amount of time and effort making sure the internees were taken care of and that their businesses and personal property were kept intact during their internment.

The Morrish Collection (as we have named it) contains nearly 2,000 documents relating to Japanese Americans and Japanese aliens and their interactions with Morrish. About 1,500 of these are letters written back and forth, while the rest are tax documents, receipts, and some of Morrish's personal letters. Morrish wrote nearly 800 individual letters to 25 families over a 3-year period (and in some cases he helped some people after the war had finished and after they were allowed to go back home). These documents have never been published before, and they give us a fresh glimpse at what was going on in the minds of these Americans who were forcibly taken away, just because of what they looked like, during World War II. It also gives us a glimpse of the tireless work that Morrish did in protecting this community from financial ruin.

The following chapter introduces the seven major things that Morrish accomplished during the war. The chapter is organized by giving a short introduction to the topics and then giving the primary sources to illustrate what Morrish was doing during the time of internment. The seven categories are: 1) helping the interned with their financial affairs, including paying their taxes; 2) visiting the properties of the interned to make sure everything was running smoothly; 3) visiting some internees when they were in Tanforan; 4) writing letters of support for some internees, especially if they wanted to leave the camps for work elsewhere or if they needed a letter from a Caucasian person so that they could join the military; 5) sending things to the internees; 6) selling personal items and leasing property; and 7) receiving gifts from those he was helping. This chapter also contains several transcribed copies of the letters (the lists do not contain every single instance when these occur in the Morrish Collection—just the highlights were chosen). Five or six examples of each category will be given. Many of the letters contain other information not related to these categories, but the letters were not edited. Following this chapter will be several reproductions of other letters in the Morrish Collection.

Financial Transactions

One of the main duties that Morrish took on for these internees was helping them with their finances. As previously mentioned, the internees still had to pay their taxes and could be fined for not paying them or for paying late. They still had to maintain their properties and pay the various insurances on them. Some also had to keep their businesses going, in hopes that they would be able to come back home and pick up where they had left off. Morrish helped them with all of these challenges.

June 13, 1942.

[A letter to Adachi about various financial transactions.]

Dear Miss Adachi:—

I had thought that I might be able to get to Tanforan today but find that I can not make it so will make an effort to do so sometime next week.

I have one or two things I wanted to write you about, however, and will talk further with you about them next time I see you. Several payments have come in from the attorney making collections and the amounts have been credited to the California Chrysanthemum Growers Association. I am no [sic] sure if you want duplicates of these sent to you there or not. If you do, I will be glad to send them on as collections come in.

I have received two or three water bills that I am not clear on just how to handle. Perhaps you can help me out:— The Belmont Farms Co. bill for $1.00, $11.45 closing bill; T. Yatabe on Valota Road $1.00, $1.00 and $2.75 closing; T. Kitiyama, Horgan Ranch, $1.55 closing. None of these folks gave me any instructions. If they are at Tanforan and you see them and they wish me to charge their account and pay their bills, I will be glad to do so.

While you were here one day, I spoke to you about a bill from the Standard Printing Co. for the Bay Nursery, Kamada Bros for $93.22. I have heard nothing from them on this and was wondering if you could give me their address so that I can make an effort to collect this for our client.

The checks that you enclosed with your letter have been credited to your two accounts as indicated on the duplicate tags that are enclosed.

A bill from the Water Company came in addressed to you in the amount of $39.67. I have sent this on to Walter Gillo for payment. I have not heard anything from him yet in regard to rent payment. If you want me to get after him on this please let me know.

Yesterday I was out at the office with the Standard Oil man to check up on a number on one of the parts of equipment that was in the office and also he wished to leave a burner that was apparently returned to him. Everything looked fine there at the ranch and the place seemed to be in very good condition.

Please remember me to the folks there and I will try and see them sometime next week.

> Yours very truly,
> J.E. Morrish
> Vice President[1]

November 19, 1942.

[A letter to George Sawamura, c/o Adachi, Topaz, Utah, about paying the taxes.]

Dear Mr. Sawamura (c/o/ Miss Adachi):—

Today I received copies of the City and County Tax bills for Wm. H. and Reo Kitagawa, City showing $136.35 covering two installments and the County $121.37 covering the two installments. It was my understanding that George Capitelli is going to pay these taxes for your account and I will stop and see him this week in regard to it.

The loan payment book that you left with me I have sent to the Title Company to have brought to date. The balance is now shown as $5012.12. Payments are to date and interest is paid to October 13, 1942.

I have been on the place a time or two lately and I think George is doing very well taking care of it. I noticed he cleaned up around and it looks fine. No doubt you have heard from him direct.

We had a fine rain this week and it has been very helpful to the gardens. The grass is coming up in the hills and it looks very pretty.

I hope this finds you and the family all fine. Kindest regards.

> Yours very truly,
> J.E. Morrish[2]
> Vice President[3]

March 17, 1944.

[Rikimaru typed a letter to Morrish with a long list of financial requests.]

Dear Mr. Morrish:

Will you please kindly do the following business for me.

1. Toru Yamane wants to know the balance of his account. His Federal Reserve Bank account numbers is NO. #####.

2. Toru Tamane wants to know his Buick (1942 early model) condition, also he would like to know the price of the car, in case he dicide [sic] to sell it. His car is in Davies Auto Company, Redwood City.

3. R. S. Yamane wants to sale [sic] his new Black cloth. He has about 650 yards and he packed it in a box and left it over our warehouse [sic]. He puts [sic] his name on top of the box so you will have no difficult time finding it. He wants to get about $275.00 for it.

4. K. Yamane wants you to sent [sic] here One Typewriter (Royal No. Y 38-107236) and One Trunk from warehouse.

Please charge all packing, express and other expense to our business to California Chrysanthemum Growers Ass'ns' account.

> Yours respectfully,
> J. I. Rikimaru

[In a handwritten note:] p.s. Kaoru Okamura wants to sell his Defense Bond. Can you sell for him? He wants to know price too. He says he keeps all his bonds in your bank's safety box.[4]

Morrish had put an "x" in the margins beside numbers 2, 3, and 4, showing when he had completed the requests.

Visiting Internee Property

Morrish spent some of his time going out and inspecting the properties of various internees, sometimes on his own initiative and other times when he was requested.

June 13, 1942.

[Morrish wrote to Naoye Mayeda, telling him he had been out to the ranch a few times and everything looked fine.]

Dear Mr. Mayeda:—
    Your letter of May 29th with check enclosed came in while I was away on a short vacation and this amount was credited to your account and I am enclosing a duplicate tag.

Mr. Hassler has been in a time or two and seems to be getting along all right, also I have been by the ranch a couple of times and it looks fine and Mr. Hassler always seems to be very busy there.

Hope everything is going along nicely with you and your family.

Yours very truly,
J.E. Morrish
Vice President[5]

June 17, 1942.

[This is a postcard from M. Yamada asking Morrish to look in on two houses.]

Dear Mr. Morrish,

How are you and all down in Redwood City? All is well down here at Turlock Ass. Center. The weather is just fine, so we are getting along nicely.

We may be sent to another relocation somewhere in another state. Other centers have got their orders already.

Hope everything is o.k. at Woodside in Hogan Ranch. I have two houses at Woodside. One on the right side also. Please when you are the [sic] house look at the other, because we stored our furniture, cars, and etc. Hope no one has been in it.

Thank you.
M. Yamada[6]

October 24, 1942.

[A letter from Morrish to Nakata about his visit to that family's property.]

Dear Mrs. Nakata:—

This morning I received your very interesting letter and I am glad to know that you are finally getting settled in the new location. Perhaps after the rainy weather starts your experience with the dust will be over; I hope so at any rate. It will be very interesting to see what is done there with the camp within the year. From what I hear the soil conditions are good there for certain things and perhaps the camp will be on its own by that time.

Glad to hear about your husband being so busy. Tell him that we young fellows have to keep busy to keep out of mischief.

I was by your place the other day and it looks very well. I know that you miss your flowers and vegetables, and you are certainly going to enjoy them again when you get back.

Glad to know the children are all right. My kindest regards to you.

Yours very truly,
J.E. Morrish
Vice President[7]

November 23, 1942.

[A letter from Morrish to Mayeda.]

Dear Miss Mayeda:—

Recently I received from the County Tax Collector a bill for $145.90 for 1942–43 taxes both 1st and 2nd installments. The bill that you sent to me and which I paid for you was in the amount of $150.50. This bill shows taxes for lot eleven—five acres Faber subdivision. Did you receive a paid bill covering the payment of $150.50. Please let me know if these bills are for the same property.

I was by the place last Sunday and noticed a good many flowers unpicked. I talked to Mr. Hasler and he told me he had lots of difficulty in getting help and that he could not get enough help to do the picking. He was quite disappointed in his net returns for the season. In reference to the rental he is about six months behind now but has promised very definitely to take care of it in the next two weeks.

Kindest regards to you.

Yours very truly,
J.E. Morrish
Vice President[8]

November 23, 1943.

[Morrish wrote a letter to George Nakano. Although the letter is not about Morrish himself visiting the Nakano property, someone else did and reported to Morrish, and he planned on looking.]

Dear George:

This morning Frank Osorio told me that yesterday when he was going by your property he noticed the door of the house was opened

and he shut it and later on met one of the boys working for Harry
Lee and spoke to him about it and thought it was rather odd that the
door was opened and they looked around and found that a
window was broken. Someone had been in the house, apparently
nothing much had been disturbed but I think perhaps we should
board the windows up and if you will care to send me the key, I will
go down and see if everything looks all right and have the windows
boarded up. This is the first difficulty of this kind that I have had
occasion to check up.

I hope this finds you and the family fine. Kindest regards.

> Yours very truly,
> J.E. Morrish
> Vice President[9]

December 20, 1943.

[A letter from Morrish to Mayeda.]

Dear Mrs. Mayeda:
Today I was out at the ranch to deliver the lease to the
Chinese boys and I looked the place over while there. As far as I
can see they are taking very good care of the place. They have just
planted the Bayshore frontage in spinach and under the stick houses
they have sweet peas coming up. The shed where your furniture is
stored is still locked and the boys have promised to watch out for things
and I believe that they will. They have never been in the place where
your furniture is and as far as I can tell no one has been in since you
left. It would be quite difficult for you to get an inventory now on lumber,
pipe, etc. They apparently are not using any of the sticks as they
are all piled up where you left them and I notice that the hose is still
inside where they kept their tools and equipment. They have quite a lot
of their own equipment that they keep in the shed next to the house. If
you can remember what the lumber, pipe, tools, hose, etc. that you left,
let me know and I can check with the boys to see if it is still there. I
wrote to Mr. Hassler several times to try to get a list from him but
I have not been able to get it.

Kindest regards to you and my best wishes to you all for a Happy Christmas.

Yours very truly,
J.E. Morrish
Vice President[10]

December 7, 1944.

[A letter from Morrish to Mr Kitagawa.]

Dear Mr. Kitagawa:

Enclosed please find debit memorandums of tax payments, which I have just cleared, paying the first and second installments of the Redwood City taxes all for 1944–1945 in the amount of $150.49. The tax receipts have been filed in your file here at the bank.

I have been out to your place several times and things look fairly good there. George is doing a good job in keeping things up and I think he has been doing very well.

Taxes will be collected from George and refunded to your account.

I hope everything has been going along nicely with you folks. Kindest regards to you.

Yours very truly,
J.E. Morrish
Vice President[11]

Going to Tanforan

As well visiting internee properties, Morrish also made numerous trips to the assembly center at Tanforan, in the city of San Bruno, California, from Redwood City.

June 16, 1942.

[Morrish was trying to organize a number of people to meet him when he was out at Tanforan.]

Dear Miss Adachi:—

We are enclosing duplicate tags showing credit to the California Chrysanthemum Growers Association, one for $50.00 covering the check I have been holding for collection and a $500.00 deposit was received from Single, Bryant, Cook & Herrington.

I am in hopes of getting up to see you sometime Thursday morning. Will try and be there around ten o'clock. Would like to see Ham Honda, H. Inouye, Mrs. Okamura and any other of the Redwood City people who happen to be around at that time of the day.

> Kindest regards to you.
> Yours very truly,
> J.E. Morrish
> Vice President[12]

June 18, 1942.

[Morrish wrote a very long letter to Miss F. Tagaki, who was not at Tanforan but was staying in Marysville, California. He mentioned, along with a number of business transactions, his visit to Tanforan.]

Dear Famiko:

This morning I received your letter of June 17 and will be glad to take care of the bills that you enclosed. I will charge the Takamum Nursery commercial account and mail a cashiers check. In regard to your P.G. & E. service, I have already arranged to have that turned off next week. I would have had it turned off before but Al Decia has been using the water for the glads and this week he told me the day before yesterday would finish the crop [*sic*]. It has not been very good money and the blooms have not been perfect.

I talked to George Boring in reference to the insurance. This is not for the house, but it is for the liability and property damage on your Oldsmobile. If you folks do store these two cars, be sure to let me know and we can get some return premiums on the car insurance, as during that period it should not be necessary for you to pay anything except fire and theft. It will be necessary, of course, for you to continue with your payments on fire insurance covering your property in Los Altos for your own protection as well as for the bank. However, [can't read this word] these policies you have paid for the insurance so that it will not be necessary to make any further payment until June, 1943. I am in hopes that you will be back by that time, but, if not, we will write you further about it.

I have been out to your ranch again with two different parties who are quite interested in the property. One of them, a Mr. Coats from Palo Alto, is expecting a friend down this weekend who would go in partners with him on a deal, and, if the party he is waiting for is as interested as he is, I think probably they will take it over. If that does not work out, there is another party, an old couple, who would be willing to go in the house on a month to month basis, paying a very small rental property of perhaps $10 to $15, just to have someone there to watch out for the property. I think this is very important and believe it to your advantage to have someone there even though you were unable to get any rent. So, unless I hear from you to the contrary and if Mr. Coats decides not to do anything, I will try and make arrangements with this couple, after checking into their reputation, etc., to live on the place so that they would be there to show the property, etc.

Would you be interested in selling your Frigidaire? I have a man who wants to buy one, and, if you want to sell it, please let me know what price and maybe we can dispose of it.

This morning I went up to Tanforan and saw a good many of the Redwood City people. I had a talk with George Tsukagawa in regard to the tulips. He advised me that all the money that he received from the crop was $132.16 plus a small check for $6.80 that Mr. Decia brought it. The $132.16 was credited through your account on May 2, and the $6.80 on May 11. George was very much disappointed on the returns on the tulips. He seems to feel that he should have payment from you, but did not press it because there was such a small payment involved, and he told me to mention to you that it would be all right either way with him. Of course, I do not know just what the returns of this crop could be, but it seems to me that it should be more than the above amount. George says definitely that he has not taken anything out of it.

The folks there at Tanforan seemed to be getting along fine. Some of them are working, and those who are not would like to be doing something.

I hope this finds you all fine.

> Very truly yours,
> J.E. Morrish
> Vice President[13]

September 10, 1942.

[Morrish wrote to Adachi and wanted her and others to be at the pavilion at 10:30 a.m. to meet with him. Morrish knew on September 10, 1942, that some people might be moved, so he wanted to go to Tanforan on September 11, 1942.]

Dear Miss Adachi:—

Today Walter Gillo sent in your rent payment of $35.00 and we have credited it to your commercial account. We are enclosing a duplicate tag. I am also enclosing a duplicate tag for credit to the California Chrysanthemum Growers Association which was received from Dun & Bradstreet for the account of Julius Epstein.

It is possible that I will be able to get up tomorrow as I wanted to see Ham Honda. I also understand that some of the folks may be moved and I would like to see them before they leave; so should you see any of the Redwood City folks thereabouts in the morning, will you please ask them to be somewhere around the Pavilion around ten thirty.

Kind Regards to you.

> Yours very truly,
> J.E. Morrish
> Vice President

September 15, 1942.

[Adachi wrote to Morrish on September 15, 1942, and she thanked him for his visit (see note above, September 10, 1942). She informed him that she was leaving on a train for Utah, sometime between 5 and 8 p.m.]

Dear Mr. Morrish:

May I thank you for your last visit here to Tanforan. It was a pleasant surprise to see you have made time to see us. I am sorry that I was not able to arrange to have more of our group there, but those that were there returned to their barracks happy. My only wish is that I may return soon and pick up my old affairs.

I am leaving for Utah tonight on a train that will leave between 5:00 and 8:00 o'clock. In leaving California there is one thing that I was not able to finish. As you know, that the collections have been coming in quite regularly, but I have not been able to distribute it to the growers. For the purpose of distributing funds due the members, I made a request to the manager of this assembly center to go home, to remove from the safe certain books and records necessary. However, I have been refused this request. Consequently, as a last resort, I am asking for your help. I want you to place my problem before Mr. Davis, our manager, and have George Tsukagawa, one of the active board member [sic] of the California Chrysanthemum Growers' Association, go to the office and get these records.

As my time is very short, may I ask you to please write or phone Mr. Davis as soon as possible. Since this my [sic] last letter from Tanforan, I want to thank you for everything you have done for me. Because I am leaving California, I will have to depend so much more on you. Do take care of yourself and the best of health always.

Sincerely,
Sumiye Adachi[14]

Letters of Support

Morrish not only helped the evacuees with their businesses, properties, and taxes, he also played a large role is helping them get out of Topaz, for either work, education, or military service. One of his earliest requests came from Mrs. T. Yatabe, on behalf of Mr. and Mrs. Rikimaru (June 1942, when they were being held at Tanforan). Of particular importance are a series of letters from Morrish to Adachi on her efforts to get permission for student relocation. At the same time Morrish was writing letters of support for Ryuji Adachi, the brother of Sumiye Adachi. Morrish was also responsible for joining a husband and his family back together. Yamane was being held at Lordsby, New Mexico, and had been separated from his entire family, who were being held at Topaz. Morrish was also the sponsor of Yamane after he was released from the camp.

June 20, 1942.

[Yatabe wrote to Morrish requesting that he write a letter of recommendation for Mr. Rikimaru, who was being held separately from his wife. The entire letter follows.]

At the time Mr. Rikimaru was interned, my husband and I called at your office to request you make a statement on Mr. Rikimaru's behalf. You consented to do so upon request from the proper authorities. The following is a paragraph from a letter from the Department of Justice which Mr. Rikimaru has forwarded to us and is the answer to his request for a re-hearing before the Alien Enemy Control Board:

"The proper procedure in this respect is to send an application to the United States Attorney (the Honorable Frank J. Hennessy, United States District Attorney at San Francisco, California) who conducted the hearing in your case in the first instance. Such application must be accompanied by substantial, factual information, in affidavit form or otherwise, relating to your character, activities, and loyalty from reliable persons who can vouch for you and have had an opportunity to observe your conduct. It is therefore within the discretion of the above mentioned official to weigh the merits of your application and either grant or deny your request."

Both Mrs. Rikimaru, who is here at Tanforan, and I realize and appreciate deeply that the recent evacuation of all Japanese from the community has added many cares to your duties in the bank and we certainly do not wish to impose on you further. However, it is Mr. Rikimaru's request that you testify on his behalf. Situated as we are, we cannot do anything ourselves, and we must ask this favor of you. It is our earnest and fervent hope that you will find it within your power to grant this request.

I would like to take this opportunity to tell you that all of us are deeply touched by your kind personal interest in our problems and everyone wished that there was some way in which we could express this heartfelt appreciation. Very sincerely yours, Kuri Yatabi, Mrs. T. Yatabe, California Chrysanthemum Growers Ass'n.

Will you please send all communications concerning the above to [and the Tanforan address of Mrs. Rikimaru is given]. She intends to collect all testimonial statements and send them together to her husband who in turn will send them on to the Honorable Frank J. Hennessy to whom they are addressed.

[In a handwritten note at the bottom:] July 1, 1943, Will you please make five copies of the testimonial statement. I understand this is required. Thank you. Kuri Yatabe[15]

February 8, 1943.

[Adachi wrote a handwritten letter to Morrish, needing proof that she had money in her account to help her relocate as a student.]

Dear Mr. Morrish:

Thank you again for your keen interest in my problems. It seems as tho' I am always imposing so much on you, and I can't get away from it.

Enclosed is a check for the amount of $100 from Walter Gillo. Please deposit it to my account. I am writing him again for a fair settlement of the account.

I am sending a request for evidence as to bank account [sic] to show that I have some money to relocate as a student.

Mr. Morrish there is so much red tape connected with relocation that I am trying to leave as a student for the middle west and get my connections.

My appreciation for what you have done for me is beyond words. Best of health always,

Sincerely, Sumiye Adachi[16]

February 13, 1943.

[Morrish wrote back and told her that he had forwarded the information about her account to the Student Relocation Center in San Francisco.]

Dear Miss Adachi:—

This morning we received your letter of Sept. 8th [note: he must mean February 8] enclosing check from Walter Gillo. This has been credited to your commercial account and we are enclosing duplicate tag.

I am forwarding the request for evidence as to your bank account direct to the National Student Relocation Center in San Francisco. I hope that you are able to work something out on this.

Please let me know if Walter Gillo owes you any more money and I will try and collect it for you.

Kindest regards.

Yours very truly,
J.E. Morrish
Vice President[17]

There is an undated letter from the National Student Relocation Council, 1830 Sutter Street, San Francisco, to the bank in Redwood City, asking for certification of the balance in the account of Sumiye Adachi.

Request For Evidence as to Bank Account
To: First National Bank
Redwood City
California
Gentlemen:

Will you please send to the NATIONAL STUDENT RELOCATION COUNCIL, 1830 Sutter Street, San Francisco, California, a certification of the balance to the credit of S. Adachi at the close of business day on the last day preceding the receipt of this request.

Please indicate on the certification that it is being sent for the file of Sumiye Adachi.

Thank you.[18]

Below is an undated letter from Dillon S. Myer, the director of the WRA, Washington, D.C., asking that Morrish give his opinion on Ryuji Adachi because he wanted to leave the relocation center "for employment, education, or residence elsewhere."

> To: T. E. Morrish [sic]
> c/o First National Bank
> Redwood City, California

Dear Sir:

Ryuji Adachi has given your name as a reference in connection with an application to leave a relocation center of this Authority for employment, education, or residence elsewhere.

We would appreciate it if you would give us your opinion of this individual with respect to such matters as the extent of Americanization through education and upbringing, general standing and reputation in the community, and occupational abilities. If you have ever employed the applicant, a statement concerning the quality of the work performed for you would be helpful.

An addressed envelope which needs no postage is included for your reply.

> Sincerely yours,
> D.S. Myer
> Director[19]

February 8, 1943.

[Morrish was writing to the WRA, Barr Building, Washington, D.C., to state that Ryuji Adachi was known to him and that he was a good citizen.]

> War Relocation Authority
> Barr Building
> Washington, D.C.

Gentlemen:—

Ryuji Adachi has been known to me for several years. I believe that he is thoroughly honest and reliable and have no reason to believe that he is other than a good citizen. He went to the local high school here and seems to have a good reputation in the community.

Yours very truly,
J.E. Morrish
Vice President[20]

February 9, 1943.

[This is a letter by K. Yamane asking Morrish to write a letter for her husband who was being kept at Lordsburg, New Mexico. She told Morrish that her kids were loyal, true Americans and had known no other life.]

Dear Mr. Morrish:

I was informed today by my husband, Tooru Yamane who is being interned at Lordsburg, New Mexico, that his case would be re-heard about 20th [*sic*] of this month.

My mother-in-law, my children, and I would appreciate it very much if you would be kind enough to send another letter to Mr. F. J. Hennesy, U.S. Attorney, San Francisco and vouch for my husband's character. He feel [*sic*] certain that your letter would be very helpful in having my husband back with us. I make this request especially for my mother-in-law who is 75 years old and who has been in poor health ever since we came to Utah. She, seeing other internees return to their families, is praying and hoping for the day when her son would be coming back to her.

As you already know, my husband has been growing flowers in Redwood City for the last 23 years and I assure you that he has done nothing which was against the United States of America. Our children know no other country but America and it has been my husband's and my own desire to bring them up as true loyal American citizens. Our three boys are just at the age where they need their father's guide [*sic*] and advice the most.

Thanking you for your kindness and with best regards, I am

Very truly yours,
Sakae Yamana[21]

February 17, 1943.

[Morrish wrote back to Yamane.]

Dear Mrs. Yamane:—
    Today we have written to Mr. Hennesey in San Francisco in regard to
your husband, Tooru Yamane. We are hopeful that he will be allowed to
join you at Topaz.
    I hope this finds you all well.

                                            Yours very truly,
                                            J.E. Morrish
                                            Vice President[22]

March 2, 1943.

[Soon after this the Federal Reserve Bank in San Francisco sent a long
letter to the First Nation Bank, stating that the accounts of Tooru Yamane,
at Lordsburg Internment Camp, must be frozen. Most of the letter is
transcribed below.]

Dear Sirs:
    The War Department has advised the Treasury Department that the
internee named above (hereinafter referred to as internee) has been
interned for the duration of the war. There is reasonable cause to believe
that such internee is a national of a blocked country, pursuant to Executive
Order No. 8389, as amended, and within the meaning of section 5(b) of the
Trading with the enemy Act, as amended, and that assets held by him, or
on his behalf, are assets in which a national of a foreign country designated
in Executive Order 3839, as amended, has an interest. Accordingly, the
Secretary of the Treasury, pursuant to the provisions of Executive Order
No. 8389, as amended, and section 5(b) of the Trading with the enemy
Act, as amended, has directed us to inform you that all of the above-
named internee's bank accounts, safe deposit boxes, and other assets held
by banks and banking institutions, are now blocked accounts and that no
payment, transfer, or withdrawal may hereafter be made therefrom except
as authorized by an appropriate license. The internee has indicated that you
are holding assets in which he has an interest, direct or not.
    In accordance with these instructions, you are directed to block all
the accounts, safe deposit boxes, securities, etc., that the above-named
internee may have with you or in which you believe he has an interest, direct or indirect. Please notify us when you have taken this action

and advise us of the name of any other business enterprise in which you believe he has a substantial interest.

These instructions do not apply to accounts in the name of a custodial officer of an internment camp in trust for interned aliens. If you maintain such account, they should not be blocked. . . .

The accounts of such internee are to be treated solely in accordance with the provisions of this letter, and all previous instructions with respect to the treatment of such accounts are rescinded.

The internee has designated your bank as the institution from which he desires to withdraw funds under the enclosed Treasury Department license, which we believe is self-explanatory. A copy of this license has been mailed to the internee. Please direct any questions to the Foreign Funds Control Department of this bank.

> Yours very truly,
> Herbert D. Armstrong
> Assistant Cashier[23]

March 5, 1943.

[Morrish wrote to Mrs. T. Yamane (probably on the same day he received the above letter), telling her that her husband's accounts had been blocked. It wasn't until March 1945 that the accounts were unfrozen.][24]

Dear Mrs. Yamane:--

Today we received a letter from the Federal Reserve Bank in San Francisco instructing us to block the account of T. Yamane also the safe deposit box registered in the name of T. Yamane and Sakae Yamane. Both the account and the safe deposit box have been blocked. The account is subject to license #33639 issued by the Federal Reserve Bank. I believe that you or Mr. Yamane received a copy of this license.

> Yours very truly,
> J.E. Morrish
> Vice President[25]

October 9, 1943.

[The investigation of Toru Yamane continued through October 1943.
Below is the official letter to Morrish from the U.S. Department of Justice,
Immigration and Nationalization Service, Detention Station, Santa Fe,
New Mexico, regarding Toru Yamane.]

Dear Sir:
   SUBJECT: Toru Yamane
   The above named alien, who is being made the subject of an investigation by this office, has stated that you can furnish this office with information relative to his residence in the United States while he was living at
Redwood City from 1921 to 1942.
   Any information which you may be able to give, including known dates
of his residence in your locality, will be of assistance to this office in clear-
ing up the status of this alien, and will be greatly appreciated.
   For your convenience in replying a franked, self-addressed envelope,
which requires no postage, is enclosed.

                                        A. L. Hector
                                        Immigration Inspector[26]

February 14, 1944.

[Four months later Toru Yamane then sent a letter to Morrish.]

Dear Mr. Morrish
   I wish to express my sincere appreciation for all you have done in the
past. Due to your kindness, I been able to return to my family on the
6th of February. My wife told me of all the favors you have done for her
and the family.
   I hope that someday we can all return to Redwood City and thank you.
   Thanking you again, I remain,

                                        Sincerely yours,
                                        Toru Yamane[27]

A few days later (February 18, 1944), Dillon S. Myer wrote to Morrish,
saying that Toru Yamane needed a reference to leave the relocation center
for "employment, education, or residence elsewhere."[28] On February 23,
1944, Morrish wrote the following letter to the WRA.

Dear Gentlemen:

Toru Yamane has been known to us for several years and during that period was a flower grower. As far as we are able to determine, he has always enjoyed a good reputation in the community and we know of nothing that would indicate he was un-American.

> Yours very truly,
> J.E. Morrish
> Vice President[29]

October 9, 1945.

[After the war was finished, Morrish was still helping out Toru Yamane. Morrish became the "sponsor" of Toru Yamane. A sponsor was a person who needed to keep tabs on someone. We are fortunate to have the "Parolee's or Internee's At-Large Agreement," filled in by Toru Yamane, assigning Morrish as his sponsor, as well as the letter releasing Morrish from this position. The At-Large Agreement was issued by the U.S. Department of Justice, Immigration and Naturalization Service.]

I, Toru Yamane [his Palo Alto, California, address is given], a national of Japan, in consideration of my (parole or internment-at-large) under regulations relating to alien enemies, hereby agree to keep in close contact with Mr. J.E. Morrish, who has agreed to act as my sponsor; and to that end I agree to make personal report to him weekly and written report once a month to F. O. Seidle, Chief, Detention, Deportation and Parole Section, Appraisers Bldg. San Francisco, Calif. I also agree to comply with all the provisions of the regulations pertaining to alien enemies and with all the terms of my (parole or internment-at-large).

The letter is then signed by Yamane. Just below this is the sponsors agreement. Morrish's name is not on it, but he signed the document. It states that Toru Yamane was an alien enemy and:

During the period that he remains liable to restrictions pertaining to alien enemies I hereby undertake to keep in close touch with him, observe his conduct and activities, and maintain knowledge of his whereabouts, to the end of assuring his compliance with the terms of (parole or internment-at-large). I also agree to render report concerning him to F. O. Seidle, Chief, Detention, Deportation and Parole Section, Appraisers Bldg. San Francisco, Calif. each month; and in case he commits any violation of the terms of (parole or internment-at-large) or if I should receive adverse information concerning said alien enemy that is or may be pertinent to the National Defense I agree to make immediate report thereof to such officer.[30]

Morrish's duty as sponsor to Toru Yamane lasted only a few months, and it was terminated on December 7, 1945.[31]

February 15, 1945.

[We can look at one more example (out of many) of a letter of recommendation that Morrish wrote. J. Rikimaru sent Morrish a letter requesting a letter of recommendation for him so that he would not be classified as a parolee (like Yamane above).]

Dear Sir:

I am once again writing to ask a special favor of you in reference to my status as a resident in the United States of America. The attainment of a normal status means as much to me as does the American citizenship which you cherish. As you know, my present status is, as yet, that of a parolee. If a parolee departs from a relocation center, he will find it necessary to report to authorities weekly, and in that way his freedom will be considerable restricted.

It has been announced by the Department of Justice that parolees may secure complete release by again securing a number of affidavits and testimonies from Caucasian individuals. Although I realize this will be an imposition on your time and efforts, I am asking this favor of you in order that my status of parolee may be changed to that of a loyal Japanese alien.

My record has been further proven loyal by letters sent to me by the Army notifying me that my name has been removed from the Military Suspension List. This has now cleared me to go to all parts of the United States, Alaska and Hawaii. I would deeply appreciate it if you could write an affidavit supporting my character, integrity, loyalty and service to this country and my desire to reside here in the United States, at your earliest convenience.

Thanking you for your many past favors in this respect, I remain,

Truly yours,
Joseph I. Rikimaru[32]

Morrish wrote to the WRA on March 5, 1945, stating that he had known Rikimaru for 11 years and that he was "of good character and I believe him to be loyal to the United States."

Sending Things to the Internees

A good part of the time Morrish was arranging to have personal property packed up and shipped to the internees. He would often have to go out to their property, search for the individual items that were being requested, arrange to have them packed up, and then arrange to have them shipped. There are a few examples we can look at.

March 25, 1942 [although this date is probably 1943, based on the internal evidence in the letter.]

[This first letter was sent by Mrs. Enomoto to Morrish to ask for a number of items. Morrish must have had this list with him when he went to find the items since there are checkmarks and notes on this letter.]

Dear Mr. Morrish:

Thank you ever so much for seeing that my Dad's furniture were [sic] stored away. He was very happy to hear that everything was taken care of so well.

About two months ago I wrote to Mrs. Lucas asking her to have sent to me some of the things stored in Redwood City, but as yet I have not received anything. I realize, with the labor shortage and gasoline ration and what not that it is very hard for her to get to Redwood City. Bill just hates to bother you with this and that and I hesitated to write to you, but I guess I will have to bother you because I need these things very much. Please have the following sent to me. Mrs. Lucas has the list but I will list them again.

Baby carriage—stored in outside warehouse, gray color folding type with mattress.

Silverware set—stored in upstairs room in cedar chest against wall. Two sets in wooden cases.

Teaspoons—In two boxes ½ dozen in each. I think. In Cedar Chest also.

Baby Bed-Mattress-Rubber pad-Baby doll pink. All in upstairs room. I think the pad, doll are on the bed.

Blankets-Comforters-sheets—There may be a few in the upstairs room. If sheets cannot be found let it go. [In a hand-written note:] Please see if you can find two pillows.

The above things are just about impossible to get here for a long time. Please have someone pack them at the nursery or have Poole Transfer Co. do it for me.

How is your garden coming along? With Spring here it must be taking shape. I think you people are so fortunate to be able to live in California. We get homesick every now and than [sic] thinking about this and that.

I hope peace will reign once more so we may all be able to go back to California.

Please extend my best regards to Mrs. Morrish,

Sincerely,
Mrs. Edes Enomoto[33]

[In a handwritten note:] Key enclosed for chest.

March 29, 1943.

[J. Matsuyama wrote to Morrish a few times, requesting that he send out personal items, first to Topaz and then to Tule Lake.]

Dear Mr. Morrish:

At the time of evacuation I was employed by Enomot and Co. and on his advise [sic] I stored my washing machine in his warehouse on Redwood Ave. The washing machine was of General Electric make and the sewing machine a Singer treadle type.

If possible could you please arrange with a transfer company in Redwood City to crate the two and send them to the above address freight C.O.D.

Thank you for your kindness.

I remain,
J [illegible] Matsuyama[34]

November 24, 1943.

[Later in that same year Matsuyama sent a letter to Morrish from Tule Lake. In it he requested quite a few things for a number of different people. Again, there are handwritten notes on this letter, probably from Morrish since it looks as if he were keeping track of the material he found. Morrish wrote back to Matsuyama in March 1944, telling him he was able to ship some of the items he requested.][35]

Dear Sir:

I am asking you again to have the following list of things sent to us again. All these things will be found in the Enomoto warehouse.

For Matsuyama—6903—A Tule Lake, Newell, California
2 trycicle [sic] (one new and one old, new trycicle [sic] take on Suzuki)
1 baby buggy

K. Tanino-
2 wooden boxes
3 paper boxes

M. Imoto-
   3 boxes

M. Kajiyama-
   1 box.
   Will you have the things belonging to K. Tanino, M. Imoto and M. Kajiyama sent to the address—
   3401-6 Tule Lake, Newell, Califn.
   In case some of the boxes need crating some more, will you please ask Poole to do it. In case they cannot do it, I wish you would ask Mr. Lucas. Please send all the things by freight. If this cannot be sent by COD, please pay for all of it from my account. Thank you very much.

Yours very truly,
J. Matsuyama [sp?][36]

December 16, 1943.

[Morrish wrote back to Matsuyama and told him (in a common complaint found throughout the Morrish Collection) that it was hard to find labor.]

Dear Mr. Matsuyama:
   Your letter of Nov. 24 came in and I have talked to the folks out at the place and find that they are very short of help and have not been able to spare the time to prepare the things you have asked for shipment, so I am hiring a young man to go out there to get the things that you are asking for in shape to ship. Several things, of course, will have to be crated and others tied up and boxed for shipping. I have tried Mr. Poole's company but they will not even pick the things up anymore as they are so busy and are having labor problems. The things in the warehouse, of course, are not sorted and the warehouse is full so someone will have to go in there and take everything out and repack the warehouse, so it will be quite a little job. I am hoping that I will be able to get this man out there this week. It may be the first of next week before he may be available.
   I hope this finds you fine. Kindest regards.

Yours very truly,
J.E. Morrish
Vice President[37]

Trying to Sell and Lease

Throughout the Morrish Collection there is correspondence requesting Morrish to sell material for the internees or to help the internees as they try to sell their property. Many times, for example, Morrish wrote to some internees telling them that he had, for example, a buyer for black cloth, which was at this point a necessary item for growing flowers in San Mateo County. He told the internees that things would not age well and that there was no point in hanging on to things, just to have them rot. Morrish would rather they have the money. Many times the internees agreed with him. As mentioned before, the internees had to pay their taxes, pay their utility bills, and maintain their property even though they were kept away. They needed the money, and although a few mentioned being worried about not having anything left when (or if) they came home, many wanted to sell their personal property, especially large-ticket items like cars, refrigerators, and clothes washers.

May 2, 1942.

[W. Enomoto wrote to Morrish, asking him to sell his truck since it would be cheaper to buy one locally rather than having it shipped out.]

Dear Mr. Morrish:

Mr. Arnold wrote me asking me for back rent. I have replied as per copy enclosed.

The gas bill you sent me is not a duplicate. This is for the current month on surplus gas. I will pay from here.

Peter Reinberg advised me that they sent in $75 to your bank. He promises to settle up within a month or so.

I wired you yesterday about sending our truck here but since, I have found that it would be more economical to buy a truck here. Please arrange to have this truck sold in any way you deem best. Whether by advertising or on consignment. Pete Towne said he will take it on consignment for about $400. He also has with him one tire in his shop that I gave him which was to go along with this truck.

I want to thank you for all those details that you have taken care of for me. I feel very fortunate in having you do so much.

Yours very sincerely,
William Enomoto[38]

[In a handwritten note:] Mr. Sunserix of International Nursery in Mt. View will come to see you about some plants for your garden. I think camellias and rhododendrons will be nice. If there are other trees you have in mind, just ask him for it. Fruits, acacia, etc.

May 7, 1942.

[William Enomoto wrote to Morrish about selling his truck and then gave him a price list of fertilizers he would sell.]

Dear Mr. Morrish:

Thank you for your letters. If Pete Towne is willing to pay me $400 now, that is satisfactory with me. I also have a credit due me of $13.95 for a brand new battery which I bought and returned. Pete will know about it because I gave it to him personally.

Regarding those fertilizers that are still there. My cost on the Rape Seed Meal of 4 1/2-5 tons was $30 per ton. The Mustard Seed Meal cost $20 per ton. The Chile Nitrate approximately 15-20 sacks about $42 a ton.

If there are any stray Bone Meal or Blood Meal and Vigoro which can be about two or three sacks of each, please feel absolutely free and use them in your garden. I had intended to send them up to your ranch.

I am sending a check to Poole Transfer Company today.

> Thanking you, I am,
> Yours sincerely,

[In a handwritten note:] You are authorized to reduce price any amount in order to liquidate. Thanks.[39]

July 18, 1944.

[Morrish was still involved with selling the personal and business items of Enomoto in 1944. The Morrish Collection contains a letter from Morrish to Shapiro (dated March 4, 1944). Morrish told him that he would be selling some personal items from the Enomoto house, and he wanted to know if Mr. Shapiro was interested in buying them.[40] Morrish must have had an offer for Enomoto's greenhouse, but in the following letter, Enomoto stated that he did not want to sell that.]

Dear Mr. Morrish,

Thank you for your letter with reference to an offer for our greenhouse. The offer is fair enough but we would like to keep the place as a nucleus to start business again in the future. There are so few opportunity or field [*sic*] for people like us that the flower business or related lines offers [*sic*] the best future as I can see it now.

The radio arrived quite some time ago and we are enjoying it very much. My portable was going on the blink.

When the paint job is done and should the painters want their money right away, please feel free to draw out of my account.

> With my deepest
> appreciation, I remain,
> Yours very truly,
> William Enomoto[41]

April 27, 1943.

[Morrish wrote a letter to Adachi, telling her that someone wanted to buy her refrigerator.]

Dear Miss Adachi,

Yesterday a Mrs. Cossuto called and said Frank Osorio told her that you may have a Frigidaire that you would be interested in selling. I told her I did not know that you had one other than what you had in your house, but I would drop you a line sometime. If any of the folks that have frigidairs [*sic*] stored there [*sic*] in the association room wish to dispose of them, set a price on them and we will do what we can in turning them into cash.

The Chinese boys out on the property are getting ready for planting now and are very busy. Frank has cleaned up around the association building and it looks quite nice. He has made no charge as he has been leaving his equipment around there in back and I asked him to run it around the building which he was glad to do.

The road going in from Woodside is in rather bad shape and I don't know what we can do about that; two or three pretty good size chuck holes.

I hope this finds you all fine. Kindest regards.

> Yours very truly,
> J.E. Morrish
> Vice President[42]

He wrote again on July 16, 1943, about people selling their refrigerators, and in November 1943 Adachi wrote to Morrish to tell him that he could use the association's money to purchase gravel to fill the potholes.[43]

August 28, 1943.

[Morrish was involved in trying to lease the houses of many of the internees. This was another way for them to make the money they needed to pay
their taxes and bills (especially since their income was cut off). One example is a series of letters between Morrish and Kitayama. In the first letter
Morrish wrote to Tasuo Kitayama to ask if he was interested in leasing
his place. Morrish told him that someone called and wanted three to four
acres. They did not need the house since it was rented to Mr. Willows.]

Dear Mr. Kitayama:
    Would you please let me know if you would be interested in leasing
your place. We have a call for approximately three or four acres and they
are interested in your property. They would like to have the pipe and
equipment, also cloth available and a packing shed for bunching. They
will not need the house and I understand that it is rented to Mr. Willows.
Let me know if you are interested and also the price you would ask.

> Yours very truly,
> J.E. Morrish
> Vice President[44]

September 11, 1943.

[Kitayama wrote back to Morrish and explained why he did not want to
lease his land.]

Dear Mr. Morrish—
    I am very sorry that I could not answer your letter immediately as I
have been in and out of the camp for the last few weeks.
    First of all I want to thank you for taking immediate care of my request
on my account. I am unable to send you my bank book as it is in the safe
deposit box. Therefore please keep record of it and when I return again to
California you can make adjustment for me.
    As for the leasing of my place I am not very interested because I've been
using that soil for quite a long time and it needs a rest for a while, thus I
want you to refuse that offer.
    In the near future I am intending to visit Chicago for a while. There
are number [sic] of people that you know are in Chicago at present. Sumi
Adachi and her brother are there too and I'm looking forward to meet [sic]
them all over there.
    Thank you again for all your favors and with kindest regard.

> Sincerely yours
> Tetsuo Kitayama[45]

December 7, 1943.

[Morrish sent another letter to Kitayama, asking him if he wanted to sell his stick house and if he wanted to sell his car.]

Dear Mr. Kitayama:

Today I had an offer of $300.00 for your stick house that stands directly in back of your house. This price, of course, would be cash and the purchaser would have to take the house down and move it to his own location. If you are interested in selling this, will you please let me hear from you right away.

We have had two or three calls for cars and I am wondering whether or not you wish to sell your car; if so, let me hear from you right away, giving me price [sic] you desire to receive.

> Yours very truly,
> J.E. Morrish
> Vice President[46]

It wasn't until March 6, 1944, that Morrish indicated that he had sold the stick house for $325.[47] As the final example, Morrish sent a letter to K. Yamada about selling some items from her business.

Dear Miss Yamada:

Yesterday I had a call for fifty pieces of black cloth also some 1 ½ inch pipe as well as stick house lumber. I'm not sure if you have any pipe that you want to sell but I notice some black cloth that you might be glad to dispose of, so let me have a price right away if you do. If you want to dispose of what lumber you have there for stick house purposes, let me know. It might be that the party interested would be willing to take yours down and pay you for it. Another winter will not help that any as last year I had to have someone pick up the sticks and straighten the house out two different times after storms. Recently somebody purchased some property facing the Woodside Road and have put a fence around there including part of your stick house. The property has been surveyed and apparently your stick house was on part of that property so to get the benefit of the lumber on that part, I think it should be taken down if we can find a party willing to buy, and supply the labor for removing. I would like to hear from you right away on this and also be sure to send the key to your car so that the purchaser can try it out.

Kindest regards.

> Yours very truly,
> J.E. Morrish
> 'Vice President[48]

She did not write back to Morrish until October 1943 with the answers to his questions.

Dear Mr. Morrish,

In answer to disposing some of our equipments [*sic*], I am listing the prices as approximately as what we figure they are worth.

Black Cloth—1 piece is 100 ft. by 10 ft. Selling price from $10 to $7.50. Comment*-Most of the cloth are getting faded but they are still good for 2 to 3 years more. Among them are sides, which are smaller. Sell at $3 to $5.

Pipes—Size 1 ½" $25 to $50 for the pile. Pile is located under the oak tree facing our house. Also some timber is under same tree.

As far as the lumber for the stick house is concerned we would like to sell for whatever we can get for the whole thing since it's pretty old and whatever they can salvage from the land they can have for $10 or $15 but for those stacked and clean we should get around $10. Please get rid of whatever you can get for the stick house. [Someone has written by hand:] Sold Jan'44 $100

The Wheels to the car are stored in the back room of the barn right behind the door. The points are in the car compartment.

Thank you very kindly.

> Yours very truly,
> K. Yamada

[In a handwritten note:] P.S. I am enclosing the keys and the pink slip too.[49]

The Morrish Collection contains a letter (dated October 16, 1943) from West Bay Motors in Redwood City saying they are sending a check for $525 for the car to K. Yamada.[50]

Receiving Gifts

While there is no concrete proof that Morrish was paid by the internees to watch over their properties and take care of their businesses, it is clear from a number of different letters that the internees thanked Morrish for all of this help by sending him various gifts all throughout the period they were interned.

November 20, 1942.

[Enomoto wrote a letter to Morrish with a number of different items, including a gift of flower bulbs.]

Dear Mr. Morrish,

I have received your letter with regards to the roof which was repaired. I will send Mr. Lauman a check.

Meanwhile, would you please look thru the large safe in the warehouse and see if the policy is there? It should be in one of the drawers and enclosed in an envelope marked "Webster St. House." [Mr. Enomoto then gave the combination to the safe.]

It is not time for bulb planting and so I have instructed A. Rynveld, a good friend of mine in San Francisco to send you some bulbs. I thought 100 Daffodils and 100 Poeticus narcissus would look nice growing wild in the grove of big trees by your house. Anemone and Ranunculi will need lots of sunshine, and the Camellia type Begonias will do well in the shady part.

You should be getting these bulbs in a week or so. They will be delivered at the bank.

I have paid all the property tax except:

San Mateo County tax [Mr. Enomoto then gave the address.]

I have written A. McSweeny for the bills because it was not amongst those you sent me.

> With my best regards,
> I remain,
> Yours sincerely,
> William Enomoto[51]

PS. If the snow should stop, I am planning to go through some of the close by southern state tomorrow.

November 24, 1942.

[While not a gift, T. Kitayama sent Morrish a handwritten note thanking him for all that he had done.]

Dear Mr. Morrish-
 I have received your letter through Miss Adachi and am appreciating your kindness for all the trouble you are going through in order to help us. We are all hoping that one day soon we may be able to thank you for all you have done for us.
 Thank you again and wish you a very happy Thanksgiving from us all at Topaz.

Very sincerely yours,
T. Kitayama[52]

January 9, 1943.

[Morrish wrote to K. Sawamura to thank him for a painting of Topaz.]

Dear Mr. Sawamura:-
 Yesterday I received the package and was very much surprised to find the painting of Topaz. I was not aware that you did this accomplishment. You certainly did a fine job and I appreciate very much your sending it to me.
 I presume you received my letter written about ten days ago. In trying to find your address, we could not find the barrack and apartment so we sent it in care of S. Adachi, and I hope she handed it to you. We wrote you in regard to the settlement of Mr. Capitella for the fertilizer. Mr. Capitella brought me the money for your taxes and I paid them. Occasionally I stop at the ranch and was there last week again and I believe George is doing a very good job. The place looks well and apparently he is doing a very good job inside as the plants look good and healthy. I believe he made fairly good for the season. Of course he is having some labor problems but he seems to have fairly good success in getting help.
 Again thanks for your painting and kindest regards to you.

Yours very truly,
J.E. Morrish,
Vice President[53]

December 7, 1943.

[K. Yamada was writing on Gila River letterhead. She wondered if other people from Horgan Ranch were selling their radios. She was also sending a Christmas gift from her father.]

Dear Mr. Morrish,

Received your letter and statement of Nov. 18. I hope you have heard from my brother about the car radio. I am sorry that we didn't mention about it in the earlier letters.

As it is too much trouble, and so we didn't do anything further in regard to the release of the house radio. We appreciate your kind consideration of getting rid of those things. In Hogan Ranch has anyone sold their radio?

Thank you for all your conscientious management of our affairs.

As a Christmas gift my father is sending you a kane [sic] made from Arizona's famous cactus and ironwood. I hope you like them. Thank you again and hope everything is fine with you.

                                        Respectfully yours,
                                        Kayuko Yamada[54]

January 17, 1944.

[Morrish wrote to S. Suzakawa, thanking him for the azalea plant and the box of candy that Walter Gillo gave to him.]

Dear Mr. Suzakawa:

Mrs. Morrish and I have been enjoying very much the very lovely azalea plant as well as the box of candy that Walter Gillo presented to us from you and Mrs. Suzakawa. Thanks to you for this remembrance. To date I have made several appointments with Walter to go out to your place and look over the pipe situation. He is a hard boy to tie down so we haven't been out yet but he has promised that he would call me this week sometime. I have asked him to take care of putting the pipe away for your [sic] and showed him on the diagram that you sent me where the pipe was situated.

I talked to Walter about the icebox which apparently he has sold as he brought in $60.00 which was credited to your account with the advice that it was for the icebox. I had presumed that he had taken the matter up with you. I asked him last week if he had and he advised me that he didn't. He stated further that the icebox is getting rusted and is detoriating [sic] and thought he had better dispose of it for you. He also told me that if you wished to have it back, he could repossess it. It might be well for you to drop him a line about this.

In your last letter you refer to the taxes. I am sure I replied to you that this matter had been taken care of and that I had advanced the amount of the taxes and Walter had reimbursed this amount plus the rent account at a later date. If this is not right, please write me again.

I hope this finds you fine. Kindest regards.

> Yours very truly,
> J.E. Morrish
> Vice President[55]

February 5, 1944.

[Morrish received another painting from J. Rikimaru, as he had from Sawamura (above).]

Dear Mr. Rikamaru [*sic*]:

Yesterday I was certainly agreeably surprised to receive that very fine painting that you folks sent to me. It is a beautiful piece of work and a very interesting subject that the artist picked on. It came in fine condition and it was so well packed. I can assure you Mrs. Morrish and I will enjoy it very much indeed and will you please express my sincere appreciation to all the folks who had anything to do with this and tell them that we shall enjoy the picture for many years to come.

The country must be very interesting at the present time, although no doubt cold. We have recently had some fine rains here and our creek in Woodside is running now for the first time this season. The bulbs and blossoming trees as well as the acacias are out now and the country is beginning to look more like spring every day.

Again many thanks to you all. My kindest regards,

> Yours very truly,
> J.E. Morrish
> Vice President[56]

April 6, 1944.

[Morrish wrote to T. Matsuyama, who had sent Morrish presents for himself and a broach for Mrs. Morrish.]

Dear Mr. Matsuyama:

Many thanks for your letter enclosing the passbook for the refund of $22.00. The entry has been made and I am returning the book to you herewith.

Yesterday I received the souvenir from Tule Lake and I certainly was very much interested in it and wish to express my appreciation to you for sending it. Mrs. Morrish also appreciates very much getting the broach pin. Both of these are most interesting and I am wondering how the work is done and whether or not you did this yourself. Both pieces came in fine shape and we will enjoy very much having them.

Again thank you and kindest regards to you.

> Yours very truly,
> J.E. Morrish
> Vice President[57]

December 24, 1945.

[Even after the war was over Morrish was still receiving presents from the former evacuees. Morrish wrote a note to Kitayama to thank him for the delivery of a rubber plant.]

Dear Mr. Kitayama:

Saturday two very nice young ladies brought us a fine rubber plant. This is just what we needed to put in the front of our fire place in the apartment. We appreciate receiving it very much.

Many thanks and a Merry Christmas to you all.

> Yours very truly,
> J.E. Morrish
> Vice President[58]

Morrish also sent Kitayama another letter, just a few days later (December 31, 1945), thanking him again for the rubber plant and saying that they "will enjoy it for a long time to come."[59]

Notes

1. 001_Adachi_003, June 13, 1942. All letters in this chapter are from the Morrish Collection.

2. 07_Kitagawa_003, Nov. 19, 1942.

3. 07_Kitagawa_003, Nov. 19, 1942.

4. 25_Yamane_028, March 17, 1944.

5. 10_Mayeda_006, June 13, 1942.

6. 24_Yamada_034, June 17, 1942.

7. 16_Nakata_007, Oct. 24, 1942.

8. 10_Mayeda_019, Nov. 23, 1942.

9. 14_Nakano_021, Nov. 23, 1943.

10. 10_Mayeda_037, Dec. 20, 1943.

11. 07_Kitagawa_014, Dec. 7, 1944.

12. 01_adachi_04, June 16, 1942.

13. 20_Takagi_059, June 18, 1942.

14. 01_adachi_037, Sept. 15, 1942.

15. 28_CA-Chrysthanthemum_Growers_025, June 30, 1942.

16. 01_Adachi_047, Feb. 8, 1943.

17. 01_Adachi_049, Feb. 13, 1943.

18. 01_Adachi_085, undated.

19. 01_Adachi_086, undated, but probably late January or early February, 1943.

20. 01_Adachi_048, Feb. 8, 1943.

21. 25_Yamane_011, Feb. 9. 1943.

22. 25_Yamane_012, Feb. 17, 1943.

23. 25_Yamane_013, March 2, 1943.

24. 25_Yamane_041, March 14, 1945.

25. 25_Yamane_014, March 5, 1943.

26. 25_Yamane_018, Oct. 9, 1943.

27. 25_Yamane_025, Feb. 14, 1944.

28. 25_Yamane_026, Feb. 18, 1944. The wording of this letter is exactly the same as that of 01_Adachi_086, given above.

29. 25_Yamane_027, Feb. 23, 1944

30. 25_Yamane_050, Oct. 9, 1945.

31. 25_Yamane_043, Dec. 7, 1945.

32. 18_Rikimaru_040, Feb. 15, 1945.

33. 02_Enomoto_026, March 25, 1942 (note that this date is incorrect).

34. 09_Matsuyama_001, March 29, 1943.

35. 09_Matsuyama_009, March 20, 1944.

36. 02_Enomoto_008, Nov. 24, 1943, but the author is Matsuyama.

37. 09_Matsuyama_007, Dec. 16, 1943.

38. 02_Enomoto_036, May 2, 1942.

39. 02_Enomoto_039, May 7, 1942.

40. 02_Enomoto_013, March 4, 1944.

41. 02_Enomoto_017, July 18, 1944.

42. 01_Adachi_055, April 27, 1943.

43. 01_Adachi_059, July 16, 1943, and 01_Adachi_066, Nov. 3, 1943.

44. 08_Kitayama_013, Aug. 28, 1943.

45. 08_Kitayama_014 , Sept. 11, 1943.

46. 08_Kitayama_018, Dec. 7, 1943.

47. 08_Kitayama_020, March 6, 1944.

48. 24_Yamada_047, Oct. 1, 1943.

49. 24_Yamada_048, Oct. 5, 1943.

50. 24_Yamada_049, Oct. 16, 1943.

51. 02_Enomoto_053, Nov. 20, 1942. The post-script states: "If the snow should stop, I am planning to go thru some of the close by southern state tomorrow." It is unclear what this means.

52. 08_Kitayama_006, Nov. 24, 1942.

53. 07_Kitagawa_006, Jan. 9, 1943.

54. 24_Yamada_055, Dec. 7, 1943.

55. 19_Suzukawa_007, Jan. 17, 1944.

56. 18_Rikimaru_003, Feb. 5, 1944.

57. 09_Matsuyama_011, April 6, 1944.

58. 08_Kitayama_053, Dec. 24, 1945.

59. 08_Kitayama_054, Dec. 31, 1945.

Original Letters with Annotations

Figure 1.A

June 13, 1942

Miss S. Adachi
Bldg. 33, Apt. 4
Tanforan
San Bruno, California

Dear Miss Adachi:-

I had thought that I might be able to get to Tanforan today but find that I can not make it so will make an effort to do so sometime next week.

I have one or two things I wanted to write you about, however, and will talk further with you about them next time I see you. Several payments have come in from the attorney making collections and the amounts have been credited to the California Chrysanthemum Growers Association. I am no sure if you want duplicates of these sent to you there or not. If you do, I will be glad to send them on as collections come in.

I have received two or three water bills that I am not clear on just how to handle. Perhaps you can help me out:- The Belmont Farms Co. bill for $1.00, $11.45 closing bill; T. Yatabe on Valota Road $1.00, $1.00 and $2.75 closing; T. Kitiyama, Horgan Ranch, $1.55 closing. None of these folks gave me any instructions. If they are at Tanforan and you see them and they wish me to charge their account and pay their bills, I will be glad to do so.

While you were here one day, I spoke to you about a bill from the Standard Printing Co. for the Bay Nursery, Kamada Bros for $93.22. I have heard nothing from them on this and was wondering if you could give me their address so that I can make an effort to collect this for our client.

The checks that you enclosed with your letter have been credited to your two accounts as indicated on the duplicate tags that are enclosed.

A bill from the Water Company came in addressed to you in the amount of $30.67. I have sent this on to Walter Gillo for payment. I have not heard anything from him yet in regard to rent payment. If you want me to get after him on this please let me know.

Figure 1.B

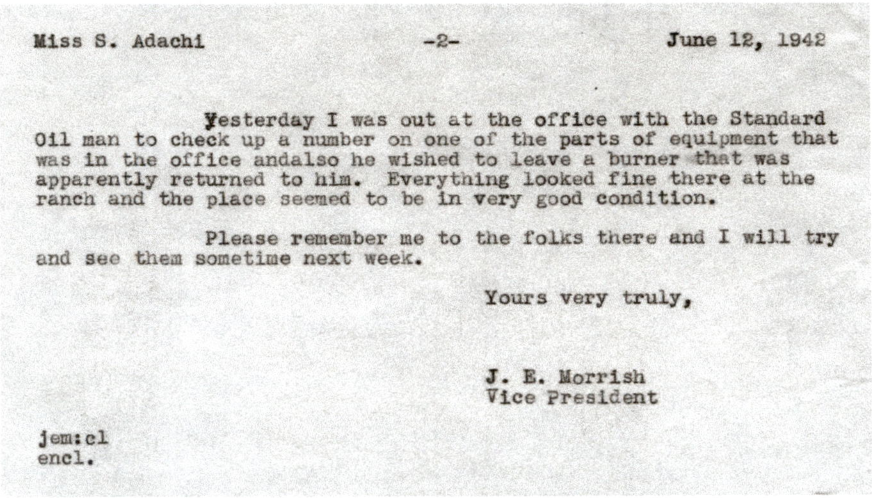

Miss S. Adachi   -2-   June 12, 1942

         Yesterday I was out at the office with the Standard
Oil man to check up a number on one of the parts of equipment that
was in the office andalso he wished to leave a burner that was
apparently returned to him. Everything looked fine there at the
ranch and the place seemed to be in very good condition.

         Please remember me to the folks there and I will try
and see them sometime next week.

         Yours very truly,

         J. E. Morrish
         Vice President

jem:cl
encl.

Figures 1.A and 1.B. An example of the shepherding of business activity that Morrish conducted as an ally on the outside.

Figure 2.A

June 25, 1942

Miss S. Adachi
Bldg. 33, Apt. 4
Tanforan
San Bruno, California

Dear Miss Adachi:-

I have talked over the rice situation again
with Mr. Green and he has offered the price of $6.90 a
hundred f.o.b. San Francisco. As far as I can determine,
it will cost approximately 35 cents to 50 cents to get
the rice to the warehouse in San Francisco; so will you
please let me know if I should sell this for you. Unless
you folks can use it in some way, I think it best to sell
as it will not improve being stored and since the ceiling
has been put upon the price, you could not get any more than
this for it and it will not be very long before the new
crop is in.

This morning Walter called me up in reference
to you rent and I find that he deposited this amount to your
account on June 6, 1942. Apparently he just took it to one
of the windows and got a duplicate tag for his receipt.

I am enclosing another water bill which has
just come in for Mr. Yatabe. I would appreciate it very
much if you would hand it to him.

Kindest regards to you all.

Yours very truly,

J. E. Morrish
Vice President

jem:cl
encl.

Figure 2.B

April 20, 194?

Miss S. Adachi
5-12-B
Topaz, Utah

Dear Miss Adachi:-

Enclosed you will find two or three tags on California
Chrysanthemum Growers Association account covering another
collection from Matrais and the collections charges for the
attorney.

I was at the office the other day and sold to Harry Lee
about sixty pounds of raffia which was in the broken box,
balance of twine, and two kegs of three penny nails. Would
you have the price on these articles so that I can make a
bill out to him. If so please let me have it, otherwise I'll
get the current price from the local stores and collect from
him. I presume you are glad to get rid of any of these supplies
that you have there and turn them into cash. I notice considerable
supply of spraying material there which no doubt deteriorates
in time and if you want to get rid of this, let me know and
give me a price on it. K. Yamada has asked me to have a couple
of packages that are stored there in the association building
sent to him in Arizona and this will be taken care of this
week.

I hope everything is going along nicely with you and
the family. Kindest regards.

Yours very truly,

J. E. Morrish
Vice President

jem:cw

Figures 2.A and 2.B. Correspondence from Mr. Morrish to the Adachi family concerning maintenance of the assets they left behind. In the earlier days of the internment, Morrish contacted them at the Tanforan Assembly Center concerning the selling of stores of rice before the price dropped, and again at the camp at Topaz, expressing concerns later in the war suggesting the sale of spraying material (chemicals? equipment?) before they deteriorated from lack of use.

Figure 3

```
                              Bldg ₃₃ apt 4
                              Tanforan Assembly Center
                              San Bruno, California




        First National Bank
        Redwood City, California

        Dear Mr. Morrish:

               Thank you very much for your letter of
        July 6, 1942.

               I am enclosing two saving withdrawal
        slips of Mrs. Okamura.  After talking it over
        with her it is her desire to have $100.00 cash
        and a new checking account started with the
        $1000.00.   I don't know whether this can be
        arrangement, but I told her that I shall try.
        Rather than carry travelers check, I figured
        that it would be more convenient for her if
        she opened a checking account.

               Yesterday we received our first pay
        and out of the pay roll my brothers and I
        were able to get the three checks which I
        am forwarding for deposit to the account of
        S. Adachi.

               Thank you again and best health always.

                              Sincerely,

                              S Adachi


        enc/ ₃checks
             ₂ withdrawal slips.
```

Figure 3. Ms. Adachi asked for assistance in depositing paychecks earned from camp work, again indicating the reliance upon Morrish for the day-to-day functioning of finances.

Figure 4

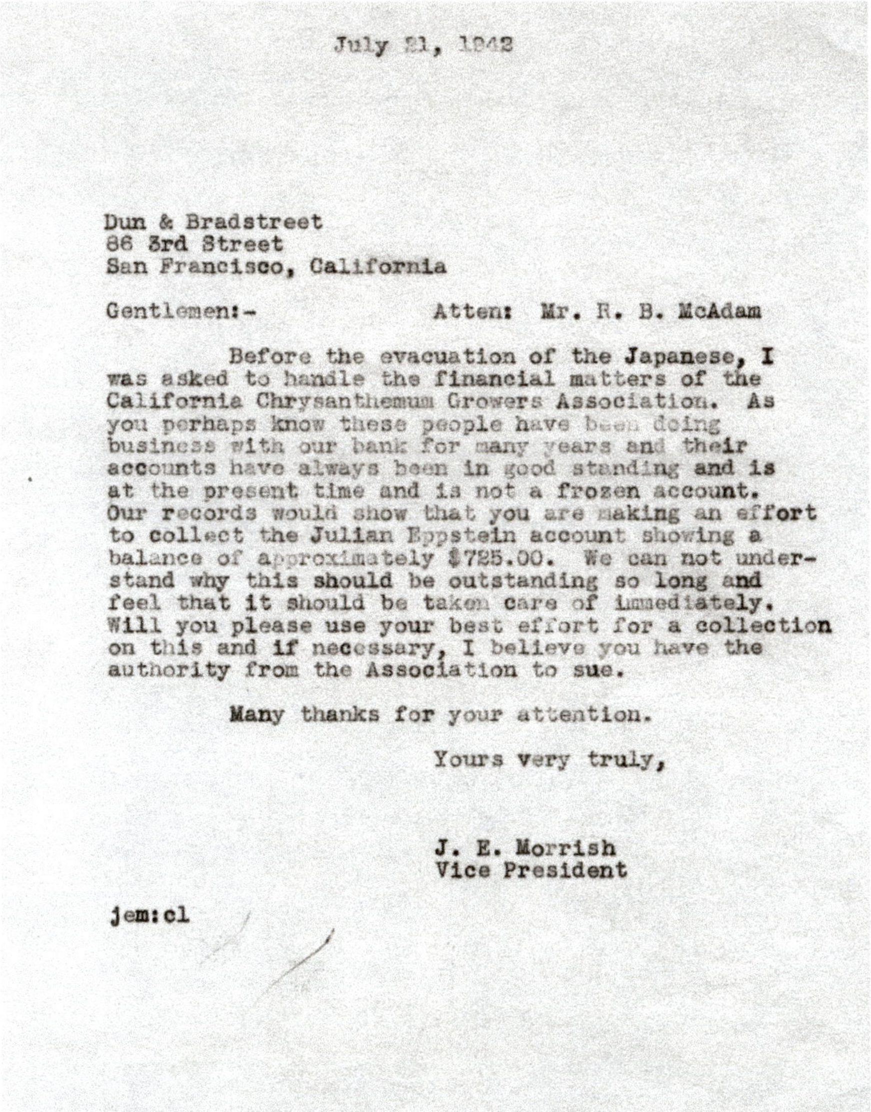

July 21, 1942

Dun & Bradstreet
86 3rd Street
San Francisco, California

Gentlemen:-   Atten: Mr. R. B. McAdam

        Before the evacuation of the Japanese, I
was asked to handle the financial matters of the
California Chrysanthemum Growers Association. As
you perhaps know these people have been doing
business with our bank for many years and their
accounts have always been in good standing and is
at the present time and is not a frozen account.
Our records would show that you are making an effort
to collect the Julian Eppstein account showing a
balance of approximately $725.00. We can not under-
stand why this should be outstanding so long and
feel that it should be taken care of immediately.
Will you please use your best effort for a collection
on this and if necessary, I believe you have the
authority from the Association to sue.

        Many thanks for your attention.

                        Yours very truly,

                        J. E. Morrish
                        Vice President

jem:cl

Figure 4. Morrish, speaking as the wartime representative of the California Chrysanthemum Growers Association, corresponded with outside businesses on behalf of the organization—in this case, Dun & Bradstreet—with a threat to sue if the client's payment was not promptly collected. Morrish made it clear that the CCGA had hired him before their removal to see after the association's affairs.

Figure 5

Mr. Morrish
First National Bank
Redwood City, California

Dear Mr. Morrish:

A new state, a new camp, a new climate is Topaz, the future jewel of the desert. I have been very busy re-establishing my self and so I find that have delayed writing to you. Amidst my confusion and organization, have meant to write but I am very sorry that the days have gone by and am just writing today.

I hope that this letter finds you in the best of health. I know that I have left with you a lot of responsiblities and can't find words to express my thanks to you. It is sure a relief to know that I have have one so capable to help me and I only wish that I can someday return to you some same favor.

Topaz is located about 15 miles from Delta, Utah and at present must declare that the dust is one thing that bother us most. I know as the days go by that it will become a better place. I must say that everyone is working very hard and the moral is so much higher that I know that it is only a matter of time. My brother has left for Idaho to help with the sugar beets. Many of the younger fellows are going to suger beets harvesting and in this small way trying to help out. There are so many opportunities for private employment that it seems that there will be very few young ones left here. I am hoping to go but with my mother here, I thought it besh if I waited until things are more settled.

Everyone from Redwood City are well and working very hard. Thank you for everything and will be writing again. I wish you the best of health, always.

Sincerely,

Sumiye Adachi

Figure 5. "A new state, a new camp, a new climate is Topaz, the future jewel of the desert." There is much meaning to be found in the first line of this first correspondence from Topaz, Utah (the Adachi's relocation camp for the duration of the war), in October 1942. It speaks to an initial feeling of utter dislocation, but with the promise that camp life would become tolerable, meaningful, and potentially patriotic. Turning Topaz into a "jewel of the desert" evokes the pioneering spirit of Americans who initially settled the frontier, claiming and settling "untamed" lands. In many cases of official internment narratives, the imagery is invoked to bring meaning and moral purpose to the act of relocation.

Figure 6.A

★ **ENOMOTO & CO., INC.** ★
CUT FLOWERS
159 FIFTH STREET WHOLESALERS, GROWERS AND SHIPPERS SAN FRANCISCO

October 19, 1942

Mr. J. E. Morrish
Redwood City, California

Dear Mr. Morrish,

I have your letter of the 16th with reference to the fertilizers.

The following is my cost and also ceiling prices prevailing in March. The ceiling price was the price millers, feed dealers, etc., were paying in carload quantities at that time.

	My cost net	Ceiling based on protein %
Tankage	$48.00 per ton	$61.50
Rape seed	29.50	33.00
Mustard seed	20.00	22.00
Chili Nitrate	42.00	

I would ½¢ principally be interested in getting my cost, or at least as close to cost as possible. Consumer's price is much hi...

As for the potash, I sold Zappettini two tons at $50.00 per ton. I think I sold him all that I had.

I paid around $10.00 per ton for the gypsum. On this, prices will have to be low because Pacific Portland Cement manufactures it, and to be competitive, there is no advantage due to freight or warehousing.

I am very glad to hear from you that the nursery is in top shape. I have known Mr. Lucas for some time, and my confidence in his ability has always been high.

Please do not hesitate to cut the prices on these fertilizers listed above because they actually are remnants from the season before, and the Rape and the mustard seal are not widely used except by Japanese chrysanthemum growers.

Incidentally, I sold the following to Zappettini:
March 31, 1942

1 ton	Ammonium Sulphate	@	52.
2 "	Sulphate of potash		50.
5 "	Superphosphate		24.50
2 "	Mixed, 8-12-6		56.25

With my best regards,

Yours very truly,

John H. Enomoto

Figure 6.B

```
                              August 30, 1944




Mr. William Enomoto
3023 Gilpin Street
Denver 5, Colorado

Dear Bill:

          I was out at the plant yesterday and the boys
talked to me about roofing the shed and boiler room. Both
of these leaked very badly last year and should be taken
care of. I think it would be quite all right to put on the
roofing paper of a good quality. They already have seven
rolls there and it will take about sixteen more rolls to cover
both buildings. I understand the rolls cost somewhere around
$3.00 each. They will be glad to furnish the labor and the
material they already have on hand, so the job should only cost
in the neighborhood of $50.00. This will put your roofing in
very good shape and I think it is a fine chance to have it done,
but I did not want to have it touched without your o.k., so
will you please advise me right away.

          Enclosed is credit memorandum for the August rent.

          The flower growers are quite active at the present
time and the chrysanthemums are getting in full swing. So far
the price has been very good but growers are worried as to
shipping as it is very difficult to get containers for shipping.
Apparently they just are not available.

          I hope this finds you and the family all fine.
Kindest regards.

                              Yours very truly,



                              J. E. Morrish
Encl.                         Vice President
jem:af
```

Figures 6.A and 6.B. One letter from Bill Enomoto dated October 1942 shows the level of detail provided for Morrish to maintain the businesses of the interned. A subsequent note from Morrish to Enomoto in August 1944 illuminates the ongoing work of long-distance property management.

Figure 7

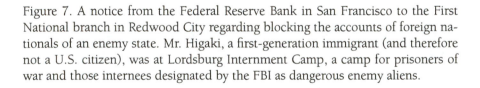

FEDERAL RESERVE BANK OF SAN FRANCISCO
FISCAL AGENT OF THE UNITED STATES
March 10, 1943

First National Bank of San Mateo County,   Re: Nobuo Higaki,
Redwood City,   Present Address: Lordsburg Internment
California.   Camp, Lordsburg, New Mexico.
                                                                   Former Address: Cor. Sequoia & Valota Road
Dear Sirs: Redwood, California.

The War Department has advised the Treasury Department that the internee named above (hereinafter referred to as internee) has been interned for the duration of the war. There is reasonable cause to believe that such internee is a national of a blocked country, pursuant to Executive Order No. 8389, as amended, and within the meaning of section 5(b) of the Trading with the enemy Act, as amended, and that assets held by him, or on his behalf, are assets in which a national of a foreign country designated in Executive Order No. 8389, as amended, has an interest. Accordingly, the Secretary of the Treasury, pursuant to the provisions of Executive Order No. 8389, as amended, and section 5(b) of the Trading with the enemy Act, as amended, has directed us to inform you that all of the above-named internee's bank accounts, safe deposit boxes, and other assets held by banks and banking institutions, are now blocked accounts and that no payment, transfer, or withdrawal may hereafter be made therefrom except as authorized by an appropriate license. The internee has indicated that you are holding assets in which he has an interest, direct or indirect.

In accordance with these instructions, you are directed to block all the accounts, safe deposit boxes, securities, etc., that the above-named internee may have with you or in which you believe he has an interest, direct or indirect. Please notify us when you have taken this action and advise us of the name of any other institution in which you believe the above-named internee has an account and of any business enterprise in which you believe he has a substantial interest.

These instructions do not apply to accounts in the name of a custodial officer of an internment camp in trust for interned aliens. If you maintain such accounts, they should not be blocked.

Pursuant to the direction of the Secretary of the Treasury, the above-named internee is entitled to the privileges of outstanding general licenses, except that he is not entitled to the privileges of any general license which by its terms is limited to a national or nationals of a country named therein, and in addition he is not entitled to the privileges of General Licenses Nos. 11, 12, 32, 33, 71, and 75. Your attention is particularly directed to the fact that by the terms of General Licenses Nos. 28, 42, and 68A, the above-named internee is excluded from their provisions.

Reports on Form TFR-300, as required under Public Circular No. 4C, should be submitted to us within 15 days from the date of this communication. The report on Series L of the form should show the property in your hands on the date of blocking.

FOR VICTORY
BUY
UNITED
STATES
SAVINGS
BONDS
AND STAMPS

Figure 7. A notice from the Federal Reserve Bank in San Francisco to the First National branch in Redwood City regarding blocking the accounts of foreign nationals of an enemy state. Mr. Higaki, a first-generation immigrant (and therefore not a U.S. citizen), was at Lordsburg Internment Camp, a camp for prisoners of war and those internees designated by the FBI as dangerous enemy aliens.

Figure 8

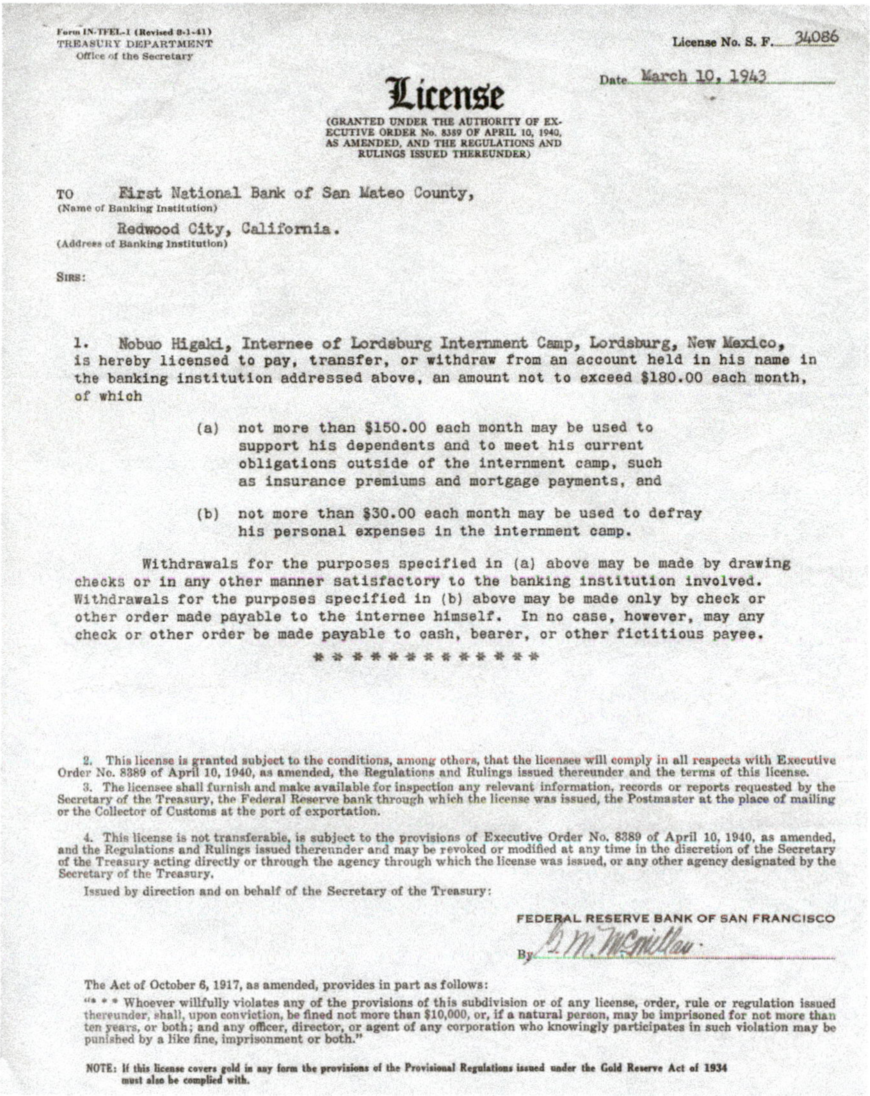

Figure 8. By March 1943, Higaki acquired a license to withdraw on March 10, 1943, under the authority of Executive Order 8389. The Treasury Department contacted Morrish's bank, stating that Nobuo Higaki, an internee of New Mexico, could "pay, transfer, or withdraw" money but only up to $180 each month, $150 for supporting his dependents and meeting obligations outside of the camp, and no more than $30 for personal expenses in the camp.

Figure 9

April 9, 1942

Western Wholesale Florists
361 Tehama Street
San Francisco, California

Gentlemen:-

        We understand that you have leased the Okamura place
on Redwood Avenue in Redwood City. Directly opposite the
Okamura place is a place owned by T. Honda with eight large
glass houses and one small house, and heating equipment, etc.
These houses have been used for growing celery and pepper
plants, as well as roses and other cut flowers. Mr. Honda is
away, and has left the matter in our charge, and we are anxious
to see the place rented. Would you be interested in leasing
these houses? We would appreciate your advice.

                      Very truly yours,

                      J. E. Morrish
                      Vice President

jem:cmc

Figure 9. Morrish managed the affairs of the Honda family by attempting to rent out their property for income. The offer was to rent nine greenhouses owned by Honda while Honda was "away."

Figure 10

May 26th, 1942

Mr. J. E. Morrish
First National Bank
Redwood City, California

Dear Mr. Morrish:

You told me over the telephone last Friday that you would write me a letter relative to the Honda plant.

I do not doubt that you will, but due to this extremely faced-about situation, caused by the Jap evacuation, I wish once more, to call your attention to several points which do not seem to have yet come to the attention of many outside of those in this business, and I might say at this point that few, very few, are doing anything about it.

There is now, and will be more so with the passing of each day, an extreme shortage of flora type bedding plants. The demand is even greater than it was last year. Production has practically stopped. The only sources of supply are from a few nurseries who have a rapidly dwindling stock, the biggest part of which was grown by the Japs before they were sent away.

I know these things, because I am the heaviest buyer of these plants on the peninsula. Many varieties I cannot find a trace of. I am buying, and paying premium prices for scrawny, seedling size plants (too small to plant yet) and scattering them about my various jobs, under trees, in garages, anyplace, to allow them another two to three weeks to develop to planting size. I am just trying to show you what is happening, unbeknowing to the public.

There _were_ six large, completely stocked trucks making the peninsula route from the growing houses, bi-weekly. Now there is not ONE. By the end of this week there wont be fifty flats of decent plants in all the nurseries in Santa

Figure 10 (*continued*)

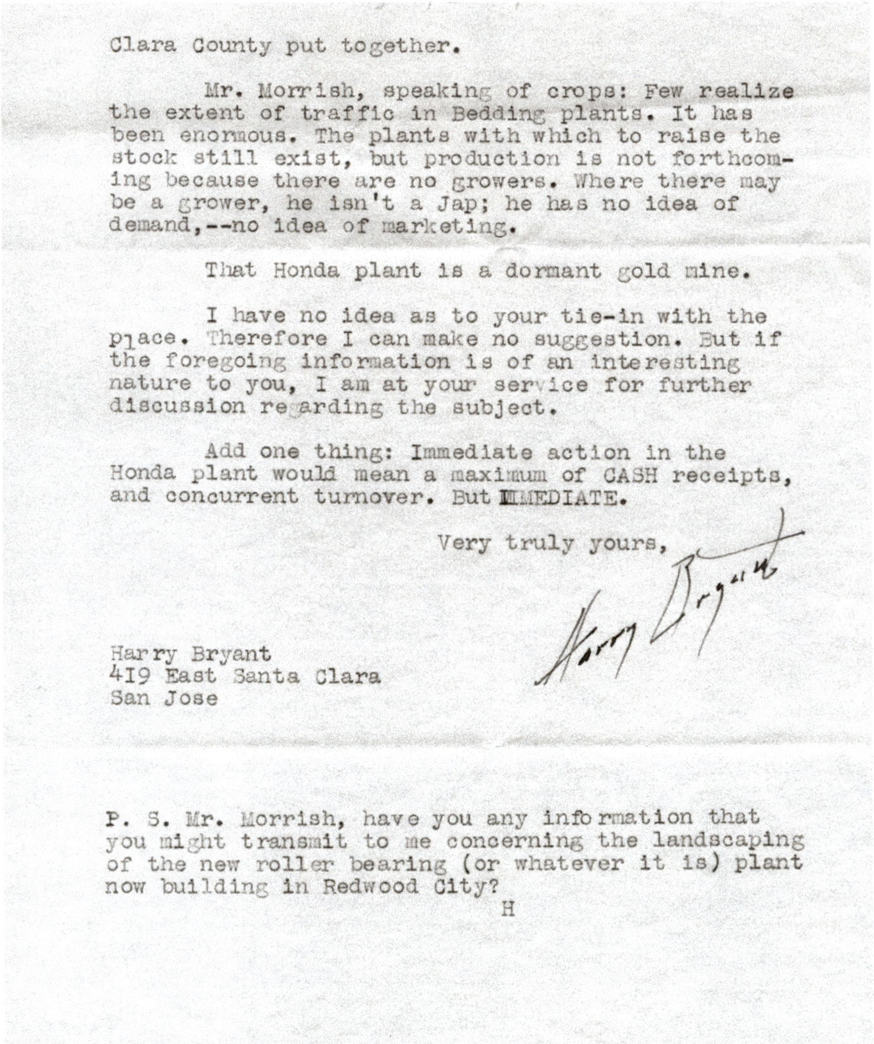

Clara County put together.

Mr. Morrish, speaking of crops: Few realize
the extent of traffic in Bedding plants. It has
been enormous. The plants with which to raise the
stock still exist, but production is not forthcoming because there are no growers. Where there may
be a grower, he isn't a Jap; he has no idea of
demand,--no idea of marketing.

That Honda plant is a dormant gold mine.

I have no idea as to your tie-in with the
place. Therefore I can make no suggestion. But if
the foregoing information is of an interesting
nature to you, I am at your service for further
discussion regarding the subject.

Add one thing: Immediate action in the
Honda plant would mean a maximum of CASH receipts,
and concurrent turnover. But IMMEDIATE.

Very truly yours,

Harry Bryant
419 East Santa Clara
San Jose

P. S. Mr. Morrish, have you any information that
you might transmit to me concerning the landscaping
of the new roller bearing (or whatever it is) plant
now building in Redwood City?
                              H

Figure 10. Morrish received correspondence from those who had previously conducted business with his interned clients as well. This letter speaks directly to the
interruption of agricultural trade (in this case, flower bulbs) as the author of the
letter, landscaper Harry Bryant, expressed his notable concern about the lack of
plants and seedlings in distribution because of the "Jap evacuation." He also described the Honda plant as a "dormant gold mine."

Figure 11

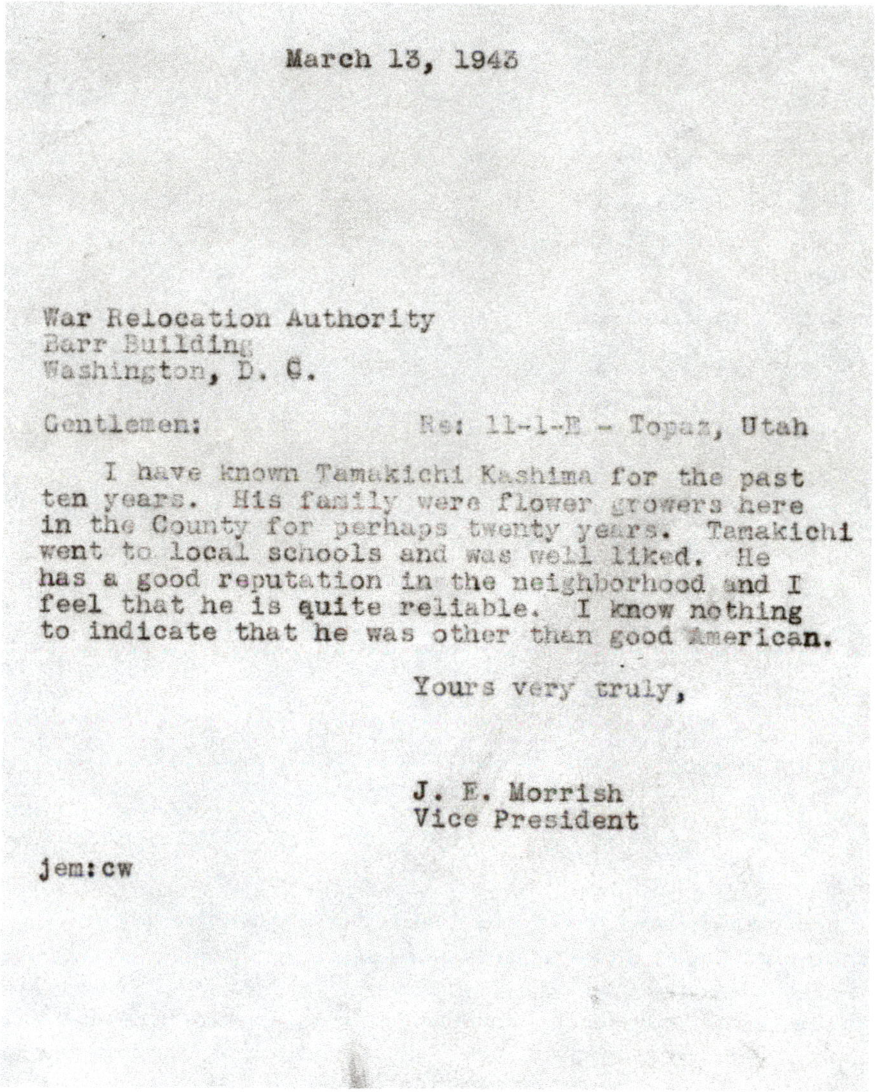

March 13, 1943

War Relocation Authority
Barr Building
Washington, D. C.

Gentlemen: Re: 11-1-E - Topaz, Utah

    I have known Tamakichi Kashima for the past
ten years. His family were flower growers here
in the County for perhaps twenty years. Tamakichi
went to local schools and was well liked. He
has a good reputation in the neighborhood and I
feel that he is quite reliable. I know nothing
to indicate that he was other than good American.

                Yours very truly,

                J. E. Morrish
                Vice President

jem:cw

Figure 11. An example of a reference letter written by Morrish on behalf of an internee at the request of the WRA. Morrish wrote in regards to Tamakichi Kashima that his family had been flower growers for 20 years and he was aware of "nothing to indicate that he was other than good American [sic]."

Figure 12

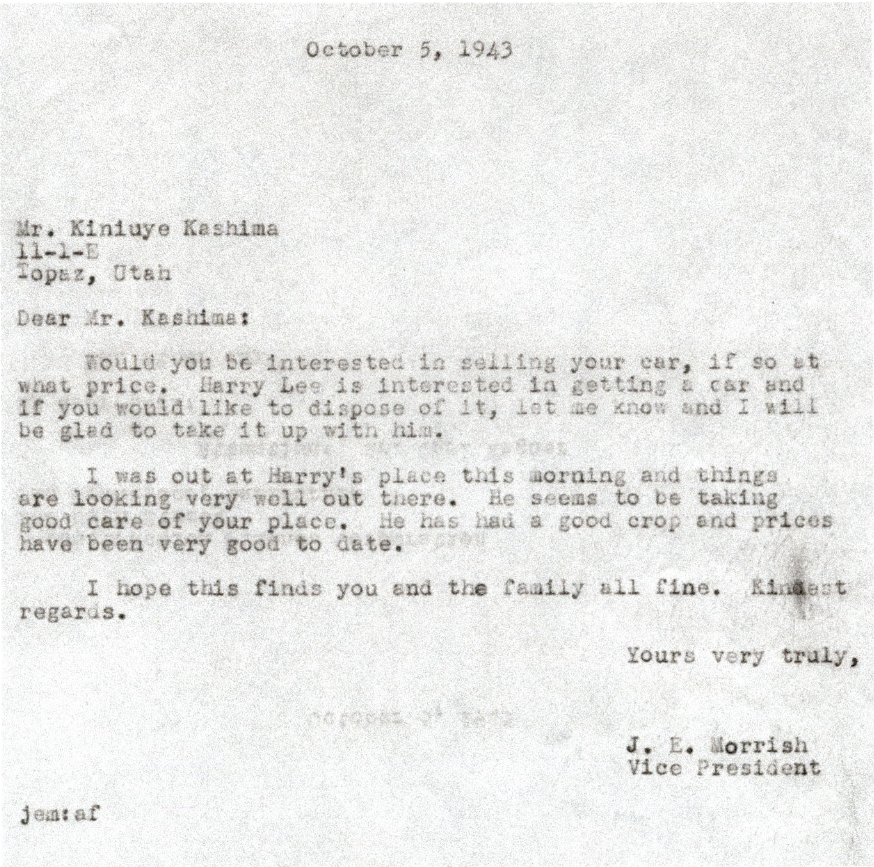

October 5, 1943

Mr. Kiniuye Kashima
11-1-E
Topaz, Utah

Dear Mr. Kashima:

Would you be interested in selling your car, if so at
what price. Harry Lee is interested in getting a car and
if you would like to dispose of it, let me know and I will
be glad to take it up with him.

I was out at Harry's place this morning and things
are looking very well out there. He seems to be taking
good care of your place. He has had a good crop and prices
have been very good to date.

I hope this finds you and the family all fine. Kindest
regards.

                                        Yours very truly,

                                        J. E. Morrish
                                        Vice President

jem:af

Figure 12. An example from late in 1943 when Morrish contacted internees about disposing of possessions still left behind, including in quite a few cases their cars. Theoretically, spare parts for automobiles would have been scarce during the war in light of ubiquitous scrap-metal drives. Further, by the end of 1943, it likely had become clear that the relocation would not be a short stay away from home, and opportunities for shoring up financial accounts would have been welcome as well.

Figure 13

STATE OF CALIFORNIA)
:
COUNTY OF SAN MATEO)

  KINUYE KASHIMA   , being duly sworn, deposes and says;

  1. I am years of age and a national of Japan residing at

               . I have resided only in the Continental
United States at all times on and since June 17, 1940.

  2. This affidavit is made in connection with my application to the
New York Life Insurance Company for them to accept my check for $21.48 drawn
on the First National Bank of San Mateo County towards payment of the
premium due February 13, 1942 on Mitsuki Kashima's policy #12 803 714 and
towards payment of the premium due February 13, 1942 on Hideyoshi Kashima's
policy #12 803 818.

  3. This application is not made directly or indirectly by, for, or
on behalf of a Japanese National who is (a) any individual, partnership,
association, corporation or other organization on the premises of which
the Treasury Department maintains a representative or guard or on the
premises of which there is posted an official Treasury Department notice
that the premises are under the control of the United States Government,
or (b) any bank, trust company, shipping concern, steamship agency, or
insurance company, or (c) any person who, on or since June 14, 1941 has
represented or acted as agent for any person located outside the Continental United States or for any person owned or controlled by persons located
outside the Continental United States, or (d) any person who on or since
June 14, 1941 has acted or purported to act directly or indirectly for the
benefit or on behalf of any blocked country, including the government
thereof, or any person who is a national of Japan by reason of any fact
other than that such person has been domiciled in, or a subject or citizen
of, Japan at any time on or since June 14, 1941.

  4. This transaction does not directly or indirectly substantially
diminish or imperil the assets within the Continental United States of any
national of Japan or otherwise prejudicially affect the financial position
of such national within the Continental United States.

                   _____
                   APPLICANT
Sworn to before me this_____day
of_____,19 .

_____
  NOTARY PUBLIC

Figure 13. An affidavit signed with a request to maintain a life insurance policy in spite of the applicant's status as a foreign national. Internees in many cases were asked to avow their loyalty and assure in writing that their financial transactions would in no way benefit Imperial Japan or harm the United States.

Figure 14

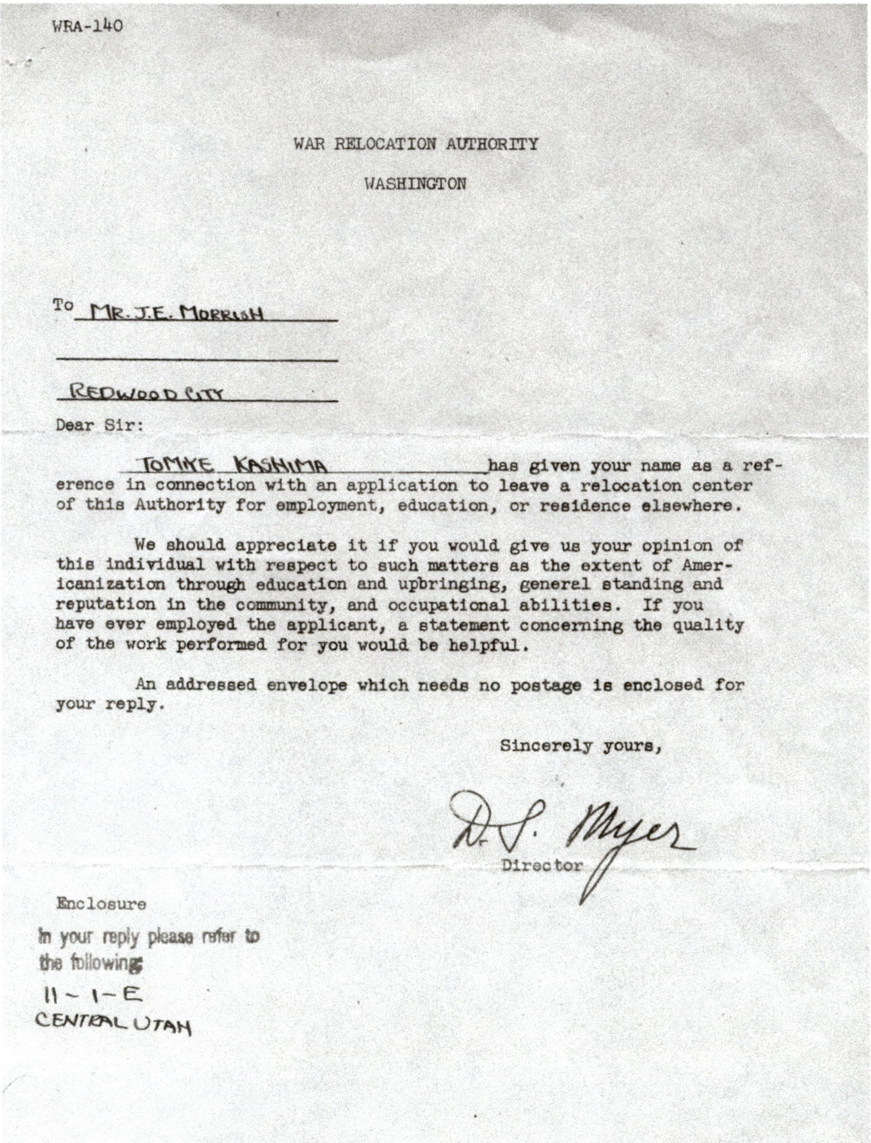

WRA-140

WAR RELOCATION AUTHORITY

WASHINGTON

To __MR. J.E. MORRISH__

__REDWOOD CITY__

Dear Sir:

__TOMYE KASHIMA__ has given your name as a reference in connection with an application to leave a relocation center of this Authority for employment, education, or residence elsewhere.

We should appreciate it if you would give us your opinion of this individual with respect to such matters as the extent of Americanization through education and upbringing, general standing and reputation in the community, and occupational abilities. If you have ever employed the applicant, a statement concerning the quality of the work performed for you would be helpful.

An addressed envelope which needs no postage is enclosed for your reply.

Sincerely yours,

D.S. Myer

Director

Enclosure

In your reply please refer to the following

11 - 1 - E
CENTRAL UTAH

Figure 14. An example of the requests made by the WRA to white citizens, like Morrish, to vouch for the character of evacuees seeking permits to leave the camps.

Figure 15

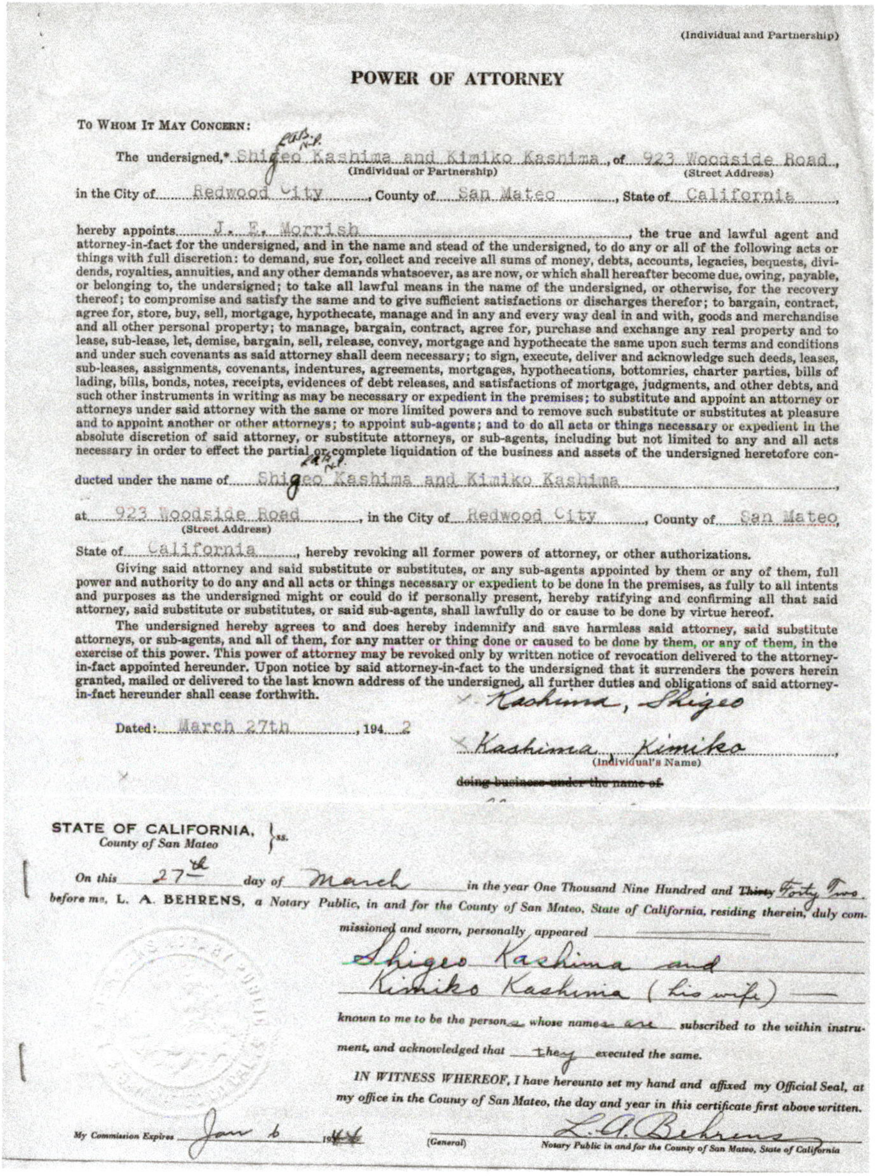

(Individual and Partnership)

POWER OF ATTORNEY

To Whom It May Concern:

The undersigned,* Shigeo Kashima and Kimiko Kashima (Individual or Partnership), of 923 Woodside Road (Street Address), in the City of Redwood City, County of San Mateo, State of California, hereby appoints J. E. Morrish, the true and lawful agent and attorney-in-fact for the undersigned, and in the name and stead of the undersigned, to do any or all of the following acts or things with full discretion: to demand, sue for, collect and receive all sums of money, debts, accounts, legacies, bequests, dividends, royalties, annuities, and any other demands whatsoever, as are now, or which shall hereafter become due, owing, payable, or belonging to, the undersigned; to take all lawful means in the name of the undersigned, or otherwise, for the recovery thereof; to compromise and satisfy the same and to give sufficient satisfactions or discharges therefor; to bargain, contract, agree for, store, buy, sell, mortgage, hypothecate, manage and in any and every way deal in and with, goods and merchandise and all other personal property; to manage, bargain, contract, agree for, purchase and exchange any real property and to lease, sub-lease, let, demise, bargain, sell, release, convey, mortgage and hypothecate the same upon such terms and conditions and under such covenants as said attorney shall deem necessary; to sign, execute, deliver and acknowledge such deeds, leases, sub-leases, assignments, covenants, indentures, agreements, mortgages, hypothecations, bottomries, charter parties, bills of lading, bills, bonds, notes, receipts, evidences of debt releases, and satisfactions of mortgage, judgments, and other debts, and such other instruments in writing as may be necessary or expedient in the premises; to substitute and appoint an attorney or attorneys under said attorney with the same or more limited powers and to remove such substitute or substitutes at pleasure and to appoint another or other attorneys; to appoint sub-agents; and to do all acts or things necessary or expedient in the absolute discretion of said attorney, or substitute attorneys, or sub-agents, including but not limited to any and all acts necessary in order to effect the partial or complete liquidation of the business and assets of the undersigned heretofore conducted under the name of Shigeo Kashima and Kimiko Kashima, at 923 Woodside Road (Street Address), in the City of Redwood City, County of San Mateo, State of California, hereby revoking all former powers of attorney, or other authorizations.

Giving said attorney and said substitute or substitutes, or any sub-agents appointed by them or any of them, full power and authority to do any and all acts or things necessary or expedient to be done in the premises, as fully to all intents and purposes as the undersigned might or could do if personally present, hereby ratifying and confirming all that said attorney, said substitute or substitutes, or said sub-agents, shall lawfully do or cause to be done by virtue hereof.

The undersigned hereby agrees to and does hereby indemnify and save harmless said attorney, said substitute attorneys, or sub-agents, and all of them, for any matter or thing done or caused to be done by them, or any of them, in the exercise of this power. This power of attorney may be revoked only by written notice of revocation delivered to the attorney-in-fact appointed hereunder. Upon notice by said attorney-in-fact to the undersigned that it surrenders the powers herein granted, mailed or delivered to the last known address of the undersigned, all further duties and obligations of said attorney-in-fact hereunder shall cease forthwith.

Kashima, Shigeo

Dated: March 27th, 1942

Kashima, Kimiko
(Individual's Name)

~~doing business under the name of~~

STATE OF CALIFORNIA, } ss.
County of San Mateo

On this 27th *day of* March *in the year One Thousand Nine Hundred and* ~~*Thirty*~~ Forty Two *before me,* L. A. BEHRENS, *a Notary Public, in and for the County of San Mateo, State of California, residing therein, duly commissioned and sworn, personally appeared* Shigeo Kashima and Kimiko Kashima (his wife) *known to me to be the person*s *whose name*s are *subscribed to the within instrument, and acknowledged that* they *executed the same.*

IN WITNESS WHEREOF, I have hereunto set my hand and affixed my Official Seal, at my office in the County of San Mateo, the day and year in this certificate first above written.

My Commission Expires Jan 6 1946

(General)

L. A. Behrens
Notary Public in and for the County of San Mateo, State of California

Figure 15. An example of J. Elmer Morrish's taking on the power of attorney for a Japanese American family during the internment.

Figure 16

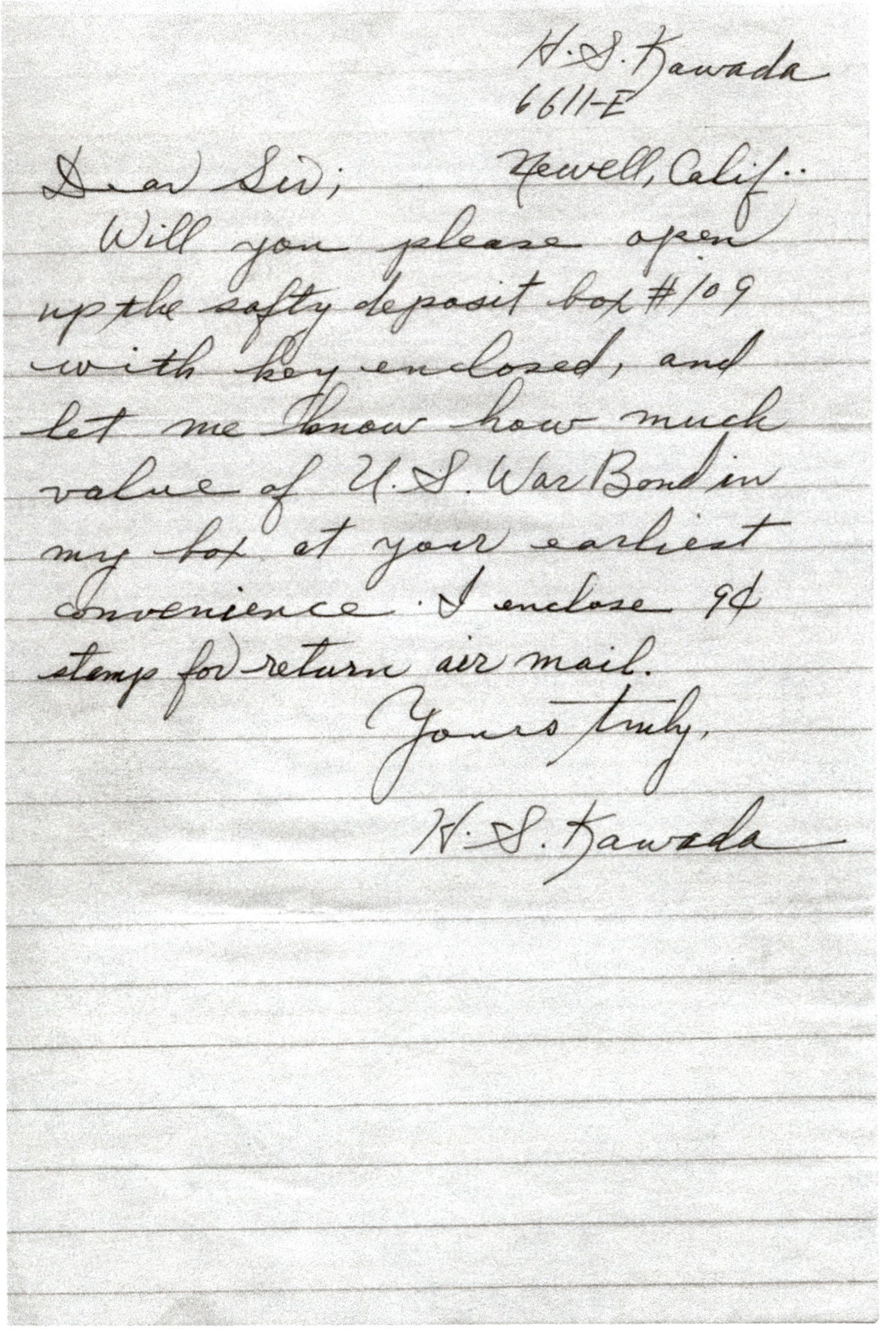

H. S. Kawada
6611-E
Newell, Calif.

Dear Sir;
Will you please open
up the safty deposit box #109
with key enclosed, and
let me know how much
value of U. S. War Bond in
my box at your earliest
convenience. I enclose 9¢
stamp for return air mail.
                    Yours truly,
                    H. S. Kawada

Figure 16. Citizens indeed: The Kawada family wrote to ask Morrish to check the value of their U.S. War Bond. Transcription follows.

FIGURE 16 TRANSCRIPTION

H.S. Kawada
6611-E
Newell, Calif.

Dear Sir,

Will you please open up the safty deposit box #109 with key enclosed, and let me know how much value of U.S. War Bond in my box at your earliest convenience. I enclose 9¢ stamp for return air mail.

Yours truly,
H.S. Kawada

Figure 17

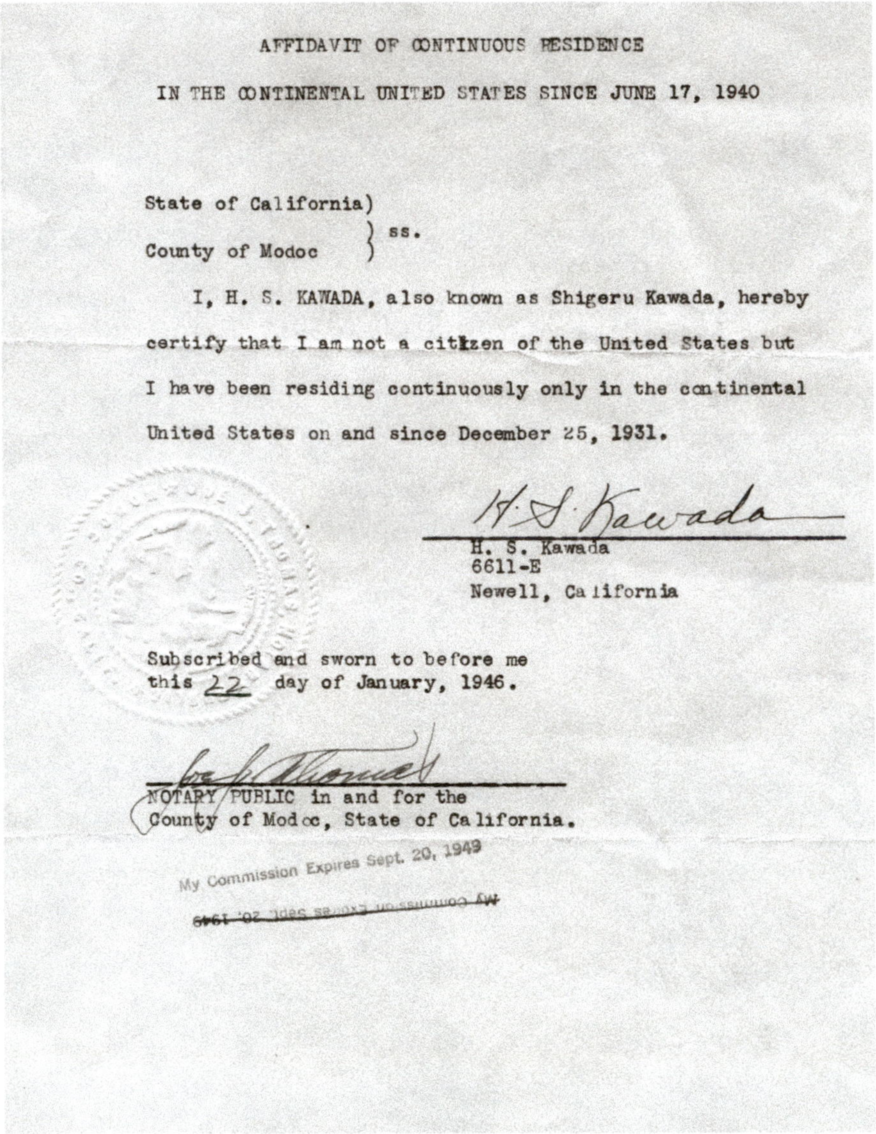

```
              AFFIDAVIT OF CONTINUOUS RESIDENCE

      IN THE CONTINENTAL UNITED STATES SINCE JUNE 17, 1940


      State of California)
                         )  ss.
      County of Modoc    )

          I, H. S. KAWADA, also known as Shigeru Kawada, hereby

      certify that I am not a citizen of the United States but

      I have been residing continuously only in the continental

      United States on and since December 25, 1931.
```

H. S. Kawada

```
                                   H. S. Kawada
                                   6611-E
                                   Newell, California

      Subscribed and sworn to before me
      this 22  day of January, 1946.
```

```
      NOTARY PUBLIC in and for the
      County of Modoc, State of California.

           My Commission Expires Sept. 20, 1949
```

Figure 17. Other ways of classifying the detained: In this affidavit of continuous residence, H. S. (Shigeru) Kawada affirmed that although he was not a citizen of the United States, he had been residing there continuously since 1931. Notary Public verified.

Figure 18

August 20, 1945

Mr. William Kitagawa
c/o Mr. Sawamura
Block 7, Topaz, Utah

Dear Bill:

Enclosed you will find three copies of lease agreement
covering your property on Redwood Avenue which has been leased to
George Capitelli. This, you will note, covers a term of approximately five years. It is going to be necessary for Mr. Capitelli to do
a great deal in the way of improvements and before starting in he
would like to have this lease taken care of. It will be necessary
for him to spend considerable money in repairs and planting several
houses. Please go over the matter carefully and if agreeable to you,
you and Reo can sign all three copies of the lease and return them
to me for delivery to Mr. Capitelli. Will you please have your sig-
natures witnessed. I will be glad to take care of the collection of
the monthly rent and credit your account here with remittances to the
title company covering your deed of trust payment. Also you can advise me as to payment of taxes, etc.

Also enclosed is a duplicate tag covering payment
from Mr. Capitelli reimbursing your account for taxes paid last year.

I hope everything is going along all right with you
and the family. Kindest regards.

If you want to sell this property I   Yours very truly,
think Mr. Capitelli would be interested
in buying providing your price is within reason and title is
satisfactory. Please advise me.
                                         J. E. Morrish
                                         Vice President

jem:af
Encl.

Figure 18. At the end of the war, Morrish forwarded the details on a five-year lease for Mr. Kitagawa's property, indicating that he would be happy to continue to collect rent on the place on his behalf. Morrish also informed Mr. Kitagawa that the renter was potentially interested in buying the property outright, as Mr. Kitagawa was among those who relocated elsewhere.

Figure 19

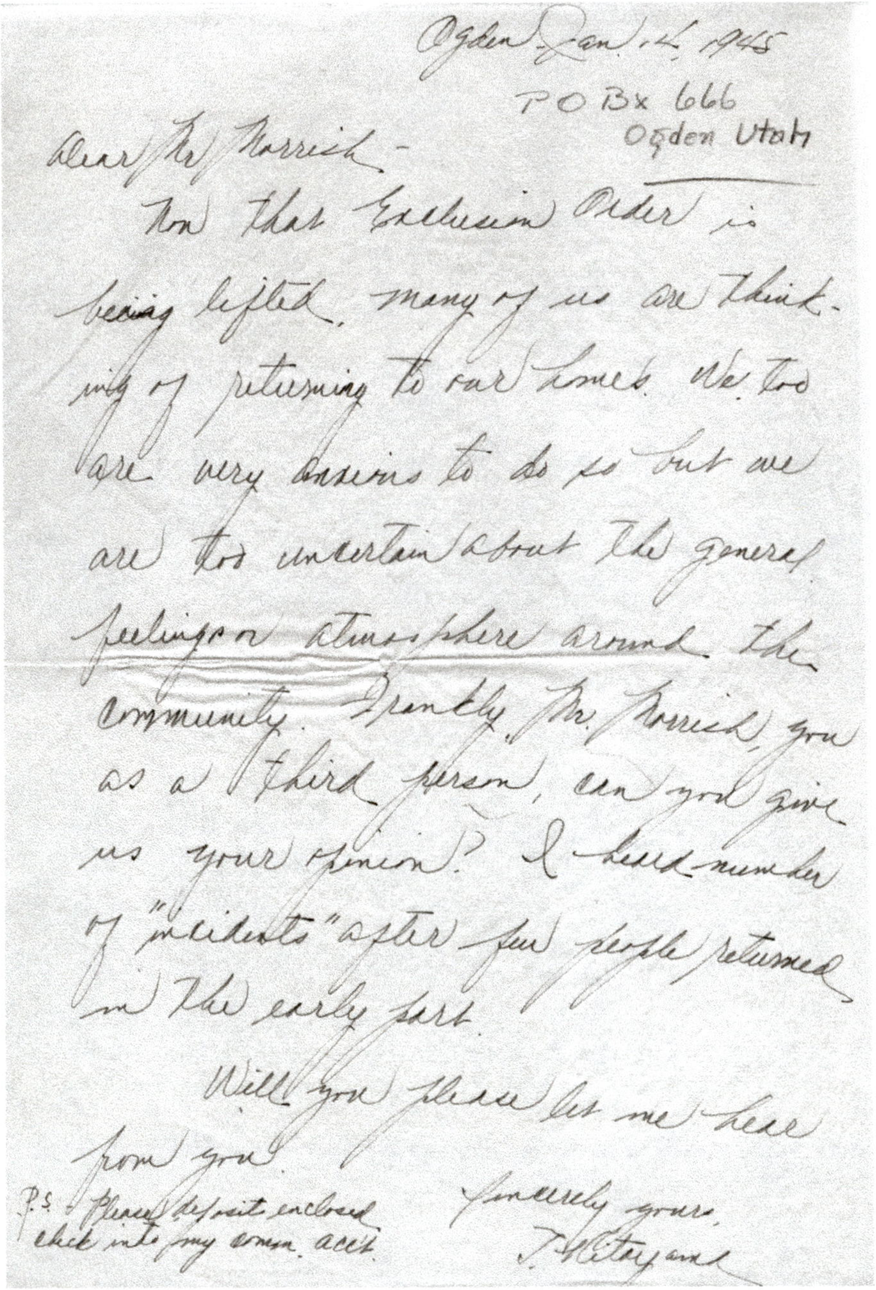

Figure 19. In January 1945, T. Kitayama wrote to Morrish to ask for his thoughts on evacuated families relocating back to Redwood City since the exclusion order had been lifted. He said that many were thinking about coming back home. Kitayama inquired after the atmosphere: "Frankly Mr. Morrish, you as a third person, can you give us your opinion? I heard number [sic] of 'incidents' after few [sic] people returned in the early part. Will you please let me hear from you." Transcription follows.

FIGURE 19 TRANSCRIPTION

Ogden, Jan. 14, 1945
PO Bx 666
Ogden Utah

Dear Mr. Morrish—

Now that Exclusion Order is being lifted, many of us are thinking of returning to our homes. We too are very anxious to do so but we are too uncertain about the general feelings or atmosphere around the community. Frankly Mr. Morrish, you as a third person, can you give us your opinion? I heard number (sic) of "incidents" after few people returned in the early part.

Will you please let me hear from you.

Sincerely yours.
T. Kitayama

p.s. Please deposit enclosed check into my comm. acc't.

Figure 20

January 17, 1945

Mr. T. Kitayama
P. O. Box 666
Ogden, Utah

Dear Mr. Kitayama:

Your letter of January 14th enclosing a check for deposit was received and duplicate tag is enclosed.

Several of the folks have been in recently, most of them on a visit and to look over their property. The only ones who have come back permanently are Sumje Adachi and her sister, who are living on the place now and their brother and Hiromike Inouye, who are living on the Stanford University campus and teaching Japanese at the university. Harumi Higaki was in last week for a few days but has gone back again.

I think the feeling locally would be for most part all right; however, there is a real problem on housing and any of the folks coming back should very definitely arrange their housing beforehand, as I think if it was necessary to move somebody, the action would not be so good. I believe, however, that wherever possible, it would be best to delay returning a few months until the general public got used to the idea of the return. Then it would be a more natural result by a few coming back at a time.

Kindest regards to you.

Yours very truly,

J. E. Morrish
Vice President

Figure 20. Morrish wrote back quickly to Mr. Kitayama, suggesting that the family wait a few months "until the general public got used to the idea of the return. Then it would be a more natural result by a few coming back at a time."

Figure 21

```
                          November 23, 1942




Miss N. Mayeda
30-10-E
Topaz, Utah

Dear Miss Mayeda:-

             Recently I received from the County
Tax Collector a bill for $145.90 for 1942-43 taxes
both 1st and 2nd installments.  The bill that you
sent to me and which I paid for you was in the
amount of $150.50.  This bill shows taxes for
lot eleven - five acres Faber Subdivision.  Did
you receive a paid bill covering the payment of
$150.50.  Please let me know if these bills are
for the same property.

             I was by the place last Sunday and
noticed a good many flowers unpicked.  I talked
to Mr. Hasler and he told me he had lots of difficulty
in getting help and that he could not get enough
help to do the picking.  He was quite disappointed
in his net returns for the season.  In reference to
the rental he is about six months behind now but
has promised very definitely to take care of it in
the next two weeks.

             Kindest regards to you.

                          Yours very truly,



                          J. E. Morrish
                          Vice President

jem:cl
```

Figure 21. In the fall of 1942, the trouble with absentee community members became more apparent. Morrish wrote to Miss N. Mayeda that many of the flowers of her property remained unpicked, owing to a problematic tenant and concomitant labor problems.

Figure 22

```
                              March 25, 1945




Mrs. N. Mayeda
30-10-E
Topaz, Utah

Dear Mrs. Mayeda:-

      Today I went out to the ranch to see if I could get
some rent from Mr. Hasler, but he is not in a position
to make any payment just at this time, however, I believe
that directly after the first of next month he can make
part payment of his delinquent rent.  I believe it is nine
months now that he is behind, but feel that he will be in a p
position to do better the coming year as apparently he has
made a fairly good connection with a group of Chinese, so
his labor will not be the problem it was last year.  This
morning he was discing the front piece to plant cauliflower.
They had spinach planted there but had to disc about half
the crop under on account of the continual rains as it turned
all yellow.  I believe that he is a good hard worker and a
very well-meaning chap, and think that probably during this
year the matter will work out all right.  It is very much
better to have someone there taking care of the place and
I feel he is doing a very good job.

      I hope this finds you all fine.  Kindest regards.

                              Yours very truly,



                              J. E. Morrish
                              Vice President


jem:cw
```

Figure 22. In March 1943 Mrs. Mayeda's renter was nine months behind on payments and was trying to get things planted with help. Morrish offered his opinion, believing the renter to be a "good chap" and explaining that it would be better to have someone there who could take care of the place. In this instance, Morrish would eventually need to obtain approval from the U.S. Department of Agriculture before leasing to a new tenant.

Figure 23.A

May 4, 1945

Dear Mr. Morris:

Just another letter to ask still another favor.

I just recieved a letter today from my mother telling me of some difficulties my father ran into in California. You see, my father left camp to prepare the way for relocating the rest of the family. He has been there now for about a month. My mother, sister and I will be joining him in about 3 weeks.

The trouble is this. The Inspector of San Mateo County came to inspect the property. I don't know what the trouble is and since my father can't speak English well, he couldn't understand either. Evidentally the property wasn't as clean as they would like it or something. Anyway they threaten to arrest my father. I know I'm asking an awful

Figure 23.A (*continued*)

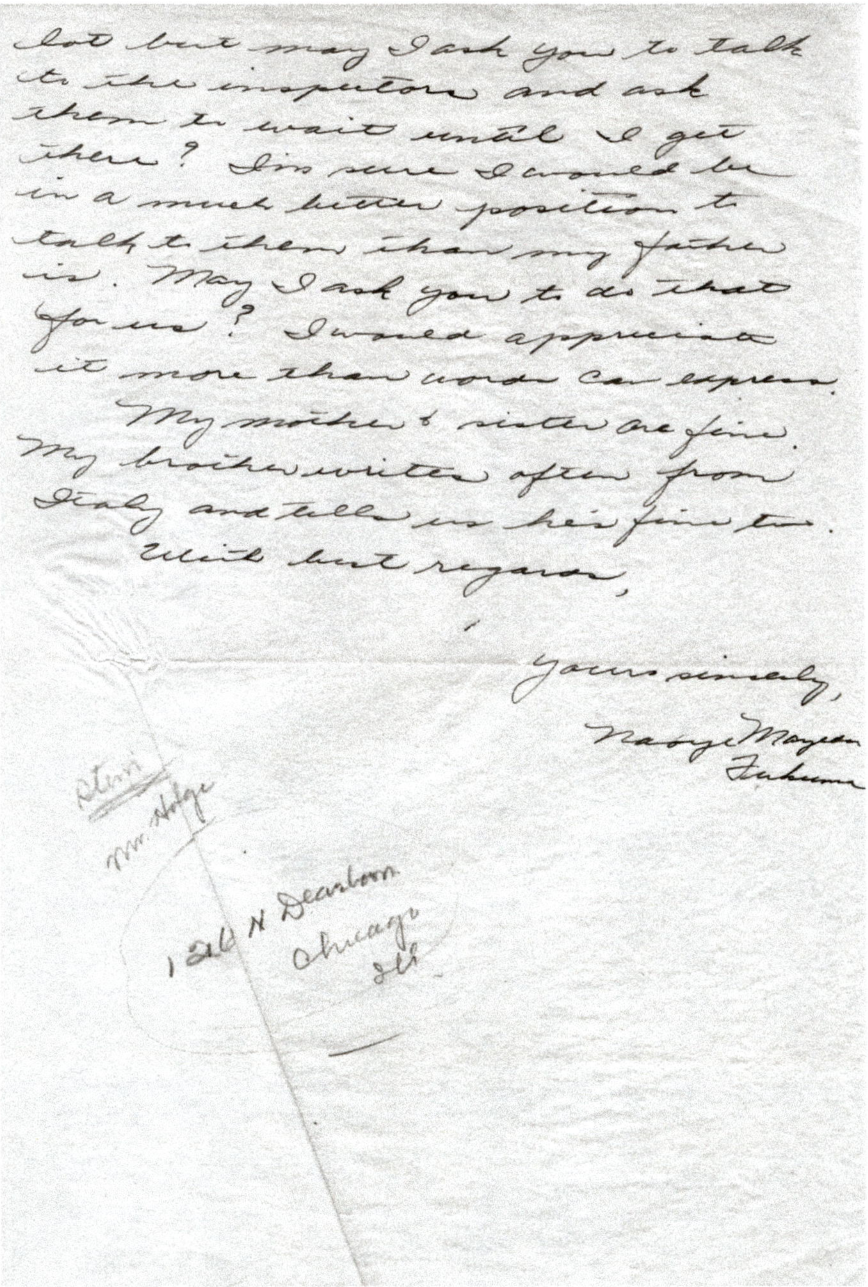

lot but may I ask you to talk to the inspectors and ask them to wait until I get there? I'm sure I would be in a much better position to talk to them than my father is. May I ask you to do that for us? I would appreciate it more than words can express.

My mother & sister are fine. My brother writes often from Italy and tells us he's fine too.

With best regards,

Yours sincerely,

Naoye Mayeda
Fukuma

Attn
Mr. Hodge

1216 N Dearborn
Chicago
Ill.

Figure 23.B

May 14, 1945

Mrs. Naoye Mayeda Fukuma
30-10-E
Topaz, Utah

Dear Naoye:

    After I received your letter of May 4th, I went out to
the ranch but could not find your father. I was advised that
he was working in Palo Alto. I contacted the County Health
Department. Today the representative of that department came
in and told me what the trouble was. Since you left the
territory, there has been set up a new sanitary district with
a sewer line on Clark Avenue and the Bayshore line. It will
be necessary to connect that with one of these lines and in
your case, I believe the Bayshore is the closest. Apparently
your father was using the outdoor toilet and a complaint was
made and the health department called and left a notice. I
am told the matter has been taken care of temporarily and
that the toilet has been torn down. The one that is still
there has been o.k.'d by them temporarily until the matter is
settled. Then it will probably be necessary for you to
connect it up with the sewer.

    You might drop your Dad a line and tell him there is
nothing to worry about. When you return, it would be best
to talk the matter over with the health department, as it
will then be necessary to make some improvement in this regard.

    I hope you hear good news from your brother in Italy and
that he is getting along fine and that he will soon be home
with you. Kindest regards.

                         Yours very truly,

                         J. E. Morrish
                         Vice President

jem:af

Figures 23.A and 23.B. Confusion from long-distance property ownership and the continued language barrier reveal fear of the return: In May 1945 Mr. Mayeda's daughter, Naoye Fukuma, wrote to Morrish, concerned that her father, in Redwood City to ready their property for the family's return, was threatened with arrest by inspectors of the property. Within ten days, Morrish responded to assure them he was not in trouble, but rather that a sanitary district had been established, and the property needed to come under compliance. Transcription follows.

Figure 23.A Transcription

May 4, 1945

Dear Mr. Morrish:

Just another letter to ask still another favor.

I just received a letter today from my mother telling me of some difficulties my father ran into in California. You see, my father left camp to prepare the way for relocating the rest of the family. He has been there now for about 1 month. My mother, sister and I will be joining him in about 3 weeks.

The trouble is this. The Inspector of San Mateo County came to inspect the property. I don't know what the trouble is and since my father can't speak English well, he couldn't understand either. Evidentally the property wasn't as clean as they would like it or something. Anyway they threatened to arrest my father. I know I'm asking an awful lot but may I ask you to talk to the inspector and ask them to wait until I get there? I'm sure I would be in a much better position to talk to them than my father is. May I ask you to do that for us? I would appreciate it more than words can express.

My mother & sister are fine. My brother writes often from Italy and tells us he's fine too.

With best regards,
Yours sincerely,
Naoye Mayeda
Fukuma

Figure 24

May 27, 1945

Dear Mr. Morris:

Last Saturday I sent you a telegram. I thought maybe I better explain that.

Before we could leave Chicago for California, we had to have definite proof that we had a place to stay and a reasonable amount of cash on hand to tide us over until we had a job. The fact that my father was there and that I was receiving letters from him evidently wasn't enough. They told me that a telegram from a banker or some one in California working in our behalf would be enough evidence. All I wanted to use the telegram for was to obtain permit & grant to travel back to California. I rushed the request to you by telegram because I wanted to take leave Chicago on the 30th of this month.

Figure 24 (*continued*)

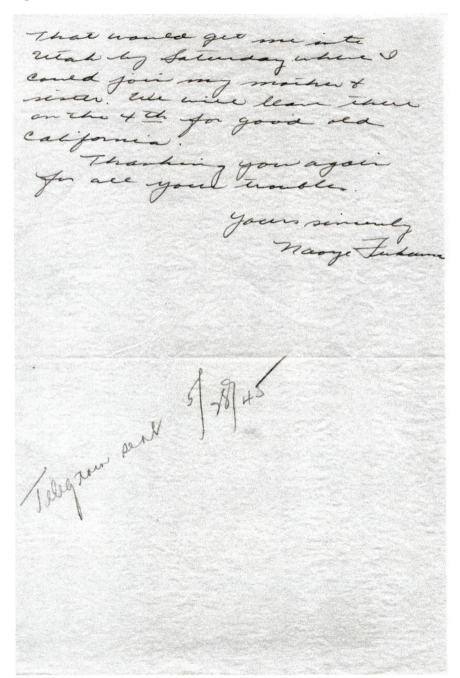

Figure 24. More difficulty in relocating back home: The Mayedas needed to have proof of a place to stay and a certain amount of cash in order to return to California. Transcription follows.

FIGURE 24 TRANSCRIPTION

May 27, 1945

Dear Mr. Morrish:

Last Saturday I sent you a telegram. I thought maybe I better explain that.

Before we could leave Chicago for California, we had to have definite proof that we had a place to stay and a reasonable amount of cash on hand to tide us over until we had a job. The fact that my father was there and that I was receiving letters from him evidentally wasn't enough. They told me that a telegram from a banker or someone in California working in our behalf would be enough evidence. All I wanted to use the telegram for was to obtain permit & grant to travel back to California. I rushed the request to you by telegram because I wanted to leave Chicago on the 30th of this month. That would get me into Utah by Saturday where I could join my mother and sister. We will leave there on the 4th for good old California.

Thanking you again for all your troubles.

Yours sincerely,
Naoye Fukuma

Figure 25.A

April 21, 1942

New York Life Insurance Company
One Montgomery Street
San Francisco, California

Gentlemen:-

        We are holding the following policies
for Japanese clients:

Pol. No. 15 420 649 - Hajime Nakano - $2,000.00
Pol. No. 7 899 437 - Hajime Nakano - $2,012.00
Pol. No. 13 041 400 - Jim H. Nakano - $1,000.00
Pol. No. 13 042 234 - Louis K. Nakano - $1,228.00

        Please advise us if there are any delin-
quent premium payments. Will you please change
your record to send premium notices to these people
in our care until further advised. The Nakano
family is away from home and have asked us to take
care of these payments for them as they become
due.

                        Very truly yours,

                        J. E. Morrish
                        Vice President

jem:cmc

Figure 25.B

NEW YORK LIFE INSURANCE COMPANY

SAN FRANCISCO CLEARING-OFFICE

403 CROCKER FIRST NATIONAL BANK BLDG.
ONE MONTGOMERY STREET, SAN FRANCISCO, CALIFORNIA

JARED M. CODY, CASHIER

April 22, 1942
File A

TELEPHONE, DOUGLAS

Mr. J.E. Morrish, Vice President
The First National Bank of San Mateo County
Redwood City, California

Dear Mr. Morrish:

We are appreciative of your cooperation and we would like very much to act on the suggestion that was made in your letter dated April 21, 1942 but it is our Company's practice not to change the record of an insured's address unless the insured furnishes a personally signed request. We suggest, therefore, that you ask Hajime Nakano, Jim H. Nakano and Louis K. Nakano to complete the enclosed Notices of Change of Address and return them to us if they no longer desire that communications concerning the policies be sent to P.O. Box 324, Redwood City, California.

Premiums on Mr. Hajime Nakano's policies #7 899 437 and 15 420 649 are paid to November 6, 1942 and December 13, 1942. Premiums on the children's policies are paid to November 15, 1942.

If there are no changes in the United States Treasury Department rulings or licenses in the meantime, the Company will require satisfactory affidavits from Louis K. Nakano and Jim H. Nakano concerning their status and activities as Japanese before we can accept payments of the premiums or transact other business with the insured. Assuming that the boys are native born citizens of the United States, we enclose affidavit forms that will be acceptable if completed and returned to us with certified copies of birth certificates. Mr. Hajime Nakano furnished a satisfactory affidavit when he paid the premium due December 13, 1941.

Yours truly,

J.M. Cody
Cashier

JMC:mjk
enclosures

TO AVOID DELAYS, PLEASE ALWAYS GIVE POLICY NUMBER WHEN WRITING THE COMPANY

Figures 25.A and 25.B. A clear example of how Morrish handled personal family business: his correspondence with the New York Life Insurance Company to have bills for the Nakano family sent to the bank while they were "away from home." As further evidence of the dynamic of handling business for the interned, the insurance company requested official affidavits regarding "their status and activities as Japanese."

Figure 26

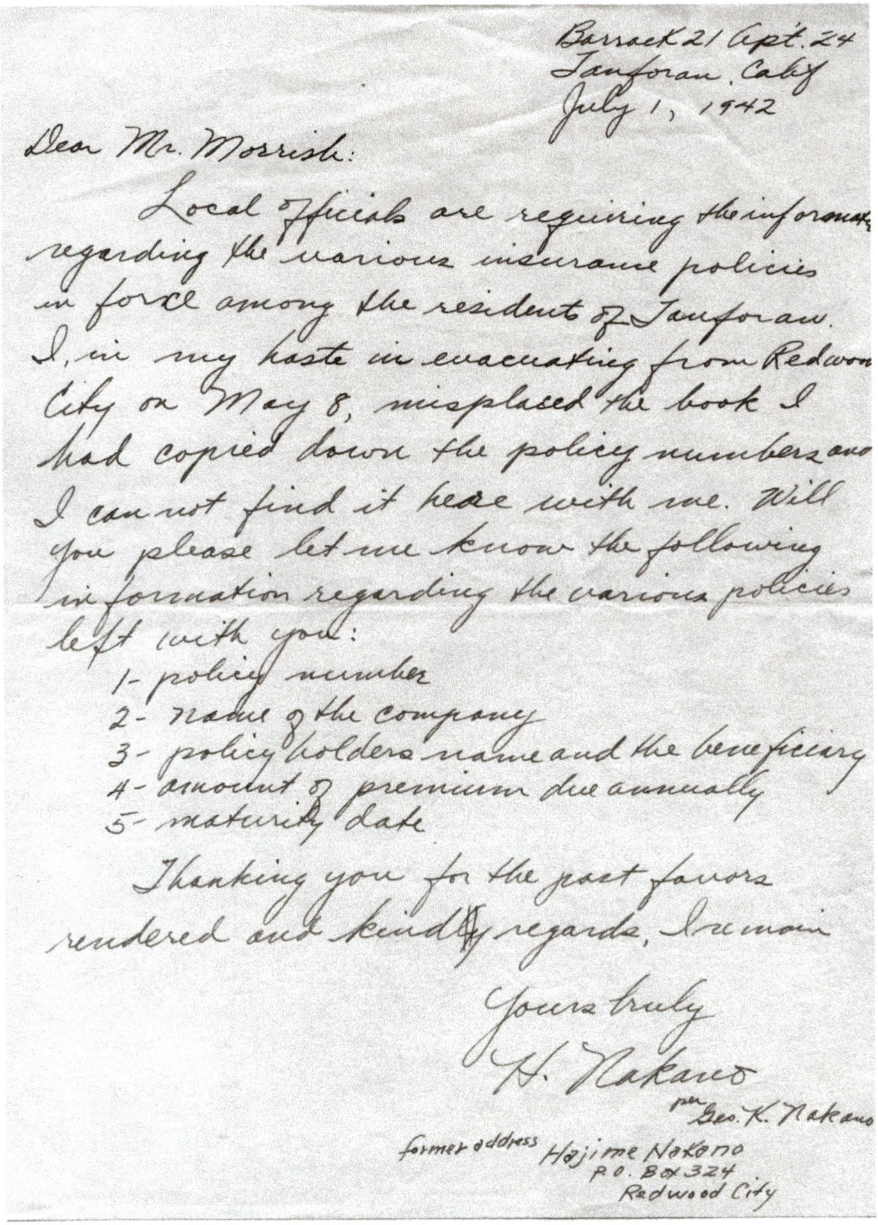

Figure 26. In July 1942 Hajime Nakano, per George Nakano, wrote from Tanforan: "Local officials are requiring information regarding the various insurance policies in force among the residents of Tanforan. I, in my haste in evacuating from Redwood City on May 8, misplaced the book. . .," and he asked Morrish to find the policies for him. Official documents were required, and in many cases internees needed assistance from those on the outside. Transcription follows.

FIGURE 26 TRANSCRIPTION

Barrack 21, Apt. 24
Tanforan, Calif.
July 1, 1942

Dear Mr. Morrish,

Local officials are requiring the information regarding the various insurance policies in force among the residents of Tanforan. I, in my haste in evacuating from Redwood City on May 8, misplaced the book I had copied down the policy numbers and I cannot find it here with me. Will you please let me know the following information regarding the various policies left with you:

1. policy number
2. name of the company
3. policy holders name and the beneficiary
4. amount of premium due annually
5. maturity date

Thanking you for the past favors rendered and kind regards, I remain

Yours truly,
H. Nakano,
per Geo. K. Nakano

Figure 27

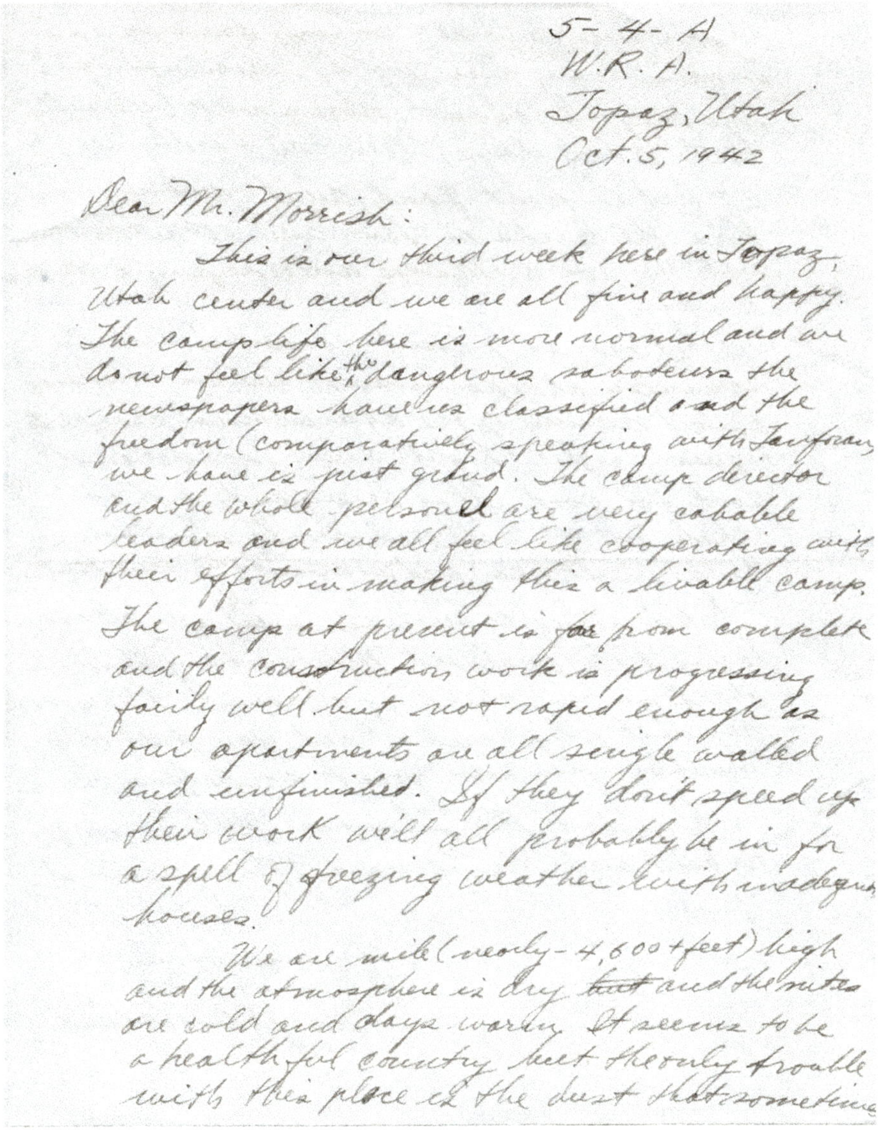

5- 4- A
W. R. A.
Topaz, Utah
Oct. 5, 1942

Dear Mr. Morrish:

This is our third week here in Topaz,
Utah center and we are all fine and happy.
The camp life here is more normal and we
do not feel like the dangerous saboteurs the
newspapers have us classified and the
freedom (comparatively speaking with Tanforan)
we have is just grand. The camp director
and the whole personnel are very capable
leaders and we all feel like cooperating with
their efforts in making this a livable camp.
The camp at present is far from complete
and the construction work is progressing
fairly well but not rapid enough as
our apartments are all single walled
and unfinished. If they don't speed up
their work we'll all probably be in for
a spell of freezing weather with inadequate
houses.

We are mile (nearly- 4,600+feet) high
and the atmosphere is dry but and the nites
are cold and days warm. It seems to be
a healthful country but the only trouble
with this place is the dust that sometimes

Figure 27 (*continued*)

chokes our throat, smarts our eyes and makes living here highly uncomfortable. This happens about once a week (usually lasts 2 to 3 days). One can hardly see 25 feet in front of and dust just simmers thru the cracks in floor and other apertures into the room. Makes housekeeping a constant drudge.

I am at present connected with the agricultural department and am making a soil survey of the agricultural prospects of this project. Right now — soil does not look too good. It is heavy and high in alkali but we will endeavor to grow some-things next year and we will try our best.

Attending to business will you please deposit the enclosed Montgomery Ward check in my checking account. Please send deposit slip and thank you for all the troubles you have gone to in helping us.

Regards to Mr. Thompson, Behrens, etc of the bank and Mr. Leonard of the agricultural office.

Yours very truly
George K. Nakano

Figure 27. In some cases, internees wrote merely to check in or to share their experiences with someone on the outside. This letter from George Nakano provides terrific detail of the family's first weeks at Topaz, giving an interesting peek into how the internees made peace with, and found their place within, the camp structure. Nakano was conducting a soil survey, and while there was an assumption that the camp would begin agricultural endeavors, Nakano reported that the soil was quite "heavy and high in alkali" but that "we will try our best." Transcription follows.

FIGURE 27 TRANSCRIPTION

5-4-A
WRA
Topaz, Utah
Oct. 5, 1942

Dear Mr. Morrish:

This is our third week here in Topaz, Utah center and we are all fine and happy. The camp life here is more normal and we do not feel like the dangerous saboteurs the newspapers have us classified and the freedom (comparatively speaking with Tanforan) we have is just grand. The camp director and the whole personel (sic) are very cabable (sic) leaders and we all feel like cooperating with their efforts in making this a livable camp. The camp at present is far from complete and the construction work is progressing fairly well but not rapid enough as our apartments are all single walled and unfinished. If they don't speed up their work we'll all probably be in for a spell of freezing weather with inadequate houses.

We are mile (sic) (nearly-4,600 + feet) high and the atmosphere is dry and the nites (sic) are cold and days warm. It seems to be a healthful country but the only trouble with this place is the dust that sometimes chokes our throat, smarts our eyes and makes living here highly uncomfortable. This happens about once a week (usually lasts 2 to 3 days). One can hardly see 25 feet in front and dust just simmers thru the cracks in the floor and other apertures into the room. Makes housekeeping a constant drudge.

I am at present connected with the agricultural department and am making a soil survey of the agricultural prospects of the project. Right now—soil does not look too good. It is heavy and high in alkali but we will endeavor to grow some things next year and we will try our best.

Attending to business will you please deposit the enclosed Montgomery Ward check in my checking account. Please send deposit slip and thank you for all the troubles you have gone to in helping us.

Regards to Mr. Thompson, Behrens, etc of the bank and Mr. Leonard of the Agricultural Office.

Yours very truly,
George K. Nakano.

Figure 28

November 23, 1943

Mr. George Nakano
5-3-F
Topaz, Utah

Dear George:

       This morning Frank Osorio told me that yesterday when he was going by your property he noticed the door of the house was opened and he shut it and lateron met one of the boys working for Harry Lee and spoke to him about it and thought it was rather odd that the door was opened and they looked around and found that a window was broken. Someone had been in the house, apparently nothing much had been disturbed but I think perhaps we should board the windows up and if you will care to send me the key, I will go down and see if everything looks all right and have the windows boarded up. This is the first difficulty of this kind that I have had occasion to check up.

       I hope this finds you and the family fine. Kindest regards.

Yours very truly,

J. E. Morrish
Vice President

jem:af

Figure 28. In late 1943 Morrish wrote to George Nakano to inform the family of a break-in on their property. Morrish, reflecting on the local climate, suggested that they board up the windows for the duration.

Figure 29

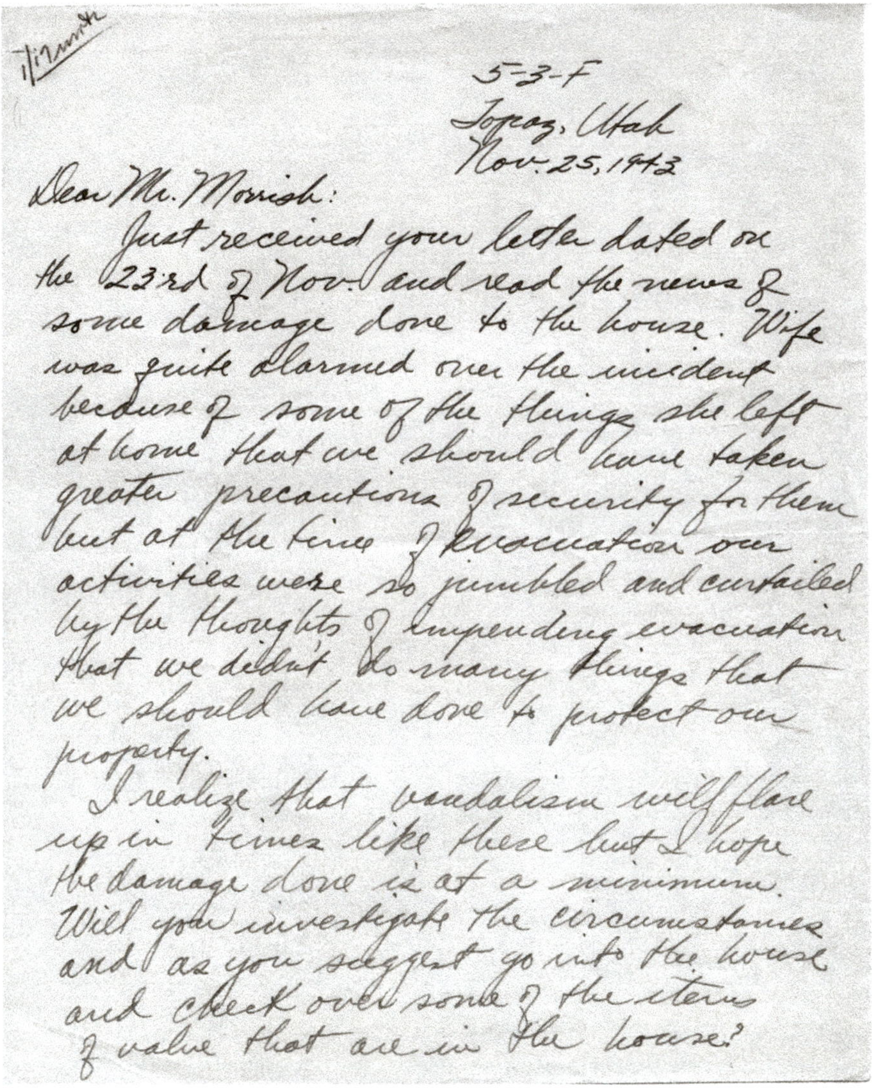

5-3-F
Topaz, Utah
Nov. 25, 1943

Dear Mr. Morish:

Just received your letter dated on the 23rd of Nov. and read the news of some damage done to the house. Wife was quite alarmed over the incident because of some of the things she left at home that we should have taken greater precautions of security for them but at the time of evacuation our activities were so jumbled and curtailed by the thoughts of impending evacuation that we didn't do many things that we should have done to protect our property.

I realize that vandalism will flare up in times like these but I hope the damage done is at a minimum. Will you investigate the circumstances and as you suggest go into the house and check over some of the items of value that are in the house?

Figure 29 (*continued*)

I will list the things of value that are in the house and the place where we left them.

1- 2 sets of silver ware in the kitchen cabinets.

2- Our bed room furniture in the room adjoining the kitchen.

3- 2 sets of dishes in a cabinet in the kitchen with door side facing the wall.

Floor Plan of the house

Kitchen — Bedroom
— closet
Living Room — Room
— Porch.
Front

In the kitchen — there are two gas stoves (one of which is my brothers) & odds and ends of no great value

In the living room are some lamps, book case, dismantled beds, couches, etc. belonging to my brother and I. In the room adjoining the living room are other odds and ends of no real value.

Only items I care a great deal for is the silver ware which are our wedding gifts and if its still there I wonder if you would take it home and safe

Figure 29 (*continued*)

guard it for me. Also in the bedroom
is a pinkish colored comforter, a black
woman's coat (in the closet) and some
shoes that we would like to have
sent up to us if possible. In fact
all the clothes in the closet would be
quite helpful to us out here as we could
use them.

When you go in the house will you
buy some mroth balls and spread
it around in the rooms.

I boarded up the back windows
but not the front ones as I thought
it would detract fo the appearance
and with Harry Lee's man around
it would be safe but if you think
to boarding up is wise please arrange
it to be done with the lumber available
on the place or buy new ones and
charg it to me. Also any other precautionary measure you see fit
to be done please arrange it to be done.

The key to house is in my safety
deposit box number 418 with my

Figure 29 (*continued*)

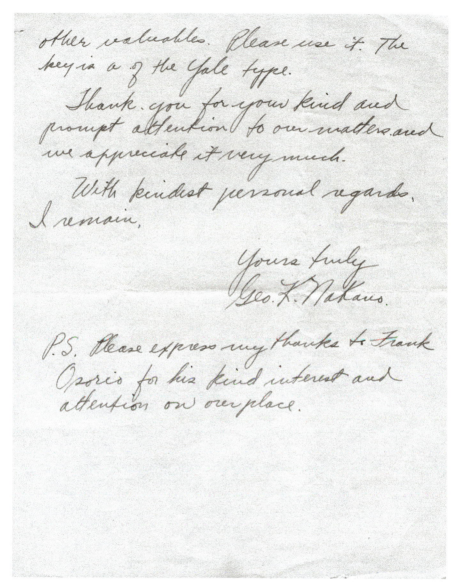

Figure 29. Within days, Nakano wrote back expressing his distress, especially concerning certain items the family had left behind in the quickness of evacuation. He drew a picture of the house and listed items that he hoped Morrish could confirm were safe. Apparently, the Nakanos too felt the evacuation would be short-lived. In the postscript, Nakano expressed his appreciation for the local resident who noticed and reported the break in. Transcription follows.

Figure 29 Transcription

5-3-F
Topaz, Utah
Nov. 25, 1943

Dear Mr. Morrish,

Just received your letter dated on the 23rd of Nov and read the news of some damage done to the house. Wife was quite alarmed over the incident because of some of the things she left at home that we should have taken greater precautions of security for them but at the time of evacuation our activities were so jumbled and curtailed by the thoughts of impending evacuation that we didn't do many things that we should have done to protect our property.

I realize that vandalism will flare up in times like these but I hope the damage done is at a minimum. Will you investigate the circumstances and as you suggest go into the house and check over some of the items of value that are in the house?

I will list the things of value that are in the house and the place where we left them.

1 – 2 sets of silverware in the kitchen cabinets
2 – Our bedroom furniture in the room adjoining the kitchen
3 – 2 sets of dishes in a cabinet in the kitchen with door side facing the
      wall.

In the kitchen—there are two gas stoves (one of which is my brothers) and odds and ends of no great value.

In the living room are some lamps, book case, dismantled beds, couches, etc., belonging to my brother and I. In the room adjoining the living room are other odds and ends of no real value.

Only items I care a great deal for is the silver ware which are our wedding gifts and if it's still there I wonder if you would take it home and safeguard it for me. Also in the bedroom is a pinkish colored comforter, a black woman's coat (in the closet) and some shoes that we would like to have sent up to us if possible. In fact all the clothes in the closet would be quite helpful to us out here as we could use them.

When you go in the house will you buy some moth balls and spread it around in the rooms.

I boarded up the back windows but not the front ones as I thought it would detract to the appearance and with Harry Lee's man around it would be safe but if you think the boarding up is wise please arrange it to be done with the lumber available on the place or buy new ones and charge it to me. Also any other precautionary measure you see fit to be done please arrange it to be done.

The key to house is in my safety deposit box number 418 with my other valuables. Please use it. The key is of the Yale type.

Thank you for your kind and prompt attention to our matters and we appreciate it very much.

With kindest personal regards, I remain,

Yours truly,
Geo. K. Nakano

P.S. Please express my thanks to Frank Osorio for his kind interest and attention on our place.

Figure 30

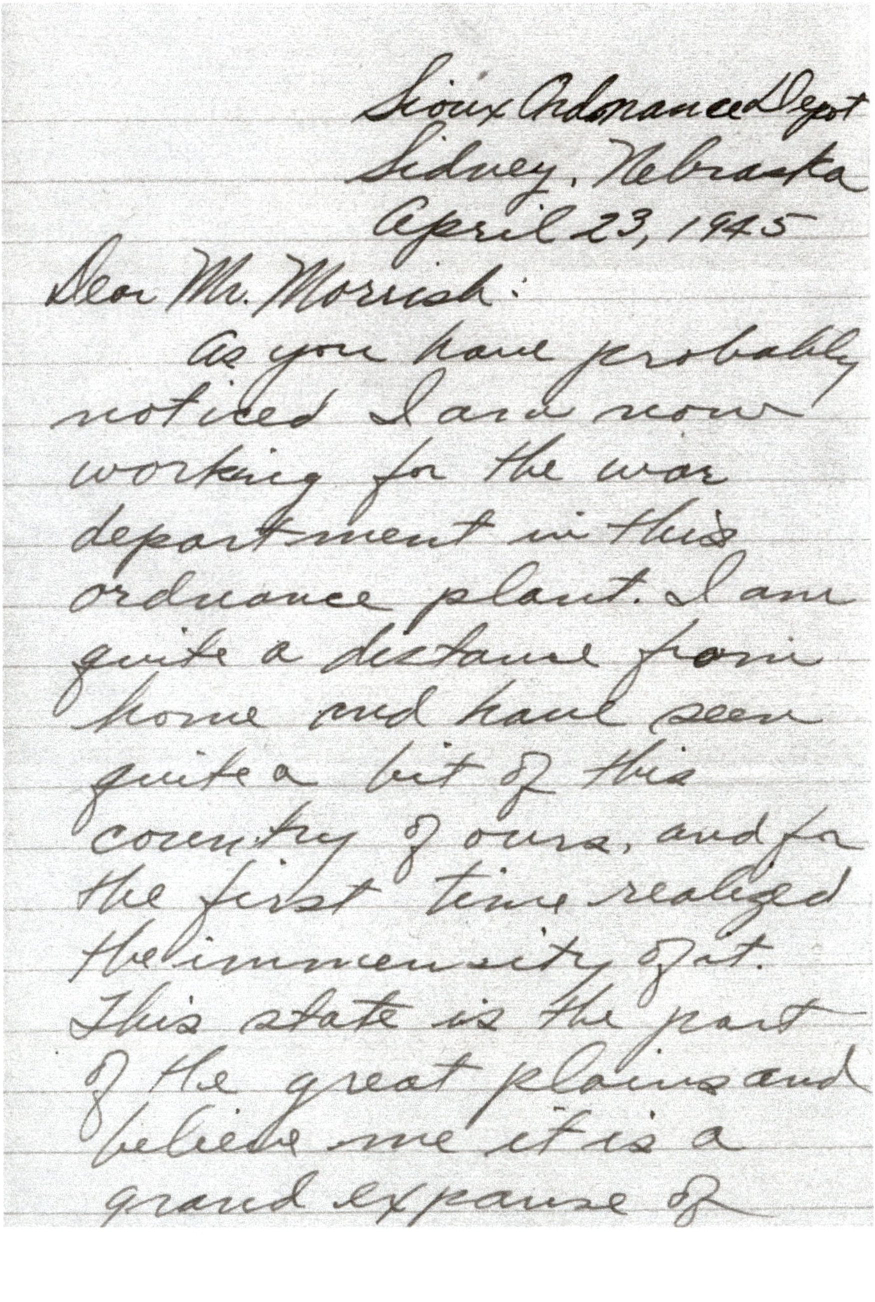

Sioux Ordnance Depot
Sidney, Nebraska
April 23, 1945

Dear Mr. Morrish:

As you have probably noticed I am now working for the war department in this ordnance plant. I am quite a distance from home and have seen quite a bit of this country of ours, and for the first time realized the immensity of it. This state is the part of the great plains and believe me it is a grand expanse of

Figure 30 (*continued*)

rolling prairie dotted
here and there with
farms. It is too barren
for me; perhaps I
come from too good of
a state but I still
consider Redwood City
the best.

Quite a few of the former
residents of Redwood City
have returned home from
what I hear. They all
seem to be doing fine.
My brother writes that
he's doing fine and I am
very happy that they
can pursue their normal
livelihood.

Mr. Morrish, will

Figure 30 (*continued*)

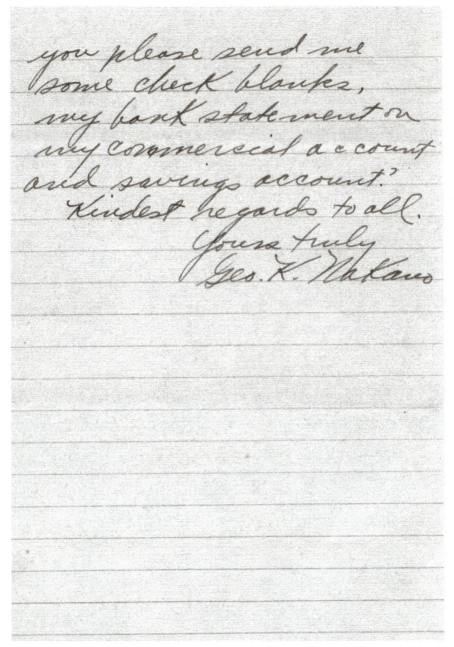

Figure 30. The documents also reveal the complexity of options for work outside of the camps, some especially interesting in light of the situation. In April 1945, George Nakano wrote to Morrish from his new address in Nebraska, where he was working for the war department. Transcription follows.

FIGURE 30 TRANSCRIPTION

Sioux Ordnance Dept.
Sidney, Nebraska
April 23, 1945

Dear Mr. Morrish:

As you have probably noticed I am now working for the war department in this ordnance plant. I am quite a distance from home and have seen quite a bit of this country of ours, and for the first time realized the immensity of it. This state is the part of the great plains and believe me it is a grand expanse of rolling prairie dotted here and there with farms. It is too barren for me; perhaps I came from too good of a state but I still consider Redwood City the best.

Quite a few of the former residents of Redwood City have returned home from what I hear. They all seem to be doing fine. My brother writes that he's doing fine and I am very happy that they can pursue their normal livelihood.

Mr. Morrish, will you please send me some check blanks, my bank statement on my commercial account and savings account?

Kindest regards to all.

Yours truly,
Geo. K. Nakano

Figure 31

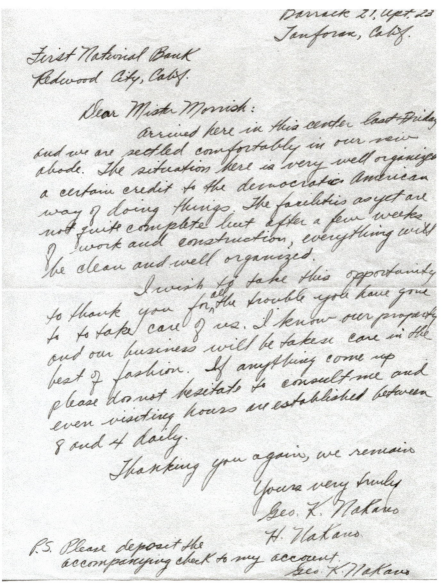

Figure 31. In a quick note to Mr. Morrish, the Nakano family checked in from Tanforan: "The situation here is very well organized, a certain credit to the democratic American way of doing things." An interesting parallel to the WRA's insistence that it would conduct the internment "as a democracy should." Transcription follows.

FIGURE 31 TRANSCRIPTION

Barrack 21, Apt. 23, Tanforan, Calif.
First National Bank
Redwood City, Calif.

Dear Mister Morrish:

Arrived here in this center last Friday and we are settled comfortably in our new abode. The situation here is very well organized, a certain credit to the democratic American way of doing things. The facilities as yet are not quite complete but after a few weeks of work and construction, everything will be clean and well organized.

I wish to take this opportunity to thank you for all the trouble you have gone to to take care of us. I know our property and our business will be taken care in the best of fashion. If anything come up (sic) please do not hesitate to consult me and even visiting hours are established between 8 and 4 daily.

Thanking you again, we remain,

Yours very truly,
Geo. K. Nakano,
H. Nakano

p.s. Please deposit the accompanying check to my account. Geo. K. Nakano.

Figure 32

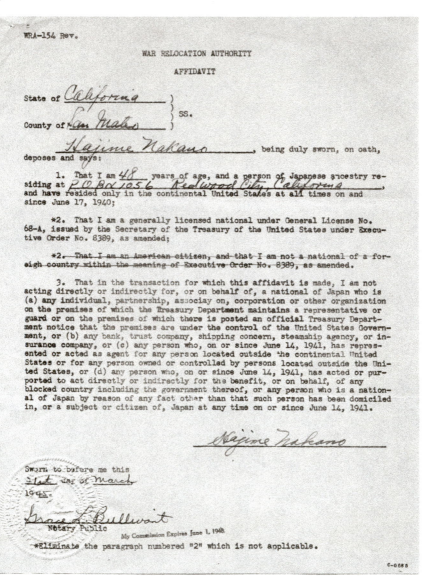

Figure 32. The WRA created documentation in the attempt to legitimize the internment and show due diligence in determining the security risks associated with the interned. This is a WRA-requested affidavit from an internee, asserting that he had not acted on behalf of an enemy national.

Figure 33

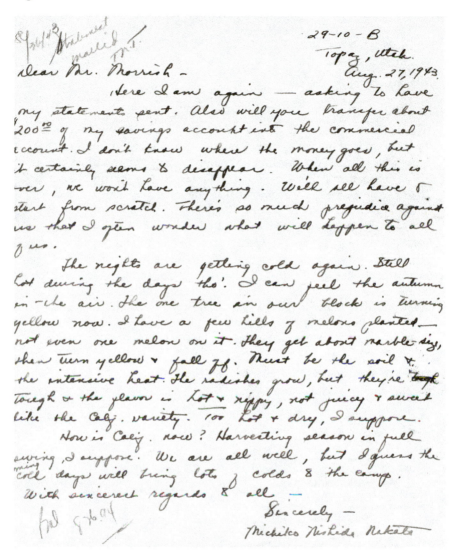

Figure 33. At times, interned families also expressed in writing their concerns about what could possibly lie in store for them. In August 1943, Mrs. Nakata wrote to Morrish to inquire about financials, then stated, "When all this is over, we won't have anything. We'll all have to start from scratch. There's so much prejudice against us that I often wonder what will happen to all of us." Transcription follows.

FIGURE 33 TRANSCRIPTION

29-10-B
Topaz, Utah,
Aug. 27, 1943.

Dear Mr. Morrish-

Here I am again—asking to have my statements sent. Also will you transfer about $200 of my savings account into the commercial account. I don't know where the money goes, but it certainly seems to disappear. When all this is over, we won't have anything. We'll all have to start from scratch. There's so much prejudice against us that I often wonder what will happen to all of us.

The nights are getting cold again. Still hot during the days tho'. I can feel the autumn in the air. The one tree in our block is turning yellow now. I have a few hills of melons planted—not even one melon on it. They get about marble-size, then turn yellow & fall off. Must be the soil and the intense heat. The radishes grow but they're tough and the flavor is hot & nippy, not juicy & sweet like the Calif. variety. Too hot & dry, I suppose.

How is Calif. now? Harvesting season in full swing, I suppose. We are all well, but I guess the coming cold days will bring lots of colds to the camp.

With sincerest regards to all—

Sincerely,
Michiko Nishida
Nakata

Figure 34

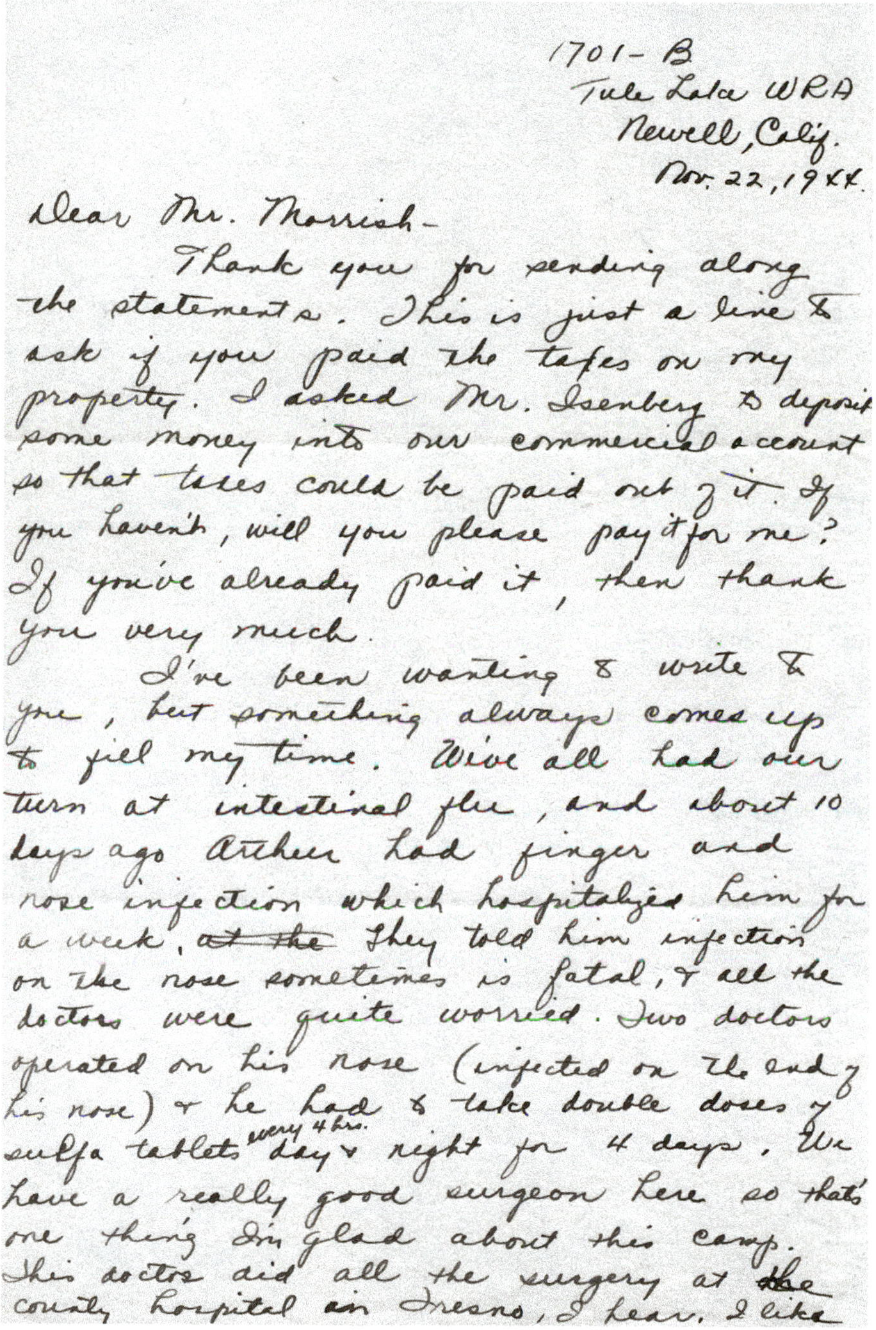

1701- B
Tule Lake WRA
Newell, Calif.
Nov. 22, 19xx.

Dear Mr. Morrish—
Thank you for sending along
the statements. This is just a line to
ask if you paid the taxes on my
property. I asked Mr. Isenberg to deposit
some money into our commercial account
so that taxes could be paid out of it. If
you haven't, will you please pay it for me?
If you've already paid it, then thank
you very much.
I've been wanting to write to
you, but ~~something~~ always comes up
to fill my time. We've all had our
turn at intestinal flu, and about 10
days ago Arthur had finger and
nose infection which hospitalized him for
a week, ~~at the~~ They told him infection
on the nose sometimes is fatal, & all the
doctors were quite worried. Two doctors
operated on his nose (infected on the end of
his nose) & he had to take double doses of
sulfa tablets every 4 hrs. day & night for 4 days. We
have a really good surgeon here so that's
one thing I'm glad about this camp.
This doctor did all the surgery at ~~the~~
county hospital in Fresno, I hear. I like

Figure 34 (*continued*)

him — he's jolly and friendly — not pompous & important looking. Incidentally — he's a Japanese & his name is Dr. Hashiba.

Another thing I want to tell you. We're so disgusted with this camp, & more & more I realize this is no place for us to stay, that we've applied for a leave clearance to another camp. After all, we're both nisei, & we've been brought up in the American system of education & thinking, & I just can't swallow what the troublemakers way of thought and living. If Japan is like this camp, I certainly don't want to go. We regret ever coming to this camp, but we've learned our lesson & I think we could be better citizens for having had a taste of it. this camp. We certainly realize our mistake in coming here. Arthur's father & his sisters & brothers are in Gila — altho' one sister & a brother & their families have relocated. His youngest brother, Tom, volunteered & is fighting in France I think. All my relatives are in Poston, & three of my cousins are in the army. One, a volunteer, was wounded in action last month in France. My aunt writes all of the time, & everybody is so glad we've made the decision to leave here. So far we have 6 relatives in the army, & more coming up.

In our application papers, we had to give 5 Caucasian references. We gave your name as one, so if you should get a letter asking about us, will you tell them about our characters? I hope it was all right. It takes quite a long time for the O.K. to come from Washington. Thank you. This will be all for this time. Regards to Mrs. Morriel

Sincerely — Michiko Nakata.

Figure 34. Conflict within the camps, and among the interned, remains a story that has not yet been fully fleshed out. One family wrote from Tule Lake, the camp that became a segregation center in the summer of 1943 for those whom the WRA had deemed "disloyal" due to protest or dissent—a step toward differentiating the status of those held in the camps. The Nakata family wrote to Morrish about being surrounded by "trouble makers," noting that "we could be better citizens for having a taste of this camp." In order to be transferred away from this camp, internees needed five "caucasian references." She also noted that for them, getting permission should be relatively easy—"after all, we are both Nisei. . . ." Later, Mrs. Nakata would write to ask for a letter on behalf of her husband, Arthur, who was listed as an "excludee" as apparently all adult males in Tule Lake were. Transcription follows.

FIGURE 34 TRANSCRIPTION

1701-B, Tule Lake WRA
Newell, Calif.
Nov. 22, 1944

Dear Mr. Morrish—

Thank you for sending along the statements. This is just a line to ask if you paid the taxes on my property. I asked Mr. Isenbery to deposit some money into our commercial account so that taxes could be paid out of it. If you haven't, will you please pay it for me? If you've already paid it, then thank you very much.

I've been wanting to write to you, but something always comes up to fill my time. We've all had our turn at intestinal flu, and about 10 days ago Arthur had finger and nose infection which hospitalized him for a week. They told him infection on the nose is sometimes fatal, & all the doctors were quite worried. Two doctors operated on his nose (infected on the end of his nose) & he had to take double doses of sulfa tablets every 4 hrs day & night for 4 days. We have a really good surgeon here so that's one thing I'm glad about this camp. This doctor did all the surgery at the county hospital in Fresno, I hear. I like him—he's jolly and friendly—not pompous & important looking. Incidentally, he's a Japanese and his name is Dr. Hashiba.

Another thing I want to tell you. We're so disgusted with this camp, & more & more I realize this is no place for us to stay, that we've applied for a leave clearance to another camp. After all, we're both Nisei, and we've been brought up in the American system of education & thinking, & I just can't swallow the trouble makers' way of thoughts and living. If Japan is like this camp, I certainly don't want to go. We regret ever coming to this camp, but we've learned our lesson and I think we could be better citizens for having had a taste of this camp. We certainly realize our mistake in coming here. Arthur's father & his sisters & brothers are in Gila—altho' (sic) one sister and a brother and their families have relocated. His youngest brother, Tom, volunteered and is fighting in France I think. All my relatives are in Poston, and three of cousins are in the army. One, a volunteer, was wounded in action last month in France. My aunt writes all of the time, and everybody is so glad we've made the decision to leave here. So far we have 6 relatives in the army, and more coming up.

In our application papers, we had to give 5 Caucasian references. We gave your name as one, so if you should get a letter asking about us, will you tell them about our characters? I hope it was all right. It takes quite a long time for the O.K. to come from Washington. Thank you. This will be all for this time. Regards to Mrs. Morris.

Sincerely, Michiko
Nakata.

Figure 35

July 7, 1945

Mrs. Michiko Nishida Nakato
1701-B Tule Lake
Newell, California

Dear Mrs. Nakato:

It was nice to get your letter of July 2nd this morning. Glad to know that you are all feeling better and I am hoping that Arthur will get good news from the Army Hearing Board.

If you folks really want to come back to your place on the highway, I can see no reason why you shouldn't do so. I have heard of no trouble whatever locally and a good many of the folks are back in their homes again and a number of the younger girls I know are out doing housework and seem to be getting along fine. I think for a while perhaps there will be a little problem with marketing that the folks will have to handle in some other way but gradually I am sure that will also be eliminated. It is possible that you folks might be able to find some place on the peninsula where Arthur could do gardening or farm work until you feel you could go back to your own place. If you are interested,in this, let me know and I will be glad to make inquiries for you. Recently two people in Hillsborough have asked me if I knew or could find a Japanese girl to do their cooking and in visiting around recently I have been to at least three homes where Japanese girls were doing domestic work.

The weather here has been fine and the mornings and evenings are nice and cool but during the day it is very pleasant.

I hope this finds you all fine. Kindest regards.

Yours very truly,

J. E. Morrish
Vice President

jem:af

Figure 35. Eventually, Morrish reported that a return to Redwood City was an entirely feasible, if not desirable, decision. In July 1945 Morrish encouraged the Nakata family to return to Redwood City, citing "no reason why you shouldn't do so." Many families had returned without trouble, except for possibly in "marketing" their businesses—due to residual anti-Japanese sentiment that he expected would pass quickly.

Figure 36

```
                                        Topaz, Utha. March 6, 1944.

Mr. J. E. Morrish,
The First Nationa Bank,
Redwood City, California.

Dear Mr. Morrish:

            I have received your letter of Feb. 10, 1944 advising me
to  sell the materials and supplies we stored in our warehouse. Well, after
I have checked among our members and found out that our stocks have been
sold already and those things in the warehouse belong to most of the indiv-
idual growers and I asked them if they want to sell the stocks and they said
they would like to keep them until after the war.

            I have just received a letter from Mr. ,Yamada a few days ago
from Rivers, Arizona where he lives now, he states that he wants to sell his
Automobile and black cloth and also said that he turned every things into
your hand. Now, do you know anything regarding this matter ? I believe that
he keeps his things in his own house or shed. He has a house and shed in
front of our Office Building.

            Mr. Maollen, of Maollen Co., of San Francisco,is using
the Hogan Ranch packing house in back of our Office Buildig and I have not
collected the rent for 1942 and 1943. I am renting the place for $30.00
a year so will you kindly collect the lot rent for $60.00 by name of The
California Chrysanthemum Growers Ass'n.

            Weather of here now getting worm and we are having mild
and sunny day evry day. We all from Redwood City are doing fine. We hope
all our old friend in Redwood City are well. I  am

                        Yours very truly,

                            J.I. Rikimaru

P.S.
        Enclosed in a receipt for Saburo Tamura's radio of Redwood City
        Police Dpartment. We were wondering if you could get the radio
        back from Mr. Collins and if you can't get it would you advice
        me what step shall I take to get it back. Please sure send the
        receipt back to me if unable to get radio back. If they returned
        the radio to you  please have it sent to Saburo Tamura  3-8-b
        Topaz, Utah. Thank you.
```

Figure 36. Some of the details within requests for assistance contain telling details of the experience: In 1944 J. Rikimaru wrote to Morrish with all manner of house-keeping requests on behalf of other internees, from selling cars to collecting rent. Of particular interest is the mention of retrieving Saburo Tamura's radio at the Redwood City Police Department, as it had been confiscated (likely as suspicious potential spy equipment) after the attack at Pearl Harbor.

Figure 37

December 31, 1944

Mr. J. E. Morrish
The First National Bank
Redwood City, California

Dear Mr. Morrish,

I have just returned from Rocky Ford, Colorado where I had to attend a friends funeral and to clear up his business matters for the family; so that is why my reply to you is so late.

Enclosed you will find the signed signature card which had Mr. Okamura's name only.

Since it is in his name he doesn't have to deposit his fund to the present commerical account so t h e withdrawl slip is not needed.

Thank you very much for the selling ot the merchandise. I have distributed the duplicate tag to the proper parties.

From now on I would like to have you keep the merchandise and not sell them anymore.

Since the re-opening of the coast, I am sure that few families who has some member in the ar med forces will be returning to Redwood City.

I wonder if you would be so kind as to give them a little assistance now and then when they find it necessary. They would certainly appreciate it I'm sure.

The weather here is still rather on the warm side as compared to the previous years. It snows now and then but not enough to make it very cold.

Hoping to find you and Mrs. Morrish in good health, I remain

Sincerely,

J. I. Rikimar u

P. S. Please remember my best regard to Mr. Thompson.

Figure 37. Nuances of relocating back to Redwood City: Mr. Rikimaru wrote as the Pacific coast was "re-opening" and asked Morrish to keep a special lookout for those families returning to Redwood City with a family member in the armed services.

Figure 38

February 15, 1945

Mr. J. Morrish
First National Bank
Redwood City, California

Dear Sir:

I am once again writing to ask a special
favor of you in reference to my status as a
resident in the United States of America. The
attainment of a normal status means as much to
me as does the American citizenship which you
cherish. As you know, my present status is,
as yet, that of a parolee. If a parolee departs
from a relocation center, he will find it necessary to report to authorities weekly, and in
that way his freedom will be considerably restricted.

It has been announced by the Department of
Justice that parolees may secure complete release
by again securing a number of affidavits and testimonies from Caucasian individuals. Although I
realize this will be an imposition on your time
and efforts, I am asking this favor of you in
order that my status of parolee may be changed
to that of a loyal Japanese alien.

My record has been further proven loyal by
letters sent to me by the Army notifying me that
my name has been removed from the Military Suspension List. This has now cleared me to go to
all parts of the United States, Alaska and Hawaii.
I would deeply appreciate it if you would write
an affidavit supporting my character, integrity,
loyalty and service to this country and my desire
to reside here in the United States, at your
earliest convenience.

Thanking you for your many past favors in
this respect, I remain,

Yours truly,

Joseph I. Rikimaru

Figure 38. The fluidity and meanings of legal statuses among internees: Joseph Rikimaru wrote to Morrish "to ask a special favor of you in reference to my status as a resident of the United States of America. The attainment of a normal status means as much to me as does the American citizenship which you cherish." As a noncitizen, Rikimaru's status upon leaving the relocation center was that of "parolee," complete with the requirement to check in with a parole office. One could be returned to "normal status" as "a loyal Japanese alien" with the appropriate letters of support.

Figure 39

> Topaz, Utah
> Sept. 32. 1943
>
> Dear Mr. J. E. Morrish:-
>
> Since I have been given a clean bill of loyalty as a american citizen of Japanese descent by the War Dept, W.R.A. and F.B.I. I have taken the opportunity in relocating for the duration or until such time we are permitted to enter Calif. again.
>
> On Oct. 4th I am leaving Topaz for Milwaukee, Wisconsin so I thought that in case you might have to contact me on business matters, thought it wise that I give you my new address -
>
> It is:-
> Charles Suzukawa
> % Mrs. A. J. Harvey
> 3580 North Lake Drive
> Milwaukee,
> Wisconsin

Figure 39 (*continued*)

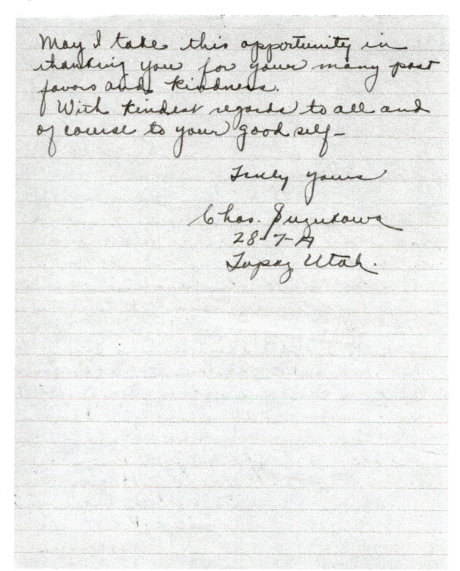

Figure 39. Charles Suzukawa, after receiving "a clean bill of loyalty" as a loyal American citizen of Japanese descent in September 1943, wrote of his choice to relocate to Milwaukee until he could return to California. Transcription follows.

FIGURE 39 TRANSCRIPTION

Topaz, Utah,
Sept. 22, 1943

Dear Mr. J.E. Morrish:

Since I have been given a clear bill of loyalty as a (sic) American citizen of Japanese descent by the War Dept., W.R.A and F.B.I, I have taken the opportunity in relocating for the duration or until such time we are permitted to enter Calif. again.

On Oct. 4th I am leaving Topaz for Milwaukee, Wisconsin. So I thought that in case you might have to contact me on business matters, though it wise that I give you my new address—it is—

Charles Suzukawa
c/o Mrs. A. J.
Harvey
3580 North Lake
Drive
Milwaukee
Wisconsin

May I take this opportunity in thanking you for your many past favors and kindness.

With kindest regards to all and of course to your good self—

Truly yours
Chas. Suzukawa
28-7-A
Topaz Utah.

Figure 40

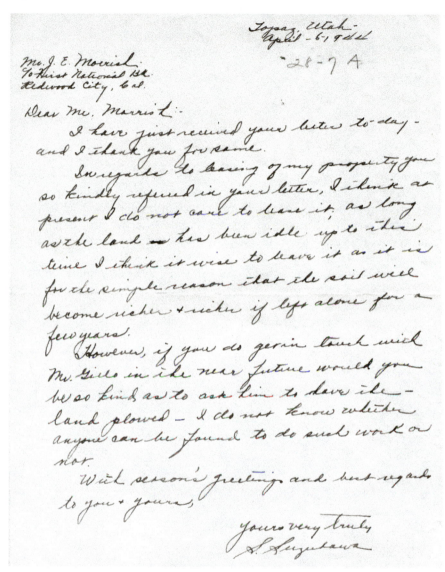

Figure 40. Agriculturalists caring for their land from away: S. Suzukawa wrote to Morrish to say he didn't want to lease his property, as the land would become "richer and richer if left alone for a few years." Transcription follows.

FIGURE 40 TRANSCRIPTION

Topaz, Utah,
April 6, 1944
28-7 A

Mr. J. E. Morrish
c/o First National Bk.
Redwood City, Cal.

Dear Mr. Morrish:

I have just received your letter to-day—and I thank you for same.

In regards to leasing of my property you so kindly referred in your letter, I think at present I do not care to lease it, as long as the land has been idle up to this time I think it wise to leave it as it is for the simple reason that the soil will become richer and richer if left alone for a few years.

However, if you do get in touch with Mr. Gillo in the near future would you be so kind as to ask him to have the land plowed—I do not know whether anyone can be found to do such work or not.

With seasons's greetings and best regards to you and yours,

Yours very truly,
S. Suzukawa

Figure 41

```
                                            P. O. Box 707
                                            Marysville, California
                                            June 1, 1942

Dear Mr. Morrish:

       Thank you very much for the bank statement you forwarded to us a few
days ago.  If you have not deducted the interest on the Deed of Trust, I
wish that you would do so from our Commercial Account at your earliest con-
venience.

       With regard to Dad's insurance policies, there are two due for pre-
mium this month.  Would you kindly write to the respective insurance com-
panies and inquire whether it is permissable to have them frozen for the
duration?  If they are not in a position to freeze the policies, Dad would
rather have them surrendered rather than to pay the premium because there
is no income at the present time.

       I forwarded the Affidavit on Lucille's policy last week.  No doubt
you have received them by this writing.  If you do not hold a birth cer-
tificate, kindly let us know at your earliest convenience and I shall have
a copy made immediately.  It is my understanding that a copy of her birth
certificate was forwarded to the insurance company at the time we first de-
cided to cash-in on her policy.

       As yet Marysville has not been ordered to evacuate, but we can never
tell just when orders will come through.  Marysville is in a very compli-
cated situation with numerous bridges and railroad tracks.  But at the
present time with shortage of farm hand we do not believe that evacuation
orders will come out for quite some time, but DeWitt of course, has the
power to do whatever he sees fit so we are waiting patiently for orders to
come at any time.

       Dad, Mother and brother are all working ten hours a day thinning
peaches.  You would be surprised at the number of jobs there are here on
the farms because most of the men here are working at the Government can-
tonment, receiving from 90 to $1.00 per hour whereas you only receive 50¢
per hour thinning peaches.  At first it was quite a hard task to learn
the art of thinning peaches rapidly, but they are gradually catching on
to their new work and working full speed and working while they can before
evacuation orders come.

       The Japanese people are all jittery as other towns in this vicinity
on the westerly side of 99-E have already evacuated.  But having come here
from the stragetic zone of 1-A, we know that we are still safe from eva-
cuation because as far as Marysville is concerned it is in 2-A, but with
the war growing from bad to worse every minute of the day we begin to won-
der how correct we are in thinking that we are free and will be free for
sometime as we guess.  Perhaps in a few days definite orders will come
out and if anything about evacuation should come through I shall notify
you immediately.

       Sincerely hope that everyone is in the very best of health as we
find ourselves here.  Please take care of yourself and the kindest regards
to Mrs. Morrish and your daughters.

                                       Very sincerely yours,

                                       Fumiko

                                       Fumiko Takagi
```

Figure 41. A rare and interesting reflection from June 1, 1942: Writing from Marysville before the family was evacuated, Fumiko Takagi described how hard the family was working and how frightened all the Japanese Americans in the area were as towns around them were evacuated. She believed that with the shortage of farm workers (because everyone had gone to work in factories) they would not be evacuated soon. At that point, the Japanese west of highway 99-E had all been evacuated.

Figure 42

```
                                              4816-C Tule Lake W. R. A.
                                              Newell, California
                                              July 30, 1943


Mr. J. E. Morrish
First National Bank
Redwood City, California

Dear Mr. Morrish:

    Thank you very much for your letter and also for the hot plate
which we received yesterday. We appreciate it very much.

    Relative to selling or leasing our property, we discussed the
matter very thoroughly and have decided to lease it to the Tau's
again next year and as long as the Tau's desire leasing it for the
duration. We figured that even though we do sell it, we would not
have use for the money at the immediate moment and since the Tau's
have started their crop going, it would be better to lease it to
them. Furthermore, we would like to sell our property for $15,000
and no less, as you well know yourself, my folks have put plenty of
money, time and effort into it. I am sure that you understand the
situation.

    Things are going along very smoothly here except that the people
in general are very excited about segregation. Tule Lake has offi-
cially been claimed as the camp for the disloyal Japanese, so we will
probably be moving into another center about November. Rumors and
gossip around the camp is that only two camps will be open and all
those leaving for the loyal camp will sooner or later be ousted to
relocate. Of course, we cannot believe such rumors, as nothing offi-
cial has been voiced by the authorities here. We are hoping to
here more of the Denver conference next week as the Project Director
will return from Denver then. I will let you know more about segre-
gation as things develop here.

    Although my leave clearance has not come through as yet, I am
planning to relocate to Philadelphia as soon as I have my family
and grandparents settled in the loyal camp. My brother and sister
will probably leave as soon as they are cleared for Chicago or there-
abouts. I, being the eldest in the family, am reluctant to leave
my parents here and not know what will happen to them after I leave.
I have been offered a job, either permanent or temporary, with the
American Friends' Society in Philadelphia. If I cannot go to Phi-
ladelphia, my next destination is Ohio. Do you have any friends or
business associates in Philadelphia or Ohio where you can recommend
me for a secretarial job? I am inquiring as I am hesitant to take
a job permanently with the AFSC as I believe their wages will not
meet my desire to fulfill the standards of living. With victory
taxes, income tax, housing, etc., I am desirous of obtaining at
least $150.00 or more per month. If you are able, please suggest
a few employers in Ohio or in Philadelphia whom I can ask for a job
or perhaps you can recommend me to a few of your friends. I shall
appreciate it very much.
```

Figure 42 (*continued*)

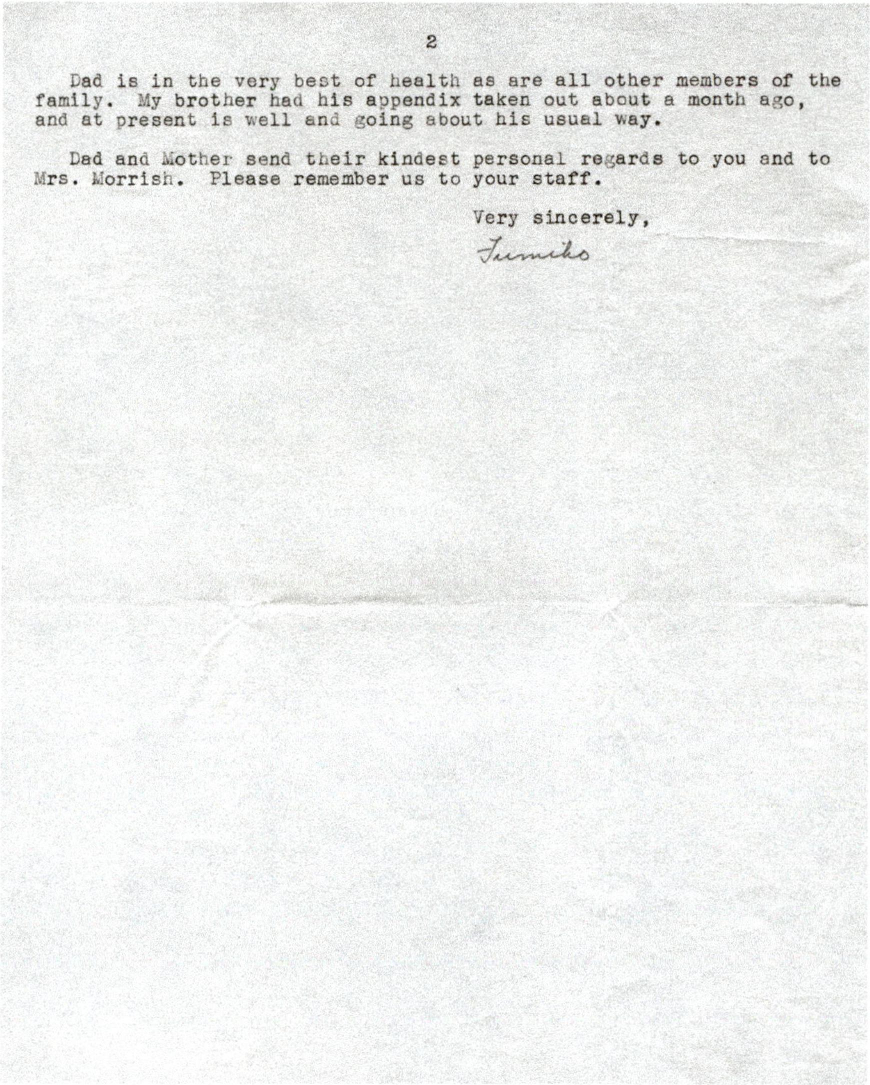

2

Dad is in the very best of health as are all other members of the family. My brother had his appendix taken out about a month ago, and at present is well and going about his usual way.

Dad and Mother send their kindest personal regards to you and to Mrs. Morrish. Please remember us to your staff.

Very sincerely,

Fumiko

Figure 42. A report on the "excitement" of the establishment of Tule Lake as a segregation center. As for where the family would be sent, Fumiko Takagi had been offered a job with the American Friends' Society in Philadelphia, a notable group of "white allies" to the internees during the war. The rest of her family would be sent to a "loyal camp"; she noted, "I, being the eldest in the family, am reluctant to leave my parents here and not know what will happen to them after I leave."

Figure 43

Dear Mr. Morrish:

Thank you very much for your letters of October 25th and November 17th. My intentions were to write much sooner than this, but have been extremely busy at the office, working day and night, consequently was unable to get around to writing you sooner than this. I hope you will understand.

Thank you very much for the letter of recommendation. That is exactly I want and I'm sure it will help me to get a good job when I am ready for relocation. Altho I thought I was ready for relocation whenever I wished, it seems that I have to have a hearing and have the Board here clear me before I can go out. The reason for the hearing is that I did not register for my leave clearance in time and so will have to have a very rigid hearing to clear myself. I'm sure that everything will work out satisfactorily as there is nothing that can hold me back from receiving my clearance.

Things are much the same here. In a few more days, it will be exactly two months since we left Tule Lake and I can assure you we are more than happy that we left when we did. I suppose you have already heard and read much about the recent Tule Lake incident. To a certain extent, the incident has reflected upon the thousands of loyal Niseis who have already relocated and also to the other nine relocation centers. I hope that everything will be smoothed out and that those rioteers of Tule will be taken out of there.

We are all well and hoping that this letter finds you and your family in good health. The weather changed overnight and we are now having very heavy rain and cold. The dirt here is just terrible; similar to adobe. It sticks to ones shoes and marks the floors of the house considerably. I can hardly wait for Spring.

Dad is working as a painter and seems to be enjoying his work. Its quite an easy job.

Hoping this letter will find you all in good health, I am

Very sincerely yours,

Fumiko Takagi

39-12-D Central Utah WRA
Topaz, Utah

Figure 43. After being relocated from the "disloyal" Tule Lake population, Fumiko Takagi wrote of the difficulty of getting permission to relocate for work: "I thought I was ready for relocation whenever I wished, it seems that I have to have a hearing and have the Board clear me. . . ." The document calls into question the meaning of being designated as "loyal."

Figure 44

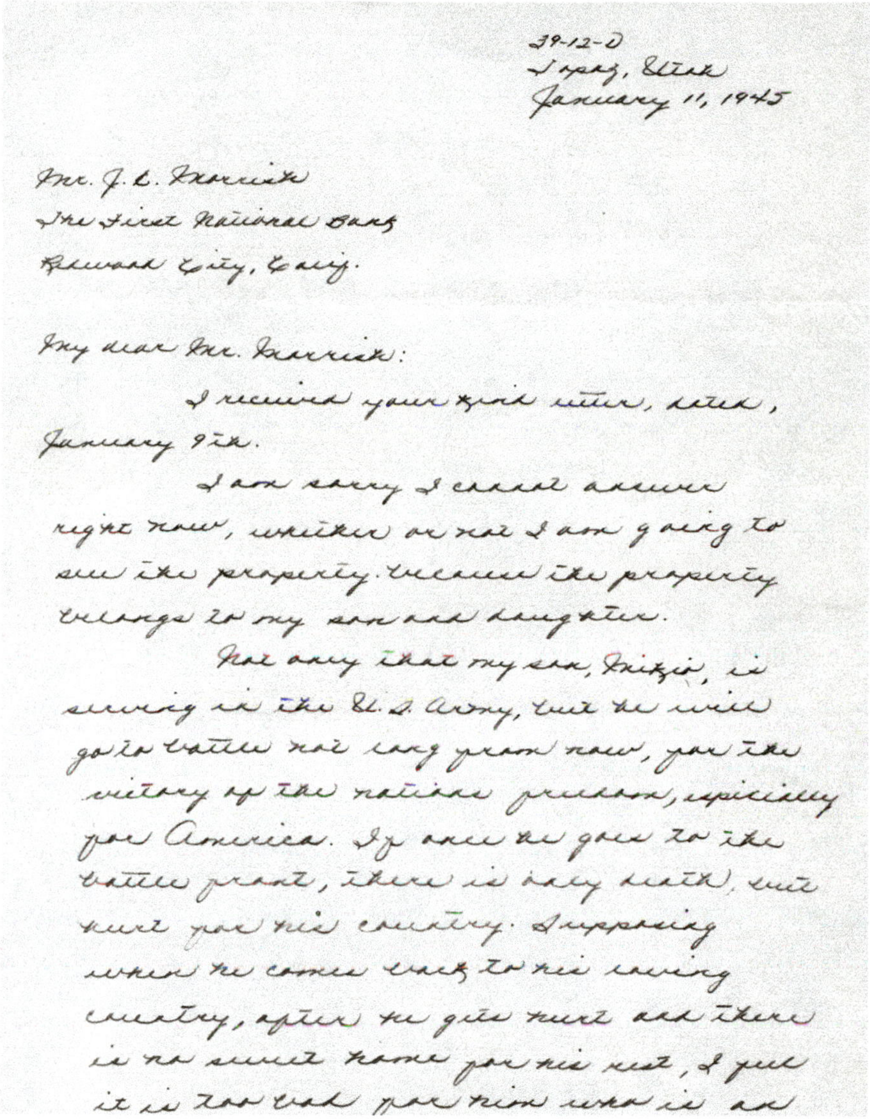

39-12-0
Topaz, Utah
January 11, 1945

Mr. J. L. Barrick
The First National Bank
Redwood City, Calif.

My dear Mr. Barrick:

I received your kind letter, dated, January 9th.

I am sorry I cannot answer right now, whether or not I am going to sell the property, because the property belongs to my son and daughter.

Not only that my son, Frizie, is serving in the U. S. Army, but he will go to battle not long from now, for the victory of the nation's freedom, especially for America. If once he goes to the battle front, there is only death, but sure for his country. Supposing when he comes back to his loving country, after he gets hurt and there is no sweet home for his rest, I feel it is too bad for him who is all

Figure 44 (*continued*)

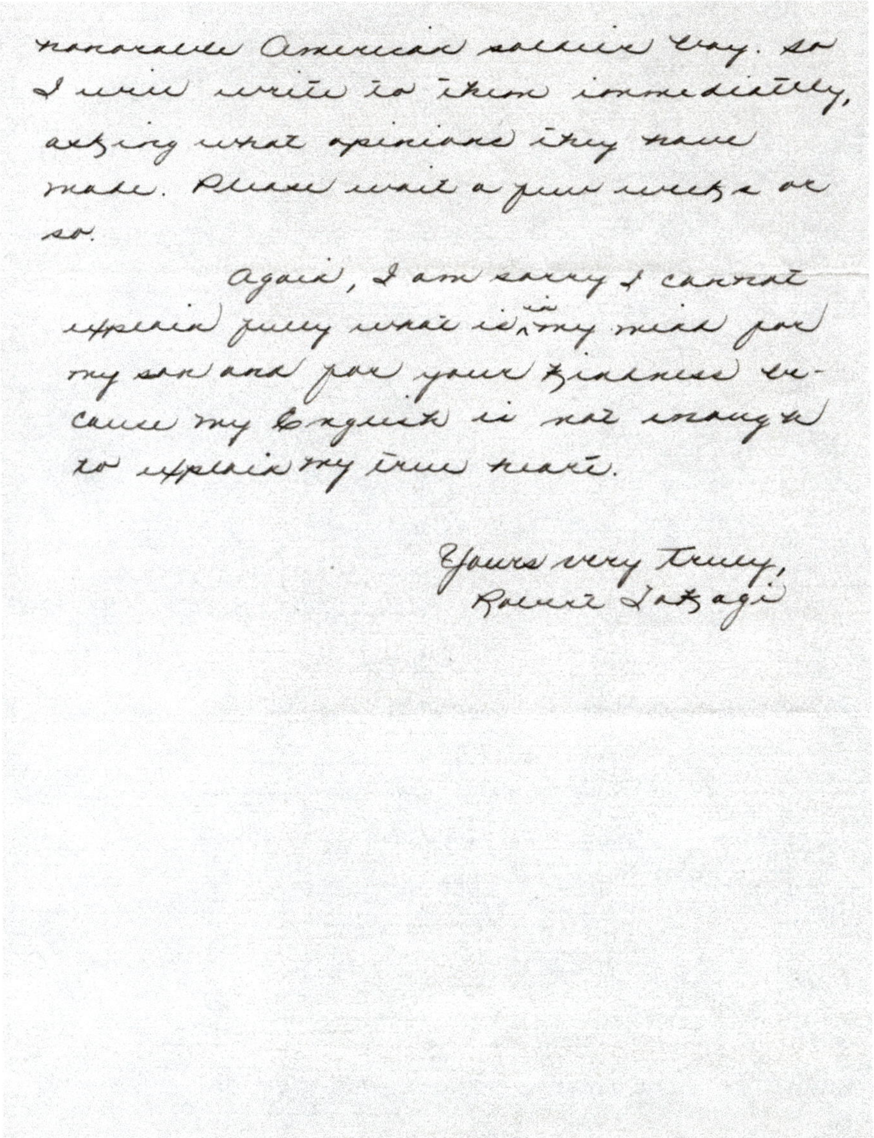

honorable American soldier way. So I will write to them immediately, asking what opinions they have made. Please wait a few weeks or so.

Again, I am sorry I cannot explain fully what is in my mind for my son and for your kindness because my English is not enough to explain my true heart.

Yours very truly,
Robert Takagi

Figure 44. On planning for life after the war: Robert Takagi wrote to Morrish, stating that he could not make a decision about selling the property because it belonged to his son and daughter. Additionally, his son, Mikio, was in the army and about to ship off to war, and Robert indicated that if he were to be hurt, when he would come back he should have a home to return to. Transcription follows.

FIGURE 44 TRANSCRIPTION

39-12-D
Topaz, Utah
January 11, 1945

Mr. J. R. Morrish
The First National Bank
Redwood City, Calif.

My Dear Mr. Morrish:

I received your kind letter, dated, January 9th.

I am sorry I cannot answer right now, whether or not I am going to sell the property, because the property belongs to my son and daughter.

Not only that my son, Mikio, is serving in the U.S. Army, but he will go in battle not long from now, for the victory of the nation's freedom, especially for America. If once he goes to the battle front, there is only death, but hurt for his country. Supposing when he comes back to his saving country, after he gets hurt and there is no sweet home for his rest, I feel it is too bad for him who is an honorable American soldier boy. So I will write to them immediately, asking what opinions they have made. Please wait a few weeks or so.

Again, I am sorry I cannot explain fully what is in my mind for my son and for your kindness because my English is not enough to explain my true heart.

Yours very truly,
Robert Takagi

Figure 45

y January, 1945

Mr. J. E. Morrish
First National Bank
Redwood City, California

My dear Mr. Morrish:

As you can understand, since the Exclusion Act has been lifted, we have been
confronted with many problems; and likewise you too have been burdened with more
than your share of troubles for our welfare and benefit. It is very difficult for
me to express my humble, yet heartfelt appreciation for your unending kindness and
sincerity in taking our problems into your hands. When I say this, Mr. Morrish,
I truly and sincerely mean it and apologize for Mother and Dad who have neglected
writing you to thank you because of their handicap in writing and speaking fluent
English. But please believe me, Mother, Dad and other members of the family as
well as myself want you to know how much we appreciate your interest in our welfare. Our welfare, which you have willingly and unselfishly taken to heart has
proven to us there is no finer person than yourself, and not another person we
can trust with our numerous problems. We bow our heads to you, Mr. Morrish, in
appreciation.

Dad has been writing me daily of new developments of our returning to California. Though I do not know definitely, it has been voiced unofficially that the
Topaz Relocation Center will close at the end of the year. No official declaration
has been made, but we have learned from experience to be on the alert for any order which may be issued between now and the tentative date set for the disbandment
of the Topaz Relocation Center.

In the event we are ordered to leave Topaz before the end of the year, we
will have no alternative but to return to our home in California. If we are firm-
ly assured our movement will not be enforced until October or between October and
December, we would not have the problem we have now of further troubling you with.
Should we, however, have to return to California before the termination of the
lease, we will have to have a place to return to. I am wondering whether it would
be possible at this late date to alter our agreement with the Tau's and insert a
phrase whereby we may return to our home on a one month notice. By this I do not
mean the complete evacuation from the premises, but from the house they are pre-
sently occupying.

It will be difficult, I know, to insert such a clause, as well as will it
be difficult for the Tau's to vacate the house on short notice. But we hope
that you and the Tau's can understand the predicament in which we find ourselves.
We understand and appreciate the fact that the Tau's will be greatly handicapped
and inconvenienced, but in view of the fact that an order from the Government is
the reason why we must impose upon them for this consideration, we beg your kind
and immediate attention to this matter. Without doubt this imposition will not
be likely that the Tau's will tolerate without much reluctance and hesitance, as
we would likewise feel the same way. We would not ask you or the Tau's to do
this had it not been for the fact that we must leave the Relocation Center, and
in this case before the termination of the lease.

Of course, it is not certain that we will have to leave the Relocation Center before October, but I am writing to you in advance in the event that such an
order is issued by the Government. We realize the obligation we owe you and the

Figure 45 (*continued*)

Mr. J. E. Morrish
5 March, 1945
Page 2

Tau's, and it is with much hesitance that I write you for consideration of our request. We know and understand the grave position in which we are placing the Tau's; please explain our regret in having to intrude in this manner.

Dad writes that he feels it will be almost impossible for Mother and he to resume business as prior to evacuation. And with Mikio in the Army and the shortage of farm help on the Coast, it is obviously a total impossibility to operate the farm on the large scale in which we have heretofore. For this reason, we would like to suggest that if the Tau's would like, they may lease our property as to date with the exception of our home. This would include the acreage, packing shed, store, etc. Dad also suggested that he and Mother would be very willing to work on the farm as their hired help. Of course, this is merely a suggestion and they have not decided on any plans definitely, but we would like to know if the Tau's would be interested in such a proposal.

We realize we are imposing you further with our problems, but we would appreciate your kind attention to this matter. Would you please forward a reply to Dad and send me a copy of the letter. Thanking you again for your many kindnesses, I am

Most sincerely,

Fumiko

FUMIKO TAKAGI

P. S. As you may recall, at the outbreak of the war, we were ordered to turn in our radios and cameras. I am wondering whether you have a receipt for my brother's camera, which I presume was turned in to the Mountain View Police Dept. If you have this receipt in our files, would you please forward it to me. Thank you.

Figure 45. The troubles with relocation continued for the Takagi family, as they negotiated where to go and what would happen when they arrived to restart their lives. Fumiko wrote, "In the event we are ordered to leave Topaz we have nowhere but our home in California to return to." Because of labor shortage and Mikio's being at war, the Takagi's were concerned about running the farm themselves and suggested letting their current Chinese tenants stay and work as their laborers.

Figure 46

```
                              1219 N. Clark St.
                              Chicago, 10, Ill.
                              March 26, 1944

Dear Mr. Morrish:

After writing to you that I would have Sumi Adachi
write to you about transfer of a certain sum from the
association account to my name, I received word from
you that you have received no word from anyone
concerning this matter. I was under the impression
that the matter would be taken care of by Sumi, but
since it has not, I have written to her again. The
problem is to see that this amount of money be trans-
fered to my account in San Jose, and to have the bank
wait a reasonable length of time before taking any
definite measures. I am trying everything in my
power to make the payments, and to comply with the
other responsibilities also.

I would appreciate your helping me get the bank to
wait, and to give me time to make this paymeny, because
the money is there in your bank.

Recently I have been reclassified into 1 A; so it looks
like I will be going into the army very shortly. This
matter brings up a problem that I would appreciate your
help. As you know, my parents, being aliens, cannot
own property. Therefore, in the event that I do not
return from war, they will not be able to inherit what
is mine. I could sell the place, but, as I have told
you before, I would like to keep the place in order
that I will have a home to come home to. There is
always the possibility that I will return, and that
is a wonderful feeling to know that a place to return
is there. My problem is will there be any protection
for my folks in the even that I die at war. I sure
wouldn't want them to let the state take the property
as the law exists now. Furthermore, would I still have
to keep the mortgage up on the property even though
I am drafted? If you could answer these questions for
me, I will be very grateful.

                              Yours very sincerely
```

Figure 46. On the trickiness of official citizenship: An internee inducted into the army was concerned about the status of his foreign national parents. In 1944 Tsukagawa wrote, "Recently I have been reclassified into 1A; so it looks like I will be going into the army very shortly. This matter brings up a problem that I would appreciate your help. As you know, my parents, being aliens, cannot own property. Therefore, in the event that I do not return from war, they will not be able to inherit what is mine. . . ." He stated that it would be great to be able to come back to a place if he survived but he wanted to protect his parents and he didn't want the state to take his property. "Furthermore, would I still have to keep the mortgage up on the property even though I am drafted? If you could answer these questions for me, I will be very grateful."

History of Morrish

The name "Morrish" occurs on many of the pages in this book. Despite this, we tried not to make him the focus. We believe that, while his actions saved many of these people more anguish than they already had, the people in the Morrish Collection played an equal part in helping themselves, and their story deserved to be told through their own words and history. That said, it seems fitting to end the book with an epilogue detailing some of the events in the life of J. Elmer Morrish. It will be clear that his actions to help Japanese Americans during World War II was not a one-off thing for Morrish. He spent his life in service to others, and his time at his bank during the war, writing letters and dealing with the financial issues of the internees, was just a part of what he did for the people of Redwood City.

Joseph Elmer Morrish (usually referred to as J. Elmer Morrish) was raised in California. Born on December 7, 1886, in Sierra City, California, he moved with his family to Berkeley in 1900. Banking was clearly in his blood as he began working at the First National Bank of Berkeley in 1905 (at the age of 19). He married his wife, Katheryn, a few years later, in 1911, and eventually they had four children. He later moved south to the San Jose Bank in 1919, where he started as an assistant cashier and ultimately moved up to be the assistant manager. Morrish was extremely active in his community throughout his life. It was noted in local newspapers that as early as 1932 he was a trustee of his local school in San Jose, the past president of the San Jose chapter of the American Red Cross, and the past president of the San Jose chapter of the American Institute of Banking. In September 1932 he and his family made the move to Redwood City; he became the manager of Redwood City's First National Bank, and in 1937 he became its vice president. When the Bank of America merged with Wells Fargo in 1955, he retained his position as vice president.

Morrish mentioned, a few times in the collection, that he was traveling during the war to various conferences. This was in part due to his elected positions in the Independent Bankers Association (he was re-elected in early 1942), including becoming its president at the end of 1944. He was also reappointed (in 1942) as the San Mateo County representative for the Committee in Public Relations of the California Bankers Association. Katheryn, his wife, died on February 4, 1953, of a heart attack.[1] His community service did not go unnoticed. In 1956 Morrish was given the honor of being named Redwood City's "Man of the Year" by the city's Chamber of Commerce. At his induction ceremony, it was stated that he was active in a number of different organizations, including being the past president of the Redwood City Kiwanis Club, the director of the Children's Health Home, the treasurer of the Hospitalized Veteran's Christmas Committee, and the treasurer of the Salvation Army Committee. His involvement with the Japanese American community was not mentioned.

His city recognized him, and so did the people he helped during the war. Many times the correspondents in the Morrish Collection expressed their wish that they wanted to thank Morrish for everything he had done. The Japanese American community got its chance in 1957, soon after his retirement from the bank. They got together, pooled their money, and sent him on a round-the-world cruise. This trip started on April 13, 1957, and ended on September 3 in New York City. The cruise also included a tour of Japan, which he certainly enjoyed. Some of the people from the Morrish Collection arranged to have relatives meet with Morrish when he was there, including a cousin of Hi Inouye who met him when he arrived in Yokohama, Japan (early May 1957). He took off three days of work in order to show Morrish around.[2] Relatives of Mr. Rikimaru then met him in Tokyo, and Mr. Rikimaru himself sent a doll to Morrish's hotel in Kyoto.

Morrish passed away on October 31, 1957, at the age of 71, just a little over a month after arriving back in Redwood City. After his death, a collection was taken up by a number of business owners in order to establish a Youth Library, named the J. Elmer Morrish Youth Library, in the Sequoia YMCA, Redwood City. A bronze plaque was installed on the door. The fundraising letter stated, "The trustees feel that this library will be a fitting memorial to Mr. Morrish as he served on the board for many years and was devoted to the interests of youth in this activity."[3] Finally, after the

Morrish Collection letters were accepted by the library, they were organized and preserved through the work of Jeanne Thivierge. The library also was awarded a grant to (among other things) build a (now defunct) website showcasing a few of the letters and to conduct oral and video interviews with survivors, with help from Thivierge and Gene Suarez. In 2003, a Buddhist temple in Palo Alto, California, organized a tribute to the life of Morrish. This brought together many of the surviving members who had been helped during World War II. Morrish lived a long and productive life. He led a life of service that was greatly appreciated by both his city and by those he helped, including the many Japanese Americans who were not only his clients but his friends.

Notes

1. Morrish Collection, Box 2, 4.

2. The personal accounts by Morrish of his round-the-world trip are held at the Redwood City Library (Archive Room, Box 2). These were sent to his secretary, Betty Farchi, and at least 45 copies were then made and sent out to the friends of Morrish. See Box 2, Folder 2 for his letter about the cousin.

3. Morrish Collection, Box 2, 3. January 17, 1958.

Bibliography

Primary Texts

"A Challenge to Democracy," War Relocation Authority, with the Office of War Information and the Office of Strategic Services, producers, 1942, https:// archive.org/details/gov.fdr.21, accessed September 27, 2016.

Deseret News (a Utah newspaper): https://news.google.com/newspapers?nid=Aul -kAQHnToC.

DeWitt, J. L. *Final Report: Japanese Evacuation from the West Coast, 1942.* Washington, D.C.: United States Government Printing Office, 1943.

Ebihara, Henry A. Notes and Observations (of Topaz), obtained from http:// digitalassets.lib.berkeley.edu/jarda/ucb/text/cubanc6714_b095h09_0001 .pdf, accessed May 1, 2016.

Executive Order 9066, http://www.ourdocuments.gov/doc.php?doc=74&page =transcript, accessed April 9, 2016.

Hayashi, Dorothy. Her diary (about Topaz), obtained from http://digitalassets.lib .berkeley.edu/jarda/ucb/text/cubanc6714_b095h09_0002_1.pdf, accessed May 1, 2016.

Hoshiyama, Fred. His diary (about Topaz), obtained from http://digitalassets.lib .berkeley.edu/jarda/ucb/text/cubanc6714_b095h09_0004.pdf, accessed May 1, 2016.

Hoshiyama, Fred. Topaz Administration (and various notes) http://digitalassets .lib.berkeley.edu/jarda/ucb/text/cubanc6714_b095h09_0006.pdf.

"Japanese Relocation," Office of War Information, Bureau of Motion Pictures producer, with the War Activities Committee of the Motion Picture Industry, 1942, https://archive.org/details/Japanese1943

Japanese Relocation.org (some of the same information as the National Archives, but with possible family members), http://www.japaneserelocation.org/.

Kikuchi, Charles. *The Kikuchi Diary: The Chronicle of an American Concentration Camp. The Tanforan Journals of Charles Kikuchi,* edited by John Modell. Urbana: University of Illinois Press, 1973.

Morrish Collection, held in the Karl A. Vollmayer Local History Room, Redwood City Public Library, Redwood City, CA. The letters are organized in files by the last name of the internees, followed by the actual letter number. For example, 01_Adachi_001 can be found in File 1 (last name Adachi), letter number one. We also made use of oral histories that were taken in 2003. These histories are also found in the Local History Room. The original organizers split the collection into two folders. Box #2 contains financial information and material about Morrish himself.

National Archives, Japanese Relocation and Internment during World War II, NARA Resources, http://www.archives.gov/research/alic/reference/military /japanese-internment.html.

National Archives search, Records about Japanese Americans Relocated during World War II, created, 1988–1989, documenting the period 1942–1946, *Record Group 210*, https://aad.archives.gov/aad/fielded-search.jsp?dt=2003 &tf=F&cat=WR26&bc=,sl.

Online Archives of California, War Relocation Authority Photographs of Japanese-American Evacuation and Resettlement, 1942–1945, http://www .oac.cdlib.org/findaid/ark:/13030/tf596nb4h0/.

Phelan, James D. "The Japanese Evil in California." *The North American Review* 210, no. 766 (September 1919): 323–328.

Proceedings of the Asiatic Exclusion League, 1907–1913. New York, NY: Arno Press, 1977.

Tanforan Totalizer, http://ddr.densho.org/ddr/densho/149/

Topaz Times, http://digitalnewspapers.org/newspaper/?paper=Topaz+Times and http://archive.densho.org/main.aspx.

U.S. War Relocation Authority, U.S. Department of the Interior. Train Route List from Topaz to Tule Lake, September, 1943 http://digitalassets.lib.berkeley .edu/jarda/ucb/text/cubanc6714_b051e06_0051.pdf.

U.S. War Relocation Authority, U.S. Department of the Interior. *Impounded People: Japanese Americans in the Relocation Centers.* Washington, D.C.: U.S. Government Printing Office, 1946.

U.S. War Relocation Authority, U.S. Department of the Interior. *WRA: The Story of Human Conservation.* Washington, D.C.: U.S. Government Printing Office, 1947.

U.S. War Relocation Authority, U.S. Department of the Interior. *The Relocation Program: A Guidebook for the Residents of Relocation Centers* vol. 6. Washington D.C.; 1943, reprinted in New York, NY: AMS Press, 1975.

U.S. War Relocation Authority, U.S. Department of the Interior. *The Wartime Handling of Evacuee Property* vol. II. Washington, D.C.: U.S. Government Printing Office, n.d.; reprinted in New York, NY: AMS Press, 1975.

Secondary Texts

Arrington, Leonard J. *The Price of Prejudice: The Japanese-American Relocation Center in Utah during World War II.* Logan, UT: The Faculty Association, Utah State University, 1962.

Austin, Allan W. *From Concentration Camp to Campus: Japanese American Students and World War II*. Urbana: University of Illinois Press, 2004.

Bailey, Thomas A. "California, Japan, and the Alien Land Legislation of 1913." *Pacific Historical Review* 1, no. 1 (March 1932): 36–59.

Bangarth, Stephanie. *Voices Raised in Protest: Defending North American Citizens of Japanese Ancestry, 1942–49*. Seattle: University of Washington Press, 2009.

Burton, Jeffery, Mary Farrell, Florence Lord, and Richard Lord. *Confinement and Ethnicity: An Overview of World War II Japanese American Relocation Sites* (Scott and Laurie Oki Series in Asian American Studies). Seattle: University of Washington Press, 2002.

Conner, Nancy Nakano. "From Internment to Indiana: Japanese Americans, the War Relocation Authority, the Disciples of Christ, and Citizen Committees in Indianapolis." *Indiana Magazine of History* 102, no. 2 (June 2006): 89–116.

Conroy, Hilary, and Sharlie Conroy Ushioda. "A Review of Scholarly Literature on the Internment of Japanese Americans during World War II: Toward a Quaker Perspective." *Quaker History* 83, no. 1 (Spring 1994): 48–52.

Daniels, Roger. *The Politics of Prejudice: The Anti-Japanese Movement in California and the Struggle for Japanese Exclusion*. Berkeley: University of California Press, 1962.

Daniels, Roger. *The Decision to Relocate the Japanese Americans*. Philadelphia, PA: J. B. Lippincott Co., 1975.

Daniels, Roger. "Incarcerating Japanese Americans." *OAH Magazine of History* 16, no. 3, World War II Homefront (Spring 2002): 19–23.

Daniels, Roger. *Guarding the Golden Door: American Immigration Policy and Immigrants Since 1882*. New York, NY: Hill and Wang, 2004.

Drinnon, Richard. *Keeper of Concentration Camps: Dillon S. Myer and American Racism*. Berkeley: University of California Press, 1987.

1872–1942: A Community Story. San Mateo, CA: The San Mateo Chapter Japanese American Citizens League, 1981.

Eisenberg, Ellen. "'As Truly American as Your Son': Voicing Opposition to Internment in Three West Coast Cities." *Oregon Historical Quarterly* 104, no. 4 (Winter 2003): 542–565.

Fiset, Louis. "Thinning, Topping, and Loading: Japanese Americans and Beet Sugar in World War II." *The Pacific Northwest Quarterly* 90, no. 3 (Summer 1999): 123–139.

Fujita-Rony, Thomas Y. "Remaking the 'Home Front' in World War II: Japanese American Women's Work and the Colorado River Relocation Center." *Southern California Quarterly* 88, no. 2 (Summer 2006): 161–204.

Gowdy-Wygant, Cecilia. *Cultivating Victory: The Women's Land Army and the Victory Garden Movement*. Pittsburgh, PA: University of Pittsburgh, 2013.

Greenberg, Cheryl. "Black and Jewish Responses to Japanese Internment." *Journal of American Ethnic History* 14, no. 2 (1995): 3–37.

Grob, G. N., ed. *Anti-American Movements in America: Proceedings of the Asiatic Exclusion League, 1907–1913*. New York, NY: Arno Press, 1977.

Hayashi, Brian Masaru. *Democratizing the Enemy: The Japanese American Internment.* Princeton, NJ: Princeton University Press, 2004.

Howard, John. "The Politics of Dancing under Japanese-American Incarceration." *History Workshop Journal* no. 52 (Autumn 2001): 122–151.

Ichioka, Yuji. "Japanese Immigrant Response to the 1920 California Alien Land Law." *Agricultural History* 58, no. 2 (April 1984): 157–178.

Inui, Kiyo Sue. "California's Japanese Situation." *Annals of the American Academy of Political and Social Science* 93, Present-Day Immigration with Special Reference to the Japanese (January 1921): 97–104.

Iwata, Masakazu. "The Japanese Immigrants in California Agriculture." *Agricultural History* 36, no. 1 (January 1962): 25–37.

Jacobs, Meg. "'How About Some Meat?': The Office of Price Administration, Consumption Politics, and State Building from the Bottom Up, 1941–1946." *The Journal of American History* 84, no. 3 (December 1997): 910–941.

Jensen, Gwenn M. "System Failure: Health-Care Deficiencies in the World War II Japanese American Detention Centers." *Bulletin of the History of Medicine* 73, no. 4 (Winter 1999): 601–628.

Kariya, Hiroji. *Kiku Kumiai, 50 Years.* Palo Alto, CA: California Chrysanthemum Growers Association, 1981.

Leonard, Kevin Allen. "'Is That What We Fought for?' Japanese Americans and Racism in California, The Impact of World War II." *The Western Historical Quarterly* 21, no. 4 (November 1990): 463–482.

Linke, Konrad. "Dominance, Resistance, and Cooperation in the Tanforan Assembly Center." *Amerikastudien/American Studies* 54, no. 4 (2009): 621–655.

Matsumoto, Valerie. *Farming the Home Place: A Japanese American Community in California, 1919–1982.* Ithaca, NY: Cornell University Press, 1993.

McWilliams, Carey. *Japanese Evacuation: Interim Report.* New York, NY: American Council Institute of Pacific Relations, 1942.

Mizuno, Takeya. "Journalism under Military Guards and Searchlights: Newspaper Censorship at Japanese American Assembly Camps during World War II." *Journalism History* 29.3 (2003): 98–106.

Muller, Eric. *Free to Die for Their Country: The Story of the Japanese American Draft Resisters in World War II.* Chicago, IL: University of Chicago Press, 2001.

Ng, Wendy. *Japanese American Internment during World War II: A History and Reference Guide.* Westport, CT: Greenwood Press, 2002.

Ngai, Mae M. "Asian American History: Reflections on the De-centering of the Field." *Journal of American Ethnic History* 25, no. 4, 25th Anniversary Commemorative Issue (Summer 2006): 97–108.

Okada, Yasuo. "The Japanese Image of the American West." *The Western Historical Quarterly* 19, no. 2 (May 1988): 141–159.

Olin, Spencer C., Jr. "European Immigrant and Oriental Alien: Acceptance and Rejection by the California Legislature of 1913." *Pacific Historical Review* 35, no. 3 (August, 1966): 303–315.

Robinson, Greg. *By Order of the President: FDR and the Internment of Japanese Americans*. Cambridge, MA: Harvard University Press, 2003.

Roxworthy, Emily. *The Spectacle of Japanese American Trauma: Racial Performativity and World War II*. Honolulu: University of Hawai'i Press, 2008.

Sackman, Doug. *Orange Empire: California and the Fruits of Eden*. Berkeley: University of California Press, 2007.

Seigel, Shizue. *In Good Conscience: Supporting Japanese Americans during the Internment*. San Mateo, CA: AACP, Inc., 2006.

Shaffer, Robert. "Cracks in the Consensus: Defending the Rights of Japanese Americans during World War II." *Radical History Review* 1998, no. 72 (Fall 1998): 84–120.

Smith, Jason Scott. "New Deal Public Works at War: The WPA and Japanese American Internment." *Pacific Historical Review* 72, no. 1 (February 2003): 63–92.

Smith, Susan. "Women Health Workers and the Color Line in the Japanese American 'Relocation Centers' of World War II." *Bulletin of the History of Medicine* 73, no. 4 (Winter 1999): 585–602.

Suzuki, Masao. "Important or Impotent? Taking Another Look at the 1920 California Alien Land Law." *The Journal of Economic History* 64, no. 1 (March 2004): 125–143.

Taylor, Sandra C. *Jewel of the Desert: Japanese American Internment at Topaz*. Berkeley: University of California Press, 1993.

Vaught, David. *Cultivating California: Growers, Specialty Crops, and Labor, 1875–1920*. Baltimore, MD: Johns Hopkins University Press, 2002.

Wollenberg, Charles. "'Dear Earl': The Fair Play Committee, Earl Warren, and Japanese Internment." *California History* 89, no. 4 (2012): 24–55, 57–60.

Yamada, Gayle K., Dianne Fukami, and Dianne Yen-Mei Wong, eds. *Building a Community: The Story of Japanese Americans in San Mateo County*. San Mateo, CA: AACP, Inc., 2003.

Index

Note: *f* indicates a figure in the book; *n* indicates a note.

About the Authors

Linda L. Ivey, PhD, is Associate Professor of History at California State University East Bay. She is a specialist in immigration and environmental U.S. history, with an emphasis on California. She has published "Ethnicity in the Land: Lost Stories in California Agriculture" in *Agricultural History* (2007); "Apples and Experts: Evolving Notions of Sustainable Agriculture" in *Global Environment* (2014); "Riotous Environments: Filipino Immigrants in the Fields of California" in the forthcoming *An Environmental History of Modern Migrations* (Routledge Press); and "Protecting the People's Mountain: Hiking and the Roots of Environmentalism in Marin County" in *Sports in the Bay Area: Golden Gate Athletics, Recreation and Community* (University of Arkansas Press, 2017).

Kevin W. Kaatz, PhD, is Assistant Professor of History at California State University East Bay. He is a specialist in digital history and the ancient world. He has published *Early Controversies and the Growth of Christianity* (Praeger, 2012) and *The Rise of Christianity: History, Documents, and Key Questions* (ABC-CLIO, 2016). He is the editor of *Voices of Early Christianity: Documents from the Origins of Christianity* (Greenwood Press, 2013) and *Documents of the Rise of Christianity: Eyewitness to History* (ABC-CLIO, forthcoming). He has also published articles in the field of early Christianity and in neuroscience.